W9-AQD-218

THE BERLITZ SELF-TEACHER:

RUSSIAN

THE BERLITZ SELF-TEACHER: RUSSIAN

EDITED BY THE STAFF OF

THE BERLITZ SCHOOLS OF LANGUAGES

UNDER THE DIRECTION OF

ROBERT STRUMPEN-DARRIE

AND

CHARLES F. BERLITZ

GROSSET & DUNLAP • *Publishers* • NEW YORK

PRINTED IN THE UNITED STATES OF AMERICA

INTRODUCTION

A very strange paradox exists in connection with languages and the learning of them. On the one hand, the ability to speak two or more languages reasonably well is *prima facie* evidence of better-than-average intelligence. On the other hand, learning a language is a very easy business. The proof of it is that every living human being who is not an utter idiot speaks one!

The trick lies in how you go about it. It would seem reasonable to use somewhat the same system to learn a new language as you did to acquire your own. This idea built up the Berlitz Schools of Languages from a one-room studio in Providence, Rhode Island, to a globe-circling institution with over 300 branches.

In a word, you learn to *speak* a language *by speaking it*—and in no other way. That is how the Russians do it, and that is how you learned English.

You will succeed with the BERLITZ SELF-TEACHER to the extent that you *speak*. Do not deceive yourself into thinking you have "arrived" when you find yourself able to read or translate the Russian text. You master Russian only in the degree to which you can express your idea in it. The ability to interpret the thoughts of others is only the first step.

One way of using the BERLITZ SELF-TEACHER is to pair off with someone else, or to organize a small group. After reading over the lesson in advance for meaning and pronunciation, each student then reads aloud, direct from the Russian text. The lesson is divided into convenient portions of agreement among the students. After each student has practiced reading aloud, one of them assumes the role of instructor and questions the others from the exercises called THINKING IN RUSSIAN. When all can answer these questions without hesitation, each student should invent ten or twelve new questions, based on the same or preceding lessons, and then put these questions to the others. Afterwards, answers to the exercise questions should be written out and corrected from the key in the appendix.

When a group of you are learning together, do not succumb to the "community-sing" temptation. Each student must speak individually, so that he can hear himself and the others, and profit thereby.

Make no mistake, however! This book is designed primarily for the student working alone. He must do exactly what pairs or groups do, covering each operation for himself. If you are embarrassed by the sound of your own voice, hide in the pantry! Put a sack over your head! No matter what form of defense mechanism you set up, see to it that you *speak out!* Do not mumble or whisper.

Your attention is directed to the glossary in the back of the book. Use it sparingly, if at all. With few exceptions, all the words are made clear in the lesson texts, and only occasionally have we sneaked a new one into the THINKING IN RUSSIAN exercises, just to keep you on your toes.

Above all, don't be frightened by the Russian alphabet. It's easier than shorthand, which millions of ordinary Americans learn each year, without undue strain.

Good luck, and have fun!

NOTE ON THE RUSSIAN ALPHABET

You are about to encounter what at first sight may look like a very complex method of writing, but which really need not frighten you at all. If you look at a page of printed Russian, it will undoubtedly look like Greek to you. This is perfectly natural in as much as the Russian or Cyrillic alphabet stems largely from the Greek. But even if you have not studied Greek, you will not find it too difficult, because you already know many of the letters. Take for example the word "America". In Russian this comes out **Америка.** With the exception of the substitutions of different letters for R and I, it looks pretty much the same, doesn't it? Now, knowing that the letter **И,** which looks like an N backwards, is an I, can you tell what **Миами** is? You are right; it is "Miami".

Therefore, instead of learning the complete new alphabet, remember only that certain letters are the same as ours; a second group looks like ours but has different values; and a third group consists of some picturesque letters which will be completely new to you. Fortunately this last group is not large.

Here are the three groups:

1. The following letters are common to both languages: **A, E, K, M, O, T.**

2. The following letters exist in English but have different values in Russian:

В	pronounced as	English	V
Н	"	"	N
Р	"	"	R
С	"	"	S
У	"	"	OO
Х	"	"	KH

   and R written backwards: **Я,** which is equivalent to "YAH" in English.

3. The following letters are equivalent to English letters or combinations of letters:

б Б	B
Г	G
Д	D
Ё	Yo (pronounced like Yo in York)
Ж	Soft J (like the S in pleasure)
З	Z
И	I (pronounced EE)
Й	Y (pronounced as the English Y in boy)
Л	L
П	P
Ф	F
Ц	Tz
Ч	Ch
Ш	Sh
Щ	Shch
Э	E (as in get)
Ю	U (as in cute)

And finally Ы pronounced somewhat like the "I" in "Shirley." You will also find the letter Ь which has no sound by itself at all, but merely implies a soft pronunciation of the preceding consonant. You can disregard the letter Ъ which occurs, on rare occasions, in the middle of some words and has no pronunciation of its own.

Here is something to encourage you! As Russian is a phonetic alphabet, you will have no spelling worries, once you have mastered the letters.

RECITE THE ALPHABET! Here are the letters of the Russian alphabet with the Russian phonetic pronunciations of their names:

а	*ah*
(Б) б	*beh*
в	*veh*
г	*ggeh*
д	*deh*
е	*yeh*
ё	*yoh*
ж	*zheh*
з	*zeh*
и	*ee*
й	*ee* KRAHT-*koh-yeh*
к	*kah*
л	*el*
м	*em*
н	*en*
о	*oh*
п	*peh*
р	*er*
с	*es*
т	*teh*
у	*oo*
ф	*ef*
х	*khah*
ц	*tseh*
ч	*chah*
ш	*shah*
щ	*shchah*
ъ	(*tv'*YOR-*dee znahk*)
ы	*yeh*-REE
ь	(*m'*YAH-*kee znahk*)
э	*eh* (*oh-boh*-ROHT-*noh-yeh*)
ю	*yoo*
я	*yah*

(See the preceding three pages for English equivalents.)

УРОК 1

Что это?
Shtoh EH-*toh?*
What is this?

Карандаш
Kah-rahn-DAHSH
Pencil

книга
*k'*NEE-*gah*
book

бумага
boo-MAH-*gah*
paper

перо
p'yeh-ROH
pen

коробка
koh-ROHB-*kah*
box

ключ.
kl'yooch.
key.

Что это?
Shtoh EH-*toh*?
What is this?

Это карандаш.
EH-*toh kah-rahn*-DAHSH.
This is the pencil.

Это карандаш?
EH-*toh kah-rahn*-DAHSH?
Is this the pencil?

Да, это карандаш.
Dah, EH-*toh kah-rahn*-DAHSH.
Yes, this is the pencil.

Это перо?
EH-*toh p'yeh*-ROH?
Is this the pen?

Нет, это не перо, это карандаш.
N'yet, EH-*toh n'yeh p'yeh*-ROH, EH-*toh kah-rahn*-DAHSH.
No, it is not the pen, it is the pencil.

REMEMBER: The present tense forms of "to be" (am, is, are) are not used in Russian as in English. In most cases they are simply omitted. Moreover, you don't have to worry when to say "a" or "the", for in Russian there is no article. For example: "this is a box" and "this is the box" are both translated by **э́то коро́бка.**

стол	**стул**	**кресло**	**лампа**	**шкаф**
stohl	*stool*	KRES-*loh*	LAHM-*pah*	*shkahf*
table	chair	arm-chair	lamp	closet

Это стул?
EH-*toh stool?*
Is this the chair?

Нет, это не стул, это стол.
N'yet, EH-*toh n'yeh stool,* EH-*toh stohl.*
No, this is not the chair, it is the table.

Это кресло?
EH-*toh* KRES-*loh*?
Is this an armchair?

Нет, это не кресло, это лампа.
N'yet, EH-*toh n'yeh* KRES-*loh*, EH-*toh* LAHM-*pah.*
No, this is not an armchair, it is a lamp.

NOTE to Student: э́то can mean "this (is)" or "it (is)". It also is used for "that is", "these are", "those are".

дверь	**окно**	**стена**	**потолок**	**пол**
dv'yehr	*ok*-NOH	*st'yeh*-NAH	*poh-toh*-LOHK	*pohl*
door	window	wall	ceiling	floor

картина	**вешалка**	**зеркало**	**полка**
kahr-TEE-*nah*	*v'*YEH-*shahl-kah*	*z'*YEHR-*kah-loh*	POHL-*kah*
picture	clothes-rack	mirror	shelf

Что это?
Shtoh EH-*toh?*
What is this?

Это дверь, окно, стена и т. д. (и так далее).
EH-*toh dv'yehr, ok*-NOH, *st'yeh*-NAH (*ee tahk* DAHL-*yeh-yeh*).
This is the door, the window, the wall, etc.

Очень хорошо!
OH-*chen khoh-roh*-SHOH!
Very good!

Спасибо!
Spah-SEE-*boh!*
Thank you!

1	2	3	4	5
один	**два**	**три**	**четыре**	**пять**
oh-DEEN	*dvah*	*tree*	*cheh*-TEE-*reh*	*p'yaht*

THINKING IN RUSSIAN

Answer the following questions aloud; then write the answers and check them on page 221.

1. Что э́то?
2. Это кни́га?
3. Это коро́бка?

4. Это стол?
5. Это зе́ркало?
6. Что э́то?

7. Это ла́мпа?
8. Это стул?
9. Что э́то?

10. Что э́то?
11. Это карти́на?
12. Это кни́га?

13. Это дверь?
14. Это ключ?
15. Что э́то?

УРОК 2

Одежда
Od-YEZH-*dah*
Clothing

Костюм *Kost*-YOOM Suit	**пиджак** *peed*-ZHAHK jacket	**жилет** *zheel*-YET vest	**брюки** *br'*YOO-*kee* trousers
рубашка *roo*-BAHSH-*kah* shirt	**галстук** GAHLS-*took* tie	**носок** *noh*-SOHK sock	**ботинок** *boh*-TEE-*nok* shoe
платье PLAHT-*yeh* dress	**блузка** BLOOZ-*kah* *blouse*	**юбка** YOOB-*kah* skirt	**чулок** *choo*-LOHK stocking
пальто *pahl*-TOH overcoat	**шляпа** *shl'*YAH-*pah* hat	**перчатка** *p'yehr*-CHAHT-*kah* glove	**платок** *plah*-TOHK handkerchief

сумка	**часы**	**карман**	**пояс**
SOOM-*kah*	*chah*-SEE	*kahr*-MAHN	POH-*yahs*
pocketbook	watch	pocket	belt

Это шляпа?
EH-*toh shl'*YAH-*pah?*
Is this a hat?

Да, это шляпа.
Dah, EH-*toh shl'*YAH-*pah.*
Yes, this is a hat.

Это платок?
EH-*toh plah*-TOHK?
Is this the handkerchief?

Нет, это не платок, это шляпа.
N'yet, EH-*toh n'yeh plah*-TOHK, EH-*toh shl'*YAH-*pah.*
No, this is not the handkerchief, this is the hat.

Что это, костюм или сумка?
Shtoh EH-*toh, kost*-YOOM EE-*lee* SOOM-*kah?*
What is this, the suit or the pocketbook?

Это костюм.
EH-*toh kost*-YOOM.
This is the suit.

Что это, пальто или пиджак?
Shtoh EH-*toh, pahl*-TOH EE-*lee peed*-ZHAHK?
What is this, the coat or the jacket?

Это не пальто и не пиджак, это рубашка.
EH-*toh n'yeh pahl*-TOH *ee n'yeh peed*-ZHAHK, EH-*toh roo*-BAHSH-*kah.*
This is not the coat and not the jacket, this is the shirt.

Костюм ли это или сумка?
Kost-YOOM *lee* EH-*toh* EE-*lee* SOOM-*kah?*
Is this the suit or the pocketbook?

Это ни костюм, ни сумка, это пальто.
EH-*toh nee kost*-YOOM, *nee* SOOM-*kah,* EH-*toh pahl*-TOH.
It is neither the suit nor the pocketbook, it is the overcoat.

6	7	8	9	10
шесть	**семь**	**восемь**	**девять**	**десять**
shest	*s'yem*	VOHS-*yem*	*d'*YEV-*yaht*	*d'*YES-*yaht*

HOW TO ASK A QUESTION: Direct questions are usually expressed in the form of a statement with a rising inflexion on the word in question:
Это часы? (EH-*toh chah*-SEE?) "Is this a watch?" or by the use of the particle **ли** placed immediately after the word in question. In this case the order of the words is reversed:
Часы ли это? (*Chah*-SEE *lee* EH-*toh?*) *"Is this a watch?"*

THINKING IN RUSSIAN

(Answers on page 221)

1. Это чулóк?
2. Это платóк?
3. Это гáлстук или сýмка?
4. Что э́то?

5. Это плáтье?
6. Часы́ ли э́то или дéньги?
7. Это карандáш?
8. Что э́то?

9. Это костю́м?
10. Это пальтó?
11. Боти́нок ли э́то?
12. Это пиджáк или брю́ки?
13. Это гáлстук?
14. Носóк ли э́то или перчáтка?
15. Это шля́па?
16. Что э́то?

УРОК 3

Какой это цвет?
Kah-KOY EH-*toh tsv'yet?*
What color is it?

Masculine

Чёрный	**белый**	**красный**	**синий**
CHOR-*nee*	*b'*YEH-*lee*	KRAHS-*nee*	SEE-*nee*
Black	white	red	blue

Feminine

чёрная	**белая**	**красная**	**синяя**
CHOR-*nah-yah*	*b'*YEH-*lah-yah*	KRAHS-*nah-yah*	SEEN-*yah-yah*
black	white	red	blue

Neuter

чёрное	**белое**	**красное**	**синее**
CHOR-*noh-yeh*	*b'*YEH-*loh-yeh*	KRAHS-*noh-yeh*	SEEN-*yeh-yeh*
black	white	red	blue

IMPORTANT NOTE: Do not think that Russian has three words for each color. It is simply that there are three genders in the Russian language: masculine, feminine, and neuter. These genders are indicated by varying endings. Do not worry too much about this, because constant practice will soon develop in you a feeling for the correct endings.

Masculine

серый	**зелёный**	**жёлтый**	**коричневый**
*s'*YEH-*ree*	*zel*-YOH-*nee*	ZHOHL-*tee*	*koh*-REECH-*n'yeh-vee*
gray	green	yellow	brown

Feminine

зелёная	**серая**	**жёлтая**	**коричневая**
zel-YOH-*nah-yah*	*s'*YEH-*rah-yah*	ZHOHL-*tah-yah*	*koh*-REECH-*n'yeh-vah-yah*
green	gray	yellow	brown

Neuter

зелёное	**серое**	**жёлтое**	**коричневое**
zel-YOH-*noh-yeh*	*s'*YEH-*roh-yeh*	ZHOHL-*toh-yeh*	*koh*-REECH-*n'yeh-voh-yeh*
green	gray	yellow	brown

Карандаш красный.
Kah-rahn-DAHSH KRAHS-*nee.*
The pencil is red.

Книга красная.
*K'*NEE-*gah* KRAHS-*nah-yah.*
The book is red.

Перо красное.
P'yeh-ROH KRAHS-*noh-yeh.*
The pen is red.

Потолок белый.
Poh-toh-LOHK *b'*YEH-*lee.*
The ceiling is white.

Бумага белая.
Boo-MAH-*gah b'*YEH-*lah-yah.*
The paper is white.

Платье белое.
PLAHT-*yeh b'*YEH-*loh-yeh.*
The dress is white.

Это чёрное перо?
EH-*toh* CHOR-*noh-yeh p'yeh*-ROH?
Is this the black pen?

Да, это чёрное перо.
Dah, EH-*toh* CHOR-*noh-yeh p'yeh*-ROH.
Yes, it is the black pen.

Это зелёная книга?
EH-*toh zel*-YOH-*nah-yah k'*NEE-*gah?*
Is this the green book?

Нет, это синяя книга.
N'yet, EH-*toh* SEEN-*yah-yah k'*NEE-*gah.*
No, it is the blue book.

Какой это галстук?
Kah-KOY EH-*toh* GAHLS-*took?*
Which tie is it?

Красный.
KRAHS-*nee.*
The red one.

Какая это перчатка?
Kah-KAH-*yah* EH-*toh* *p'yehr*-CHANT-*kah?*
Which glove is it?

Чёрная.
CHOR-*nah-yah.*
The black one.

Какое это перо?
Kah-KOH-*yeh* EH-*toh* *p'yeh*-ROH?
Which pen is it?

Жёлтое.
ZHOHL-*toh-yeh.*
The yellow one.

Это серый пиджак?
EH-*toh* *s'*YEH-*ree* *peed*-ZHAHK?
Is this the gray jacket?

Нет, это коричневый.
N'yet EH-*toh* *koh*-REECH-*n'yeh-vee.*
No, it is the brown one.

ATTENTION: **ё** is usually pronounced like "yo" in "York." However, after the letters **ж, ч, ш,** and **щ** it is pronounced "o" **жёлтый** (ZHOHL-*tee*) — "yellow," **чёрный** (CHOR-*nee*) "black," **шёлк** (*shohlk*) — "silk," **щётка** (SHCHOHT-*kah*) "brush." The **ё**-syllable is always stressed.

Ботинок чёрный.
Boh-TEE-*nok* CHOR-*nee.*
The shoe is black.

Рубашка белая.
Roo-BAHSH-*kah* *b'*YEH-*lah-yah.*
The shirt is white.

Платье серое.
PLAHT-*yeh* *s'*YEH-*roh-yeh.*
The dress is gray.

Какой этот ботинок?
Kah-KOY EH-*tot* *boh*-TEE-*nok?*
What color is this shoe?

Этот ботинок чёрный.
EH-*tot* *boh*-TEE-*nok* CHOR-*nee.*
This shoe is black.

Какая эта рубашка?
Kah-KAH-*yah* EH-*tah* *roo*-BAHSH-*kah?*
What color is this shirt?

Эта рубашка белая.
EH-*tah* *roo*-BAHSH-*kah* *b'*YEH-*lah-yah.*
This shirt is white.

Какое это платье?
Kah-KOH-*yeh* EH-*toh* PLAHT-*yeh?*
What color is this dress?

Это платье серое.
EH-*toh* PLAHT-*yeh* *s'*YEH-*roh-yeh.*
This dress is gray.

NOTE to Student: Какóй means "what kind of," "which." Here we translate it as "what color." Notice how **какóй** varies with a feminine or neuter noun.

Какого цвета этот воротник?
Kah-KOH-*voh tsv'*YEH-*tah* EH-*tot voh-rot*-NEEK?
What color is this collar?

Этот воротник белый.
EH-*tot voh-rot*-NEEK *b'*YEH-*lee.*
This collar is white.

Какого цвета эта перчатка?
Kah-KOH-*voh tsv'*YEH-*tah* EH-*tah p'yehr*-CHAHT-*kah?*
What color is this glove?

Эта перчатка жёлтая.
EH-*tah p'yehr*-CHAHT-*kah* ZHOHL-*tah-yah.*
This glove is yellow.

Какого цвета это платье?
Kah-KOH-*voh tsv'*YEH-*tah* EH-*toh* PLAHT-*yeh?*
What color is this dress?

Это платье синее.
EH-*toh* PLAHT-*yeh* SEEN-*yeh-yeh.*
This dress is blue.

NOTE to Student: After having learned **какóй, какáя, какóе** "which" you may well ask what about **какóго.** It is the masculine genitive case form meaning "of what", "of which". **IMPORTANT NOTE: э́тот** (masc.), **э́та** (fem.), **э́то** (neutr.) mean "this." Notice the meaning of the following constructions:

Это белый воротник.
EH-*toh b'*YEH-*lee voh-rot*-NEEK.
This is the white collar.

Этот белый воротник.
EH-*tot b'*YEH-*lee voh-rot*-NEEK.
This white collar.

Этот воротник белый.
EH-*tot voh-rot*-NEEK *b'*YEH-*lee.*
This collar is white.

11
одиннадцать
oh-DEEN-*nahd-tsaht.*

12
двенадцать
dv'yeh-NAHD-*tsaht.*

13
тринадцать
tree-NAHD-*tsaht.*

14
четырнадцать
cheh-TEER-*nahd-tsaht.*

15
пятнадцать
p'yaht-NAHD-*tsaht.*

Чёрный карандаш длинный или короткий?
CHOR-*nee kah-rahn*-DAHSH DLEEN-*nee* EE-*lee koh*-ROHT-*kee?*
Is the black pencil long or short?

Длинное ли жёлтое платье или короткое?
DLEEN-*noh-yeh lee* ZHOHL-*toh-yeh* PLAHT-*yeh* EE-*lee koh*-ROHT-*koh-yeh?*
Is the yellow dress long or short?

Коричневая книга широкая.
Koh-REECH-*n'yeh-vah-yah k'*NEE-*gah shee*-ROH-*kah-yah.*
The brown book is wide.

Красная книга узкая.
KRAHS-*nah-yah k'*NEE-*gah* OOZ-*kah-yah.*
The red book is narrow.

Окно широкое.
Ok-NOH *shee*-ROH-*koh-yeh.*
The window is wide.

Дверь узкая.
Dv'yehr OOZ-*kah-yah.*
The door is narrow.

Улица широкая.
OO-*lee-tsah shee*-ROH-*kah-yah.*
The street is wide.

Длинный ли чёрный карандаш?
DLEEN-*nee lee* CHOR-*nee kah-rahn*-DAHSH?
Is the black pencil long?

Да, он длинный.
Dah, ohn DLEEN-*nee.*
Yes it is long.

Длинная ли чёрная коробка?
DLEEN-*nah-yah lee* CHOR-*nah-yah koh*-ROHB-*kah?*
Is the black box long?

Нет, она короткая.
N'yet, oh-NAH *koh*-ROHT-*kah-yah.*
No, it is short.

Длинное ли жёлтое платье?
DLEEN-*noh-yeh lee* ZHOHL-*toh-yeh* PLAHT-*yeh?*
Is the yellow dress long?

Нет, оно короткое.
N'yet, oh-NOH *koh*-ROHT-*koh-yeh.*
No, it is short.

Коричневая книга длинная и широкая.
Koh-REECH-*n'yeh-vah-yah k'*NEE-*gah* DLEEN-*nah-yah ee shee*-ROH-*kah-yah.*
The brown book is long and wide.

Она большая.
Oh-NAH *bol*-SHAH-*yah.*
It is large.

Красная книга короткая и узкая.
KRAHS-*nah-yah k'*NEE-*gah koh*-ROHT-*kah-yah ee* OOZ-*kah-yah.*
The red book is short and narrow.

Она маленькая.
Oh-NAH MAHL-*yen-kah-yah.*
It is small.

Чёрное платье длинное или короткое?
CHOR-*noh-yeh* PLAHT-*yeh* DLEEN-*noh-yeh* EE-*lee koh*-ROHT-*koh-yeh?*
Is the black dress long or short?

Оно длинное.
Oh-NOH DLEEN-*noh-yeh.*
It is long.

Ленинград большой.
Leh-neen-GRAHD *bol*-SHOY.
Leningrad is large.

Москва большая.
Mosk-VAH *bol*-SHAH-*yah.*
Moscow is large.

Минск маленький.
Meensk MAHL-*yen-kee.*
Minsk is small.

Большой ли город Минск?
Bol-SHOY *lee* GOH-*rod Meensk?*
Is Minsk a large city?

Нет, он не большой.
N'yet, ohn n'yeh bol-SHOY.
No, it is not large.

IMPORTANT NOTE: **Он** means "he," **oнá**—"she," **онó**—"it." Did you notice that in Russian you use the pronouns **он** and **онá** referring not only to animate beings but also to things? **Стол**—"table" is masculine and, therefore, in referring to it you use the masculine pronoun **он**—"he." **Кни́га** "book" is feminine. Accordingly, referring to it you use **онá**—"she". As you have also noticed, the gender of a town may be masculine, feminine or neuter.

Большая ли Америка или маленькая?
Bol-SHAH-*yah lee Ah*-MEH-*ree-kah* EE-*lee* MAHL-*yen-kah-yah?*
Is America large or small?

Она большая.
Oh-NAH *bol*-SHAH-*yah.*
It is large.

Египет большой?
Yeh-GGEE-*pet bol*-SHOY?
Is Egypt large?

Да, большой.
Dah, bol-SHOY.
Yes, it is large.

Советский Союз маленький?
Sov-YET-*skee Soh*-YOOZ MAHL-*yen-kee?*
Is the Soviet Union small?

Нет, он большой.
N'yet, ohn bol-SHOY.
No, it is large.

Крым маленький.
Kreem MAHL-*yen-kee.*
The Crimea is small.

Китай большой.
Kee-TIGH *bol*-SHOY.
China is large.

Сибирь большая.
See-BEER *bol*-SHAH-*yah.*
Siberia is large.

16
шестнадцать
shest-NAHD-*tsaht*

17
семнадцать
s'yem-NAHD-*tsaht*

18
восемнадцать
vos-yem-NAHD-*tsaht*

19
девятнадцать
d'yev-yaht-NAHD-*tsaht*

20
двадцать
DVAHD-*tsaht*

THINKING IN RUSSIAN

(Answers on page 222)

1. Дли́нная ли кра́сная кни́га?
2. Широ́кая ли она́?
3. Она́ больша́я?
4. Коро́ткая ли зелёная кни́га?
5. Узкая ли она́?
6. Ма́ленькая ли она́?
7. Како́го цве́та больша́я кни́га?
8. Како́го цве́та ма́ленькая кни́га?
9. Како́го цве́та дли́нное пла́тье?
10. Оно́ кра́сное?
11. Чёрное пла́тье дли́нное?
12. Коро́ткое ли оно́?
13. Како́го цве́та коро́ткое пла́тье?
14. Чёрное ли оно́ или зелёное?
15. Широ́кое окно́ си́нее или кра́сное?
16. Како́го цве́та у́зкое окно́?
17. Се́рое ли оно́?
18. Широ́кое ли кра́сное окно́?
19. Широ́кое ли си́нее окно́ или у́зкое?
20. Большо́е ли си́нее окно́?
21. Кра́сное окно́ ма́ленькое?
22. Ма́ленькое окно́ кра́сное или жёлтое?
23. Большо́е окно́ зелёное или си́нее?

УРОК 5

Кто это?
Ktoh EH-*toh?*
Who is it?

Господин; гражданин
*Gos-poh-*DEEN*; grahzh-dah-*NEEN.

Gentleman; citizen.

госпожа; гражданка; дама
*gos-poh-*ZHAH*; grahzh-*DAHN*-kah;* DAH-*mah.*

Mrs.; citizen (fem.); lady.

человек	**мужчина**
*cheh-lov-*YEK	*moozh-*CHEE*-nah*
person, man	man

женщина	**барышня**
ZHENSH-*chee-nah*	BAH-*reesh-n'yah*
woman	young lady, girl

Кто этот господин?
Ktoh EH-*tot gos-poh-*DEEN*?*
Who is this gentleman?

Это господин Берлиц.
EH-*toh gos-poh-*DEEN *Berlitz.*
This is Mr. Berlitz.

Кто этот мужчина?
Ktoh EH-*tot moozh-*CHEE*-nah?*
Who is this man?

Кто эта дама?
Ktoh EH-*tah* DAH-*mah?*
Who is this lady?

Это госпожа Берлиц.
EH-*toh gos-poh-*ZHAH *Berlitz.*
This is Mrs. Berlitz.

Это господин Павлов.
EH-*toh gos-poh-*DEEN PAHV-*lov.*
It is Mr. Pavlov.

Кто эта женщина?
Ktoh EH-*tah* ZHENSH-*chee-nah?*
Who is this woman?

Это госпожа Петрова.
EH-*toh gos-poh*-ZHAH *Pet*-ROH-*vah.*
It is Mrs. Petrov.

Это гражданин Павлов.
EH-*toh grahzh-dah*-NEEN PAHV-*lov.*
It is citizen Pavlov.

Это гражданка Петрова.
EH-*toh grahzh*-DAHN-*kah Pet*-ROH-*vah.*
It is "citizeness" Petrov.

Кто эта барышня?
Ktoh EH-*tah* BAH-*reesh-n'yah?*
Who is that young lady?

Это Катя Шипшева.
EH-*toh* KAHT-*yah* SHIP-*sheh-vah.*
It is Kate Shipshev.

IMPORTANT NOTE: In the Russia of today, "citizen" has replaced "Mr." as form of address. The word **това́рищ** (*toh*-VAH-*reeshch*) "comrade" is also used, but is for all practical purposes restricted to Communist party members among themselves. Here is a safe rule to follow: if in the USSR use **граждани́н;** elsewhere use **господи́н.**

Вы — господин Раевский?
Vwee gos-poh-DEEN *Rah*-YEV-*skee?*
Are you Mr. Rayevsky?

Нет, я — Егоров.
Nyet, yah Yeh-GOH-*rov.*
No, I am Yegorov.

WATCH OUT!—Don't call yourself "Mister" **(господи́н)** or "Mrs." **(госпожа́)** in Russian, when you introduce yourself.

Кто там идёт?
Ktoh tahm eed-YOHT?
Who is going there?

Это господин Зубов.
EH-*toh gos-poh*-DEEN ZOO-*bov.*
It is Mr. Zoubov.

Куда он идёт?
Koo-DAH *ohn eed*-YOHT?
Where is he going?

Он идёт сюда.
Ohn eed-YOHT *s'yoo*-DAH.
He is coming here.

Где г-жа Фомина?
Gd'yeh gos-poh-ZHAH *Foh-mee*-NAH?
Where is Mrs. Fomin?

Она здесь, она никуда не идёт.
Oh-NAH *zd'yes, oh*-NAH *nee-koo*-DAH *n'yeh eed*-YOHT.
She is here, she isn't going anywhere.

NOTE: Никуда́ means "nowhere." Notice the double negation. The literal translation is: "she is not going nowhere."

Куда идёт г. Харитонов?
Koo-DAH *eed*-YOHT *gos-poh*-DEEN *Khah-ree*-TOH-*nov?*
Where is Mr. Kharitonov going?

Он идёт домой.
Ohn eed-YOHT *doh*-MOY.
He is going home.

NOTE to Student: In spite of the fact that **идёт** (*eed*-YOHT) may mean "goes" or "comes," the Russians really know whether they are coming or going. It is used only when the circumstances will make the meaning obvious. As we shall see later, there are prefixes which make the meaning definitely "goes" or "comes."

Кто вы?
Ktoh vwee?
Who are you?

Я Корнилов.
Yah Kor-NEE-*lov.*
I am Mr. *Kornilov.*

Кто я?
Ktoh yah?
Who am I?

Вы капитан Марков.
Vwee kah-pee-TAHN MAHR-*kov.*
You are Captain Markov.

Я — русский.
Yah—ROOS-*skee.*
I am Russian.

Вы — американец.
Vwee—ah-meh-ree-KAHN-*yets.*
You are an American.

Он — татарин.
Ohn tah-TAH-*reen.*
He is a Tartar.

NOTE to Student: In a sentence where the word "is" or "are" or "am" is omitted a dash is placed before a predicate noun to separate it from the subject. If the subject is a pronoun (**я, вы,** etc.) the dash is optional. For example: "I am a Russian": **я ру́сский** or **я—ру́сский.** "Moscow is a city": **Москва́—го́род.**

Этот господин — англичанин?
EH-*tot gos-poh*-DEEN—*ahn-glee*-CHAH-*neen?*
Is this gentleman an Englishman?

Нет, он не англичанин, он мексиканец.
N'yet, on n'yeh ahn-glee-CHAH-*neen, on mek-see*-KAHN-*yets.*
No, he is not an Englishman, he is a Mexican.

Эта дама — американка.
EH-*tah* DAH-*mah—ah-me-ree*-KAHN-*kah.*
This lady is an American.

Госпожа Браун — англичанка.
Gos-poh-ZHAH *Brown—ahn-glee*-CHAHN-*kah.*
Mrs. Brown is an Englishwoman.

Антонов — китаец?
Ahn-TOH-*nov—kee*-TAH-*yets?*
Is Mr. Antonov a Chinese?

Нет, он не китаец, он русский.
N'yet, on n'yeh kee-TAH-*yets, on* ROOS-*skee.*
No, he is not a Chinese, he is Russian.

NOTE on Nationalities: In English the word "Russian" is written with a capital "R"; in Russian it is written with a small "**р.**" A Russian is **ру́сский,** an American **америка́нец,** an Englishman **англича́нин,** a Frenchman **францу́з,** (*frahn*-TSOOZ) a German **не́мец** (*n'*YEM-*yets*); but a Russian woman is **ру́сская** (ROOS-*skah-yah*) and American, English, French, and German women are **америка́нка, англича́нка, францу́женка** (*frahn*-TSOO-*zhen-kah*), **не́мка** (*n'*YEM-*kah*) respectively. You will encounter other nationalities in the text.

Мой карандаш красный.
Moy kah-rahn-DAHSH KRAHS-*nee.*
My pencil is red.

Ваш карандаш зелёный.
Vahsh kah-rahn-DAHSH *zel*-YOH-*nee.*
Your pencil is green.

Моя книга красная.
Moh-YAH *k'*NEE-*gah* KRAHS-*nah-yah.*
My book is red.

Ваша книга зелёная.
VAH-*shah k'*NEE-*gah zel*-YOH-*nah-yah.*
Your book is green.

Моё перо красное.
Moh-YOH *p'yeh*-ROH KRAHS-*noh-yeh.*
My pen is red.

Ваше перо зелёное.
VAH-*sheh p'yeh*-ROH *zel*-YOH-*noh-yeh.*
Your pen is green.

Ваш ли это карандаш?
Vahsh lee EH-*toh kah-rahn*-DAHSH*?*
Is this your pencil?

Нет, это не мой карандаш.
N'yet, EH-*toh n'yeh moy kah-rahn*-DAHSH.
No, it is not my pencil.

Чей этот карандаш?
Chay EH-*tot kah-rahn*-DAHSH*?*
Whose is this pencil?

Это ваш карандаш.
EH-*toh vahsh kah-rahn*-DAHSH.
It is your pencil.

Чья эта шляпа?
Ch'yah EH-*tah shl'*YAH-*pah?*
Whose is this hat?

Это моя шляпа.
EH-*toh moh*-YAH *shl'*YAH-*pah.*
It is my hat.

Чьё это пальто?
Ch'yoh EH-*toh pahl*-TOH*?*
Whose is this coat?

Это моё пальто.
EH-*toh moh*-YOH *pahl*-TOH.
It is my coat.

NOTE to Student: Observe how the following possessive pronouns vary according to the gender of the word they modify.

	Masculine	Feminine	Neuter
"my"	**мой**	**моя́**	**моё**
"your"	**ваш**	**ва́ша**	**ва́ше**
"whose"	**чей**	**чья**	**чьё**

Какой карандаш красный?
Kah-KOY *kah-rahn*-DAHSH KRAHS-*nee?*
Which pencil is red?

Мой карандаш красный.
Moy kah-rahn-DAHSH KRAHS-*nee.*
My pencil is red.

Чей воротник белый?
Chay voh-rot-NEEK *b'*YEH-*lee?*
Whose collar is white?

Мой воротник белый.
Moy voh-rot-NEEK *b'*YEH-*lee.*
My collar is white.

Чья рубашка синяя?
Ch'yah roo-BAHSH-*kah* SEEN-*yah-yah?*
Whose shirt is blue?

Ваша рубашка синяя.
VAH-*shah roo*-BAHSH-*kah* SEEN-*yah-yah.*
Your shirt is blue.

Чьё пальто зелёное?
Ch'yoh pahl-TOH *zel*-YOH-*noh-yeh?*
Whose coat is green?

Ваше пальто зелёное.
VAH-*sheh pahl*-TOH *zel*-YOH-*noh-yeh.*
Your coat is green.

Какой мой воротник?
Kah-KOY *moy voh-rot*-NEEK*?*
What color is my collar?

Ваш воротник белый.
Vahsh voh-rot-NEEK *b'*YEH-*lee.*
Your collar is white.

Какого цвета ваша рубашка?
Kah-KOH-*voh tsv'*YEH-*tah* VAH-*shah roo*-BAHSH-*kah?*
What color is your shirt?

Она синяя.
Oh-NAH SEEN-*yah-yah.*
It is blue.

Чья шляпа чёрная?
*Ch'yah shl'*YAH-*pah* CHOR-*nah-yah?*
Whose hat is black?

Ваша шляпа чёрная.
VAH-*shah shl'*YAH-*pah* CHOR-*nah-yah.*
Your hat is black.

21	22	23
двадцать один	**двадцать два**	**двадцать три**
DVAHD-*tsaht oh*-DEEN	DVAHD-*tsaht dvah*	DVAHD-*tsaht tree*

24	25
двадцать четыре	**двадцать пять**
DVAHD-*tsaht cheh*-TEE-*reh*	DVAHD-*tsaht p'yaht*

THINKING IN RUSSIAN

(Answers on page 222)

1. Кто вы?
2. Вы америка́нец? (Вы америка́нка?)
3. Вы учи́тель и́ли учени́к?
4. Вы — ру́сский (вы — ру́сская)?
5. Кто я?
6. Гали́на Ула́нова — америка́нка и́ли ру́сская?
7. Кто Гали́на Ула́нова?
8. Госпожа́ Чан-Кай-Шек италья́нка и́ли китая́нка?
9. Толсто́й — испа́нец?
10. Како́го цве́та мой га́лстук?
11. Кака́я ва́ша шля́па?
12. Чей э́то пи́джак?
13. Чья э́то кни́га?
14. Чьё э́то пальто́?
15. Генера́л Мака́ртур япо́нец?
16. Генера́л Ма́ршалл францу́з?

УРОК 6

Где?

Gd'yeh?

Where?

Книга на столе.
*K'*NEE-*gah-nah stol*-YEH.
The book is on the table.

Бумага в книге.
Boo-MAH-*gah v k'*NEEG-*yeh.*
The paper is in the book.

Платок в кармане.
Plah-TOHK *v kahr*-MAHN-*yeh.*
The handkerchief is in the pocket.

Кошка на диване.
KOHSH-*kah nah dee*-VAHN-*yeh.*
The cat is on the sofa.

IMPORTANT NOTE: You have just encountered what Russians laughingly call the PREPOSITIONAL case. The prepositional case is never used without a preposition. After the prepositions **в** "in" and **на** "on" it is used to denote the location of a thing. In most cases, nouns of all genders change their endings to **-е** in the prepositional case. For example: **дом** (m.) "house"—**в до́ме** (*v* DOM-*yeh*) "in the house"; **коро́бка** (f.) "box"—**в коро́бке** (*v koh*-ROHB-*keh*) "in the box"; **село́** (n.) "village"—**в селе́** (*v sel*-YEH) "in the village." Exceptions to this rule are feminine nouns ending in **-ь** and **ия.** They change their endings to **-и** instead of **-е.** Thus: **степь** (*st'yep*) "steppe," "prairie," **в степи́** (*v st'yeh*-PEE) "in the steppe"; **а́рмия** (AHR-*mee-yah*) "army," **в а́рмии** (*v* AHR-*mee-ee*) "in the army." (For details see Appendix, pages 261 and 262).

REMEMBER in particular that the names of conutries ending in **-ия** take **-и** instead of **-е: Росси́я** (*Ros*-SEE-*yah*) "Russia"—**в Росси́и** (*v Ros*-SEE-*ee*) "in Russia"; **Брази́лия** (*Brah*-ZEE-*lee-yah*) "Brazil"—**в Брази́лии,** "in Brazil."

Рим в Италии.
Reem v Ee-TAH-*lee-ee.*
Rome is in Italy.

Париж во Франции.
Pah-REEZH *vo* FRAHN-*tsee-ee.*
Paris is in France.

Киев в Малороссии.
KEE-*yev v Mah-loh*-ROHS-*see-ee.*
Kiev is in Little Russia.

Сан Франциско в Калифорнии.
Sahn Frahn-TSEES-*koh v Kah-lee*-FOHR-*nee-ee.*
San Francisco is in California.

Коробка под столом.
Koh-ROHB-*kah pod stoh*-LOHM.
The box is under the table.

Перчатка под книгой.
P'yehr-CHAHT-*kah pod k'*NEE-*goy.*
The glove is under the book.

Стул перед столом.
*Stool p'*YEH-*red stoh*-LOHM.
The chair is in front of the table.

За столом стена.
Zah stoh-LOHM *st'yeh*-NAH.
Behind the table is the wall.

Стол между стулом и стеной.
*Stohl m'*YEZH-*doo* STOO-*lom ee st'yeh*-NOY.
The table is between the chair and the wall.

Лампа висит над столом.
LAHM-*pah vee*-SEET *nahd stoh*-LOHM.
The lamp hangs above the table.

Стол под лампой.
Stohl pod LAHM-*poy.*
The table is under the lamp.

Кошка под диваном.
KOHSH-*kah pod dee*-VAH-*nom.*
The cat is under the sofa.

А где попугай?
Ah gd'yeh poh-poo-GUY?
And where is the parrot?

Попугай в клетке?
Poh-poo-GUY *v kl'*YET-*keh?*
Is the parrot in the cage?

Нет, он за клеткой.
*N'yet, ohn zah kl'*YET-*koy.*
No, he is behind the cage.

The **INSTRUMENTAL CASE:** In the preceding sentences the instrumental case is used after the prepositions **пéред** "in front of," **за** "behind," **над** "above," **под** "under" and **мéжду** "between." There are still other prepositions which require the instrumental as you will see later.

Masculine and neuter nouns form the instrumental in **-ом** or **-ем** depending on whether their endings are hard or soft. Thus: **стол** (*stohl*) "table," **за столóм** (*zah stoh*-LOHM) "behind the table," **пóле** (POHL-*yeh*) "field," **над пóлем** (*nahd* POHL-*yem*) "above the field."

Feminine nouns ending in **-а** change it to **-ой** (or **-ою**): **за стенóй** (*zah st'yeh*-NOY) or **за стенóю** (*zah st'yeh*-NOH-*yoo*) "behind the wall". Those ending in **-я** take **-ей** or **-ею: няня** (*n'*YAHN-*yah*) "nurse" **с няней** (*s n'*YAHN-*yay*) or **с нянею** (*s' n'*YAHN-*yeh-yoo*) "with the nurse."

Я стою перед столом.
Yah stoh-YOO *p'*YEH-*red stoh*-LOHM.
I am standing in front of the table.

Стол передо мной.
*Stohl p'*YEH-*reh-doh mnoy.*
The table is in front of me.

Стул стоит за мной.
Stool stoh-EET *zah mnoy.*
The chair stands behind me.

Я стою перед стулом.
Yah stoh-YOO *p'*YEH-*red* STOO-*lom.*
I am standing in front of the chair.

Вы сидите перед роялем.
Vwee see-DEET-*yeh p'*YEH-*red roh*-YAHL-*yem.*
You are standing in front of the piano.

Рояль перед вами.
Roh-YAHL *p'*YEH-*red* VAH-*mee.*
The piano is in front of you.

Я сижу перед столом.
Yah see-ZHOO *p'*YEH-*red stoh*-LOHM.
I am sitting in front of the table.

Вы сидите за столом.
Vwee see-DEET-*yeh zah stoh*-LOHM.
You are sitting behind the table.

Где стол?
Gd'yeh stohl?
Where is the table?

Стол между нами.
*Stohl m'*YEZH-*doo* NAH-*mee.*
The table is between us.

Потолок над нами.
Poh-toh-LOHK *nahd* NAH-*mee.*
The ceiling is above us.

Пол под нами.
Pohl pohd NAH-*mee.*
The floor is below us.

NOTE on PERSONAL PRONOUNS: **Мной** or **мно́ю,** (*mnoy* or MNOH-*yoo*), **ва́ми** (VAH-*mee*), and **на́ми** (NAH-*mee*) are the instrumental cases of **я** (*yah*) "I", **вы** (*vwee*) "you", and **мы** (*mee*) "we" respectively.

Синяя шляпа лежит перед вами на столе.
SEEN-*yah-yah shl'*YAH-*pah l'yeh*-ZHEET *p'*YEH-*red* VAH-*mee nah stol*-YEH.
The blue hat lies on the table in front of you.

Этот карандаш синий.
EH-*tot kah-rahn*-DAHSH SEE-*nee*.
This pencil is blue.

Тот карандаш красный.
Toht kah-rahn-DAHSH KRAHS-*nee*.
That pencil is red.

Эта книга русская.
EH-*tah k'*NEE-*gah* ROOS-*skah-yah*.
This book is Russian.

Та книга испанская.
*Tah k'*NEE-*gah ees*-PAHN-*skah-yah*.
That book is Spanish.

Это окно большое.
EH-*toh ok*-NOH *bol*-SHOH-*yeh*.
This window is large.

То окно маленькое.
Toh ok-NOH MAHL-*yen-koh-yeh*.
That window is small.

Одна перчатка здесь, а другая там.
Od-NAH *p'yehr*-CHAHT-*kah zd'yes ah droo*-GAH-*yah tahm*.
One glove is here and the other is there.

Я тут в комнате, а мой приятель там на улице.
Yah toot v KOHM-*naht-yeh, a moy pree*-YAHT-*yel tahm nah* oo-*lee-tseh*.
I am here in the room, and my friend is there in the street.

NOTE to Student: "а" usually means "and" as in the above sentences. After a negation **"а"** means "but." Thus:
Киев не в Сибири, а в Малороссии.
KEE-*yev n'yeh v See*-BEE-*ree, ah v Mah-loh*-ROHS-*see-ee*.
Kiev is not in Siberia, but in Little Russia.

Здесь ли господин Берлиц?
Zd'yes lee gos-poh-DEEN *Berlitz?*
Is Mr. Berlitz here?

Да, он тут.
Dah, ohn toot.
Yes, he is here.

Г-жа Толстая в России?
Gos-poh-ZHAH *Tol*-STAH-*yah v Ros*-SEE-*ee?*
Is Mrs. Tolstoy in Russia?

Нет, она в Америке.
N'yet, oh-NAH *v Ah*-MEH-*ree-keh*.
No, she is in America.

Где генерал Тимошенко?
Gd'yeh ggen-yeh-RAHL *Tee-moh*-SHEN-*koh?*
Where is General Timoshenko?

Он в Москве.
*Ohn v mosk-v'*YEH.
He is in Moscow.

NOTE on Russian Names: Did you notice that Mrs. Tolstoy is in Russian Tolstaya? The reason for this is that Russian surnames ending in **-ой, -ый, -ов, -ев, -ин,** and **-ский, ской,** are masculine while the respective feminine forms are **-ая -ова, -ева, -ина, -ская.**

Толстой (*Tol*-STOY) "Mr. Tolstoy," **Толстая** (*Tol*-STAH-*yah*) "Mrs. Tolstoy," **Чехов** (CHEH-*khov*) "Mr. Chekhov," **Чехова** (CHEH-*khoh-vah*) Mrs. Chekhov," **Пушкин** (POOSH-*keen*) "Mr. Pushkin," **Пушкина** (POOSH-*kee-nah*) "Mrs. Pushkin."

Names in **-енко** have no different forms for the two genders: **г. Короленко** (*gos-poh*-DEEN *Koh-rol*-YEN-*koh*) "Mr. Korolenko"; **г-жа Короленко** (*gos-poh*-ZHAH *Koh-rol*-YEN-*koh*) "Mrs. Korolenko."

Тифлис на Кавказе.
Teef-LEES *nah Kahv*-KAHZ-*yeh.*
Tiflis is in the Caucasus.

Уфа на Урале.
Oo-FAH *nah Oo*-RAHL-*yeh.*
Ufa is in the Urals.

THINKING IN RUSSIAN

(Answers on page 222)

1. Где кни́га, под столо́м и́ли на столе́?
2. Под сту́лом ли она́?
3. Где шля́па, на сту́ле и́ли под сту́лом?
4. Где перча́тка, в шля́пе и́ли под шля́пой?
5. Учи́тель под сту́лом?
6. Где он, под столо́м и́ли на столе́?
7. Пе́ред ва́ми ли он и́ли за ва́ми?
8. Что пе́ред столо́м?
9. Что на сту́ле?
10. Что над ва́ми?
11. Что ме́жду учи́телем и коро́бкой?
12. В шля́пе ли перо́ и́ли под шля́пой? Где оно́?
13. Что виси́т над столо́м?
14. На столе́ ли перо́ и́ли на сту́ле?
15. Что там?
16. Кто тут?
17. Где Япо́ния?
18. Где Ки́ев?
19. Где Малоро́ссия?
20. Где Баку́?

УРОК 7

Что делает учитель?

*Shtoh d'*YEH-*lah-yet oo*-CHEET-*yel?*

What does the teacher do?

Учитель берёт книгу.
Oo-CHEET-*yel b'yehr*-YOHT *k'*NEE-*goo.*
The teacher takes the book.

Учитель берёт карандаш.
Oo-CHEET-*yel b'yehr*-YOHT *kah-rahn*-DAHSH.
The teacher takes the pencil.

Он кладёт книгу на стол.
Ohn klahd-YOHT *k'*NEE-*goo nah stohl.*
He puts the book on the table.

Он кладёт карандаш в коробку.
Ohn klahd-YOHT *kah-rahn*-DAHSH *v koh*-ROHB-*koo.*
He puts the pencil into the box.

IMPORTANT NOTE: In the last lesson we saw that **на столé** means "on the table," **в корóбке** "in the box," indicating mere *position* (locative or prepositional case). Here, **на стол, в корóбку** is used to mark the *action* of putting something onto the table, into the box (accusative case). When the car *is in* the garage you say **в гарáже** (locative), but if you *put* the car into the garage, you say **в гарáж** (accusative).

Что берёт учитель?
*Shtoh b'yehr-*YOHT *oo-*CHEET-*yel?*
What does the teacher take?

Берёт ли он перо?
*B'yehr-*YOHT *lee ohn p'yeh-*ROH*?*
Does he take the pen?

Нет он не берёт перо.
*N'yet, ohn n'yeh b'yehr-*YOHT *p'yeh'*ROH.
No, he is not taking the pen.

Он берёт карандаш.
*Ohn b'yehr-*YOHT *kah-rahn-*DAHSH.
He is taking the pencil.

Кладёт ли учитель карандаш на стол?
*Klahd-*YOHT *lee oo-*CHEET-*yel kah-rahn-*DAHSH *nah stohl?*
Does the teacher put the pencil on the table?

Нет, он кладёт карандаш в коробку.
*N'yet, ohn klahd-*YOHT *kah-rahn-*DAHSH *v koh-*ROHB-*koo.*
No, he puts the pencil into the box.

Кто берёт карандаш?
*Ktoh b'yehr-*YOHT *kah-rahn-*DAHSH*?*
Who takes the pencil?

Учитель берёт карандаш.
*Oo-*CHEET-*yel b'yehr-*YOHT *kah-rahn-*DAHSH.
The teacher takes the pencil.

WATCH OUT! — The ending of the verb shows who is performing the action. In the present tense an **-у** or **-ю** at the ond of a verb indicate the first person: **я беру́**—"I take," **я говорю́**—"I speak." A **-те** ending indicates "you"; **вы идёте**—"you go," **вы говори́те**—"you speak." A **-т** ending indicates the third person "he, she, it or they": **он идёт**—"he goes," **она́ говори́т**—"she speaks," **они берут**—*oh-*NEE *b'yeh-*ROOT — "they take".

Я учитель. Я беру мел. Возьмите, пожалуйста, перо.
*Yah oo-*CHEET-*yel. Yah b'yeh-*ROO *m'yel. Voz-*MEET-*yeh, poh-*ZHAH-*looy-stah pyeh-*ROH.
I am the teacher. I take the chalk. Please, take the pen.

Вы берёте перо.
*Vwee b'yehr-*YOHT-*yeh p'yeh-*ROH.
You are taking the pen.

Положите, пожалуйста, перо в ящик.
*Poh-loh-*ZHEET-*yeh, poh-*ZHAH-*looy-stah, p'yeh-*ROH *v* YAHSH-*cheek.*
Please, put the pen into the drawer.

HELPFUL HINT: You may wonder what relation **возьми́те** has to **беру́**. As a matter of fact, **возьми́те** is from another verb used as the imperative for "take." In the same manner the imperative **положи́те** is not related to **кладу́** but is borrowed from another verb. Fortunately for the student, however, there are not many exceptions of this kind.

Что я делаю теперь?
*Shtoh yah d'*YEH-*lah-yoo t'yep*-YEHR?
What am I doing now?

Беру ли я газету?
B'yeh-ROO *lee yah gahz*-YEH-*too?*
Am I taking the newspaper?

Да, вы берёте газету.
Dah, vwee b'yehr-YOHT-*yeh gahz*-YEH-*too.*
Yes, you are taking the newspaper.

Кладёте ли вы перо в ящик?
Klahd-YOHT-*yeh lee vwee p'yeh*-ROH *v* YASH-*cheek?*
Do you put the pen into the drawer?

Да, я кладу перо в ящик.
Dah, yah klah-DOO *p'yeh*-ROH *v* YAHSH-*cheek.*
Yes, I put the pen into the drawer.

Куда вы кладёте перо?
Koo-DAH *vwee klahd*-YOHT-*yeh p'yeh*-ROH?
Where do you put the pen?

Я кладу его в ящик.
Yah klah-DOO *yeh*-VOH *v* YAHSH-*cheek.*
I put it into the drawer.

Куда вы кладёте сумку?
Koo-DAH *vwee klahd*-YOHT-*yeh* SOOM-*koo?*
Where do you put the pocketbook?

Я кладу её в шкаф.
Yah klah-DOO *yeh*-YOH *v shkahf.*
I put it into the closet.

NOTE on Accusative: The accusative of masculine nouns denoting inanimate things and of all neuter nouns is the same as the nominative, thus: **дом** "house" (nom.), **я ви́жу дом**—"I see a house" (acc.); **перо́**—"pen" (nom.), **я беру́ перо́**—"I take the pen" (acc.).

The accusative of masculine nouns indicating animate beings (persons, animals) ends in **-а** (after hard consonants) or in **-я** (following soft consonants), for example: **челове́к**—"man" (nom.), **я вижу челове́ка** (yah VEE-*zhoo cheh-lov*-YEH-*kah*) "I see a man" (acc.); **конь** (kohn) "horse" (nom.), **я вижу коня** (*yah* VEE-*zhoo kon*-YAH) "I see the horse" (acc.).

The accusative of feminine nouns varies according to their endings. Nouns ending in **-а** have **-у** in the accusative. Those ending in **-я** have **-ю**, while the accusative of those ending in **-ь** is the same as the nominative. Thus: **муха** (MOO-*khah*) "fly" (nom.), accusative: **муху** (MOO-*khoo*), **я ловлю муху** (*yah lovl*-YOO MOO-*khoo*)—"I am catching the fly."

кухня (KOOKH-*n'yah*) "kitchen," accusative: **кухню** (KOOKH-*n'yoo*)—**я иду в кухню** (*yah ee*-DOO *v* KOOKH-*n'yoo*)—"I am going to the kitchen."

степь (*st'yep*) "steppe," "prairie," accusative: **степь** (*st'yep*), **я люблю степь** (*yah l'yoobl*-YOO *st'yep*)—"I love the prairie."

Учитель стоит у окна.
Oo-CHEET-*yel stoh*-EET *oo ok*-NAH.
The teacher is standing by the window.

Вы его видите.
Vwee yeh-VOH VEE-*deet-yeh.*
You see him.

Он открывает окно.
*Ohn ot-kree-*VAH*-yet ok-*NOH.
He opens the window.

Он его открывает.
*On yeh-*VOH *ot-kree-*VAH*-yet.*
He is opening it.

Ольга играет на рояле.
OHL-*gah ee-*GRAH*-yet nah roh-*YAHL*-yeh.*
Olga plays the piano.

Вы её слышите.
*Vwee yeh-*YOH SLEE*-sheet-yeh.*
You hear her.

NOTE to Student: The accusative of the personal pronoun **он, онá, онó**—"he," "she," "it,' has, as in English, three forms, according to the gender of the object it represents: **его** (*yeh-*VOH) m.—"him," **её** (*yeh-*YOH) f.—"her," and **его** (*yeh-*VOH) n.—"it." Note that the masculine and neuter forms are the same.

Сумка на столе.
SOOM*-kah nah stol-*YEH.
The pocketbook is on the table.

Вы её берёте со стола.
*Vwee yeh-*YOH *b'yehr-*YOHT*-yeh soh stoh-*LAH.
You are taking it from the table.

Зеркало в ящике.
Z'YEHR*-kah-loh v* YAHSH*-cheek-yeh.*
The mirror is in the drawer.

Вы его берёте из ящика.
*Vwee yeh-*VOH *b'yehr-*YOHT*-yeh eez* YAHSH*-chee-kah.*
You are taking it from the drawer.

WATCH OUT!—Did you notice that in the above two sentences two different Russian prepositions are used where we say in English "from." It depends on whether the object is lying "on" something, or "in" something.

Учитель идёт в коридор.
*Oo-*CHEET*-yel eed-*YOHT *v koh-ree-*DOHR.
The teacher goes to the corridor.

Куда он идёт?
*Koo-*DAH *ohn eed-*YOHT?
Where is he going?

Он выходит из комнаты.
*On vwee-*KHOH*-deet eez* KOHM*-nah-tee.*
He leaves the room.

Откуда он выходит?
*Ot-*KOO*-dah ohn vwee-*KHOH*-deet?*
From where does he leave?

Вы идёте в комнату.
*Vwee eed-*YOHT*-yeh v* KOHM*-nah-too.*
You are going into the room.

Вы входите в комнату.
Vwee VKHOH*-deet-yeh v* KOHM*-nah-too.*
You are entering the room.

Кто выходит из комнаты, а кто входит?
*Ktoh vwee-*KHOH*-deet eez* KOHM*-nah-tee, ah ktoh* VKHOH*-deet?*
Who is leaving the room and who is entering?

Я вхожу в комнату, а учитель выходит из комнаты.
*Yah vkhoh-*ZHOO *v* KOHM-*nah-too, ah oo-*CHEET-*yel vwee-*KHOH-*deet eez* KOHM-*nah-tee.*
I am entering the room and the teacher is leaving the room.

Откуда вы приходите?
*Ot-*KOO-*dah vwee pree-*KHOH-*deet-yeh?*
From where are you coming?

Оттуда, из коридора.
*Ot-*TOO-*dah, eez koh-ree-*DOH-*rah.*
From there, from the corridor.

Куда вы приходите?
*Koo-*DAH *vwee pree-*KHOH-*deet-yeh?*
Where are you coming?

Сюда, в комнату.
*S'yoo-*DAH, *v* KOHM-*nah-too.*
Here, into the room.

Куда идёт учитель?
*Koo-*DAH *eed-*YOHT *oo-*CHEET-*yel?*
Where is the teacher going?

Туда, в коридор.
*Too-*DAH, *v koh-ree-*DOHR.
There, into the corridor.

Идите сюда, ко мне.
*Ee-*DEET-*yeh s'yoo-*DAH *koh mn'yeh.*
Come here to me.

Идите туда, к окну.
*Ee-*DEET-*yeh too-*DAH *k ok-*NOO.
Go there to the window.

Учитель приносит стул.
*Oo-*CHEET-*yel pree-*NOH-*seet stool.*
The teacher brings a chair.

Он несёт стул.
*Ohn n'yes-*YOHT *stool.*
He carries the chair.

Куда он его несёт?
*Koo-*DAH *ohn yeh-*VOH *n'yes-*YOHT*?*
Where does he carry it?

В комнату.
V KOHM-*nah-too.*
Into the room.

Принесите, пожалуйста стул.
*Preen-yeh-*SEET-*yeh, poh-*ZHAH-*looy-stah, stool.*
Please bring a chair.

Спасибо.
*Spah-*SEE-*boh.*
Thank you.

Откройте, пожалуйста, окно и дверь.
*Ot-*KROYT-*yeh, poh-*ZHAHL'*stah, ok-*NOH *ee dv'yehr.*
Please, open the window and the door.

Что вы делаете?
*Shtoh vwee d'*YEH-*lah-yet-yeh?*
What are you doing?

Я открываю окно и дверь.
*Yah ot-kree-*VAH-*yoo ok-*NOH *ee dv'yehr.*
I am opening the window and the door.

Пожалуйста, закройте окно.
*Poh-*ZHAH-*looy-stah, zah-*KROYT-*yeh ok-*NOH.
Please close the window.

Что вы делаете?
SHTOH *vwee d'*YEH-*lah-yet-yeh?*
What are you doing?

Я закрываю окно.
*Yah zah-kree-*VAH-*yoo ok-*NOH.
I am closing the window.

Спасибо.
*Spah-*SEE-*boh.*
Thank you.

Учитель идёт к окну.
*Oo-*CHEET-*yel eed-*YOHT *k ok-*NOO.
The teacher goes to the window.

Он у окна.
*Ohn oo ok-*NAH.
He is at the window.

Вы идёте к двери.
*Vwee eed-*YOHT-*yeh k dv'*YEH-*ree.*
You are going to the door.

Вы у двери.
*Vwee oo dv'*YEH-*ree.*
You are at the door.

Учитель идёт от окна к доске.
*Oo-*CHEET-*yel eed-*YOHT *ot ok-*NAH *k dos-*KEH.
The teacher goes from the window to the blackboard.

Он около доски.
Ohn OH-*koh-loh dos-*KEE.
He is near the blackboard.

Вы идёте от двери к столу.
*Vwee eed-*YOHT-*yeh ot dv'*YEH-*ree k stoh-*LOO.
You are going from the door to the table.

Возьмите перо и тетрадку и пишите.
*Voz-*MEET-*yeh p'yeh-*ROH *ee t'yet-*RAHD-*koo ee pee-*SHEET-*yeh.*
Take a pen and notebook and write.

Мы сидим за столом и читаем газету.
*Mee see-*DEEM *zah stoh-*LOHM *ee chee-*TAH-*yem gah-*ZEH-*too.*
We are sitting at the table and reading the newspaper.

Над столом висит лампа.
*Nahd stoh-*LOHM *vee-*SEET LAHM-*pah.*
The lamp is hanging above the table.

Под столом лежит собака.
*Pohd stoh-*LOHM *l'yeh-*ZHEET *soh-*BAH-*kah.*
The dog lies under the table.

Где мы?
Gd'yeh mee?
Where are we?

Мы тут, за столом.
*Mee toot, zah stoh-*LOHM.
We are here, at the table

А где собака?
*Ah gd'yeh soh-*BAH-*kah?*
And where is the dog?

И она здесь, под столом.
*Ee oh-*NAH *zd'yes, pohd stoh-*LOHM.
It is also here, under the table.

ATTENTION: Observe the difference in meanings in the following words:

куда́ — to where? (whither?)

туда́ — to there (thither)

сюда́ — to here (hither)

А где кошка?
Ah gd'yeh KOHSH-*kah?*
And where is the cat?

Она лежит там, около камина.
Oh-NAH *l'yeh*-ZHEET *tahm,* OH-*koh-loh kah*-MEE-*nah.*
It is lying there near the fire place.

Где чёрная книга?
Gd'yeh CHOR-*nah-yah k'*NEE-*gah?*
Where is the black book?

Она вот тут, на рояле.
Oh-NAH *voht toot, nah roh*-YAHL-*yeh.*
It is right here on the piano.

А где красная?
Ah gd'yeh KRAHS-*nah-yah?*
And where is the red one?

Она там, на подоконнике.
Oh-NAH *tahm, nah pod-oh*-KOHN-*nee-keh.*
It is there on the window sill.

Где зонтик?
Gd'yeh ZOHN-*teek?*
Where is the umbrella?

Вот здесь, на диване.
Voht zd'yes nah dee-VAHN-*yeh.*
Right here on the sofa.

Пожалуйста, поставьте его в угол.
Poh-ZHAH-*looy-stah, poh*-STAHV-*t'yeh yeh*-VOH *v* OO-*gol.*
Please, put it into the corner.

Что вы делаете?
*Shtoh vwee d'*YEH-*lah-yet-yeh?*
What are you doing?

Я ставлю зонтик в угол.
Yah STAHV-*l'yoo* ZOHN-*teek v* OO-*gol.*
I am putting the umbrella into the corner.

ONE WORD IN ENGLISH— TWO IN RUSSIAN:
тут and **здесь** both mean "here."

Куда вы идёте?
Koo-DAH *vwee eed*-YOHT-*yeh?*
Where are you going?

Я иду в сад.
Yah ee-DOO *v sahd.*
I am going to the garden.

Куда вы едете?
Koo-DAH *vwee* YED-*yet-yeh?*
Where are you going?

Я еду за город.
Yah YEH-*doo* ZAH-*goh-rod.*
I am going out of town.

Едет ли Тимошенко в Москву?
YED-*yet lee Tee-moh*-SHEN-*koh v Mosk*-VOO?
Does Timoshenko go to Moscow?

Нет, он едет в Сибирь.
N'yet, ohn YED-*yet v See*-BEER.
No, he is going to Siberia.

THINKING IN RUSSIAN

(Answers on page 223)

1. Что де́лает учи́тель?
2. Берёт ли учи́тель кни́гу?
3. Кладёт ли он кни́гу на сто́л?
4. Берёт ли учи́тель коро́бку?
5. Сиди́т ли учи́тель?

6. Открыва́ет ли учи́тель окно́?
7. Что де́лает учи́тель?
8. Что окрыва́ет учи́тель, окно́ и́ли дверь?
9. Открыва́ете ли вы дверь?
10. Открыва́ет ли учи́тель дверь?

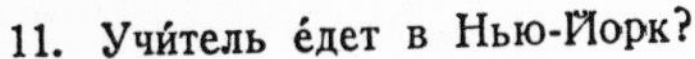

11. Учи́тель е́дет в Нью-Йорк?
12. Едет ли он в Ло́ндон?
13. Куда́ е́дет учи́тель?
14. Больша́я ли Москва́ или ма́ленькая?
15. Едете ли вы в Москву́?
16. Кто е́дет в Москву́, вы или учи́тель?

УРОК 8

Я считаю
Yah shchee-TAH-*yoo*
I count

1	1	1
один	**одна**	**одно**
oh-DEEN	*od*-NAH	*od*-NOH
one (masc.)	one (fem.)	one (neut.)

2	2
два	**две**
dvah	*dv'yeh*
two (m. and n.)	two (fem.)

NOTE to Student: With the exception of **оди́н** and **два** Russian numerals have only one form for all genders in their respective cases. **Оди́н** has a special ending for every gender: **оди́н** (masculine), **одна́** (feminine), and **одно́** (neuter). **Два** has two different endings: **два** (masculine and neuter) and **две** (feminine).

3	4	5	6	7
три	**четыре**	**пять**	**шесть**	**семь**
tree	*cheh*-TEE-*reh*	*p'yaht*	*shest*	*s'yem*

8	9	10	11
восемь	**девять**	**десять**	**одиннадцать**
VOHS-*yem*	*d'*YEV-*yaht*	*d'*YES-*yaht*	*oh*-DEEN-*nahd-tsaht*

12	13	14
двенадцать	**тринадцать**	**четырнадцать**
dv'yeh-NAHD-*tsaht*	*tree*-NAHD-*tsaht*	*cheh*-TEER-*nahd-tsaht*

15	16	17
пятнадцать	**шестнадцать**	**семнадцать**
p'yaht-NAHD-*tsaht*	*shest*-NAHD-*tsaht*	*s'yem*-NAHD-*tsaht*

18	19	20
восемнадцать	**девятнадцать**	**двадцать**
vos-yem-NAHD-*tsaht*	*d'yev-yaht*-NAHD-*tsaht*	DVAHD-*tsaht*

21	21	21
двадцать один	**двадцать одна**	**двадцать одно**
DVAHD-*tsaht oh*-DEEN	DVAHD-*tsaht od*-NAH	DVAHD-*tsaht od*-NOH

22	22	23
двадцать два	**двадцать две**	**двадцать три**
DVAHD-*tsaht dvah*	DVAHD-*tsaht dv'yeh*	DVAHD-*tsaht tree*

30	40	50	60
тридцать	**сорок**	**пятьдесят**	**шестьдесят**
TREED-*tsaht*	SOH-*rok*	*p'yaht-d'yes*-YAHT	*shest-d'yes*-YAHT

70	80	90	100
семьдесят	**восемьдесят**	**девяносто**	**сто**
*s'*YEM-*d'yes-yaht*	VOHS-*yem-d'yes-yaht*	*d'yev-yah*-NOH-*stoh*	*stoh*

200	300	400	500
двести	**триста**	**четыреста**	**пятьсот**
*dv'*YEH-*stee*	TREE-*stah*	*cheh*-TEE-*reh-stah*	*p'yaht*-SOHT

600	700	800	900	1000
шестьсот	**семьсот**	**восемьсот**	**девятьсот**	**тысяча**
shest-SOHT	*s'yem*-SOHT	*vos-yem*-SOHT	*d'yev-yaht*-SOHT	TEES-*yah-chah*

Сколько стоит ваш галстук?	**Он стоит два доллара.**
SKOHL-*koh* STOH-*eet vahsh* GAHLS-*took?*	*Ohn* STOH-*eet dvah* DOHL-*lah-rah.*
How much does your tie cost?	It costs two dollars.
Сколько стоит ваша шляпа?	**Она стоит пять долларов.**
SKOHL-*koh* STOH-*eet* VAH-*shah shl'*YAH-*pah?*	*Oh*-NAH STOH-*eet p'yaht* DOHL-*lah-rov.*
How much does your hat cost?	It costs five dollars.

YOU WILL WONDER why the endings of the word **дóллар** differ after the numerals **два** and **пять.** The reason is that the Russians use a special form of the plural called dual after the numerals 2, 3, and 4, while they use the genitive plural after all numerals over 4. However after numerals ending in 2, 3, or 4, the dual is used. Fortunately the endings of the dual coincide with those of the genitive singular of the respective nouns. E.g.: **два столá**—"2 tables", **пять столóв**—"5 tables", 22 **столá**—"22 tables".

THE PLURAL OF NOUNS

While in English there is practically only one ending ("s") denoting the plural, Russian nouns form the plural in various ways.

PLURALS IN -ы

Masculine nouns ending in a hard consonant and masculine and feminine nouns ending in **-a** have **-ы** in the plural:

стол	(m.)	"table",	nom. pl.:	**столы́**	gen.:	**столóв**
мужчи́на	(m.)	"man",	nom. pl.:	**мужчи́ны**	gen.:	**мужчи́н**
жéнщина	(f.)	"woman",	nom. pl.:	**жéнщины**	gen.:	**жéнщин**

Notice that the nouns ending in **-a** have no special endings in the genitive plural. The stem is the genitive.

PLURALS IN -и

The above rule does not apply to nouns whose stems end in **г, к, х, ж, ч, ш, щ.** Such nouns and also nouns ending in a soft consonant (i.e. followed by **ь**) or ending in **я** or **й** take **и** in the plural.

карандáш	(m.)	"pencil",	nom. pl.:	**карандаши́**	gen.:	**карандашéй**
кни́га	(f.)	"book",	nom. pl.:	**кни́ги**	gen.:	**книг**
конь	(m.)	"horse",	nom. pl.:	**кóни**	gen.:	**конéй**
степь	(f).	"steppe",	nom. pl.:	**стéпи**	gen.:	**степéй**
герóй	(m.)	"hero",	nom. pl.:	**герóи**	gen.:	**герóев**
áрмия	(f.)	"army",	nom. pl.:	**áрмии**	gen.:	**áрмий**
тётя	(f.)	"aunt",	nom. pl.:	**тёти**	gen.:	**тёть**

PLURALS IN **-а**

Almost all neuter nouns ending in **-о** take **-а** in the plural:

сло́во	(n.) "word",	nom pl.:	**слова́**	gen.:	**слов**
село́	(n.) "village",	nom pl.:	**сёла**	gen.:	**сёл**

Also some masculine nouns ending in a hard consonant form their plural in **-а** which is always stressed:

дом	(m.) "house",	nom. pl.: **дома́**	gen.: **домо́в**
го́лос	(m.) "voice",	nom. pl.: **голоса́**	gen.: **голосо́в**
господи́н	(m.) "gentleman", "Mr."	nom. pl.: **господа́**	gen.: **госпо́д**

PLURALS IN **-я**

Neuter nouns ending in **-е** have **-я** in the nom. plural:

по́ле	(n.) "field",	nom. pl.:	**поля́**	gen.:	**поле́й**
зда́ние	(n.) "building",	nom. pl.:	**зда́ния**	gen.:	**зда́ний**

Also some masculine nouns ending in a soft consonant or in **-й** take **-я** in the plural:

учи́тель	(m.) "teacher"	nom. pl.: **учителя́**	gen.: **учителе́й**
край	(m.) "edge; country"	nom. pl.: **края́**	gen.: **краёв**

PLURALS IN **-ья**

A few masculine and neuter nouns take **-ья** in the plural:

стул	(m.) "chair"	nom. pl.:	**сту́лья**	gen.:	**сту́льев**
перо́	(n.) "pen"	nom. pl.:	**пе́рья**	gen.:	**пе́рьев**

You will meet other less frequent plural endings and the other cases (dative, accusative etc.) of the plural in the text. For particulars we refer to pages 259 and 260.

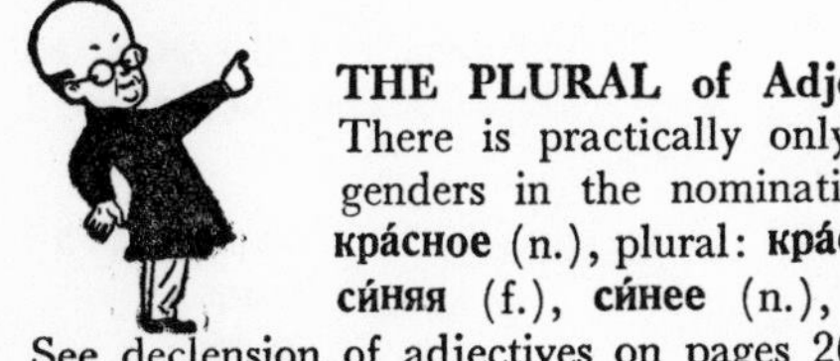

THE PLURAL of Adjectives is not complicated at all. There is practically only one ending: **-ые** or **-ие** for all genders in the nominative: **кра́сный** (m.), **кра́сная** (f.), **кра́сное** (n.), plural: **кра́сные** (for all genders), **си́ний** (m.), **си́няя** (f.), **си́нее** (n.), plural: **си́ние** (for all genders). See declension of adjectives on pages 267, 268 and 269.

Что они делают?	**Они кладут книги на стол.**
*Shtoh oh-*NEE *d'*YEH*-lah-yoot?*	*Oh-*NEE *klah-*DOOT *k'*NEE*-ggee nah stohl.*
What are they doing?	They are putting the books on the table.

Господа, откройте, пожалуйста, книги и читайте.
*Gos-poh-*DAH, *ot-*KROYT-*yeh, poh-*ZHAH-*looy-stah, k'*NEE-*ggee ee chee-*TIGHT-*yeh.*
Gentlemen, please open your books and read.

Что делают Иванов и Павлов?
*Shtoh d'*YEH-*lah-yoot Ee-vah-*NOHV *ee* PAHV-*lov?*
What are Ivanov and Pavlov doing?

Они открывают книги.
*Oh-*NEE *ot-kree-*VAH-*yoot k'*NEE-*ggee.*
They are opening the books.

ANOTHER HELPFUL HINT: Notice that the ending of the first person plural (after **мы**) always ends in an **-м,** while that of the third person always ends with a **т.**

Что мы делаем?
*Shtoh mee d'*YEH-*lah-yem?*
What are we doing?

Мы берём книги со стола.
*Mee b'yehr-*YOHM *k'*NEE-*ggee soh stoh-*LAH.
We are taking the books from the table.

Какой это карандаш?
*Kah-*KOY EH-*toh kah-rahn-*DAHSH?
Which pencil is this?

Это красный карандаш.
EH-*toh* KRAHS-*nee kah-rahn-*DAHSH.
This is the red pencil.

Какие это карандаши?
*Kah-*KEE-*yeh* EH-*toh kah-rahn-dah-*SHEE?
Which pencils are these?

Это красные карандаши.
EH-*toh* KRAHS-*nee-yeh kah-rahn-dah-*SHEE.
These are the red pencils.

Какая это шляпа?
*Kah-*KAH-*yah* EH-*toh shl'*YAH-*pah?*
Which hat is it?

Это серая шляпа.
EH-*toh s'*YEH-*rah-yah shl'*YAH-*pah.*
It is the gray hat.

Какие это шляпы?
*Kah-*KEE-*yeh* EH-*toh shl'*YAH-*pee?*
Which hats are these?

Это серые шляпы.
EH-*toh s'*YEH-*ree-yeh shl'*YAH-*pee.*
These are the gray hats.

Это перо чёрное.
EH-*toh p'yeh-*ROH CHOR-*noh-yeh.*
This pen is black.

Эти перья чёрные.
EH-*tee p'*YEHR-*yah* CHOR-*nee-yeh.*
These pens are black.

Сколько книг на столе?
SKOHL-*koh k'neeg nah stol-*YEH?
How many books are on the table?

На столе пять книг.
*Nah stol-*YEH *p'yaht k'neeg.*
There are five books on the table.

Много ли вы знаете русских слов?
MNOH-*goh lee vwee* ZNAH-*yet-yeh* ROOS-*skeekh slohv?*
Do you know many Russian words?

Я знаю слов пятьсот.
Yah ZNAH-*yoo slohv p'yaht-*SOHT.
I know about 500 words.

Сколько километров от Одессы до Киева?
SKOHL-*koh kee-lom-*YET-*rov ot Oh-*DES-*see doh* KEE-*yeh-vah?*
How many kilometers are there from Odessa to Kiev?

Километров 600.
*Kee-lom-*YET-*rov shest-*SOHT.
About 600 kilometers.

Сколько стульев в этой комнате?
SKOHL-*koh* STOOL-*yev v* EH-*toy* KOHM-*naht-yeh?*
How many chairs are there in this room?

Три стула.
Tree STOO-*lah.*
Three chairs.

NOTICE the order of words in the preceding sentences. If the numeral is put after the noun, the meaning is "about," "approximately":

три́дцать рубле́й means "30 roubles"
рубле́й три́дцать means "about 30 roubles"

В комнате жарко.
V KOHM-*naht-yeh* ZHAHR-*koh.*
It is hot in the room.

Откройте окна и двери.
*Ot-*KROYT-*yeh* OHK-*nah ee dv'*YEH-*ree.*
Open the windows and the doors.

Сколько в комнате окон и дверей?
SKOHL-*koh v* KOHM-*naht-yeh oh-*KOHN *ee dv'yeh-*RAY?
How many windows and doors are there in the room?

Два окна и одна дверь.
*Dvah ok-*NAH *ee od-*NAH *dv'yehr.*
Two windows and one door.

Сколько там людей?
SKOHL-*koh tahm l'yood-*YAY?
How many people are there?

Человек двадцать.
*Cheh-lov-*YEK DVAHD-*tsaht.*
About twenty people.

ATTENTION!—The plural for the word **челове́к** is **лю́ди.** But after numerals (over 4) you use the genitive plural **челове́к** instead of **люде́й** both for men and women.

Там два челове́ка	There are two people there.
Там де́сять челове́к	There are ten people there.
Там мно́го люде́й	There are many people there.

Сколько лет вы живёте в Нью Йорке?
SHOHL-*koh l'yet vwee zheev-*YOHT-*yeh v New* YOR-*keh?*
How many years are you living in New York?

Года три.
GOH-*dah tree.*
About three years.

REMEMBER THIS: The plural of **год** — "year" is **гóды,** but after numerals (over 4) you say **лет: два гóда,** but **пять лет.**

Сколько на столе тетрадок?
SKOHL-*koh nah stol*-YEH *t'yet*-RAH-*dok?*
How many exercise-books are on the table?

Три тетрадки.
Tree t'yet-RAHD-*kee.*
Three exercise books.

Тут два стола, а стульев нет.
Toot dvah stoh-LAH, *ah* STOOL-*yev n'yet.*
There are two tables but no chairs.

Мой костюм стоит пятьдесят долларов.
Moy kost-YOOM STOH-*eet p'yaht-d'yes*-YAHT DOHL-*lah-rov.*
My suit costs fifty dollars.

Моё пальто стоит сорок два доллара.
Moh-YOH *pahl*-TOH STOH-*eet* SOH-*rok dvah* DOHL-*lah-rah.*
My coat costs forty-two dollars.

WATCH OUT! Don't confound **стóит** and **стои́т.** The former means "it costs," the latter "(he, she, it) stands." The difference lies only in the stress. The respective infinitives are **стóить** "to cost" and **стоя́ть** "to stand."

THINKING IN RUSSIAN

(Answers on page 223)

1. Счита́йте. Что вы де́лаете?
2. Я счита́ю: 1, 2, 3, . . . и т. д. Что я де́лаю?
3. Что де́лает учи́тель?
4. Что он счита́ет?
5. Ско́лько сту́льев в э́той ко́мнате?
6. Есть здесь стол?
7. Что на столе́?
8. Ско́лько вы зна́ете ру́сских слов?
9. Ско́лько сто́ит америка́нская газе́та?
10. Ско́лько це́нтов в до́лларе?
11. Эта кни́га сто́ит сто до́лларов?
12. Сто́ит ли до́ллар сто рубле́й?
13. В э́той ко́мнате мно́го око́н?
14. Кака́я э́то ци́фра?
15. Ско́лько в э́той ко́мнате двере́й?
16. Ско́лько лет вы живёте в Нью-Йо́рке?

УРОК 9

Говорите ли вы по-русски?
*Goh-voh-*REET*-yeh lee vwee poh-*ROOS*-skee?*
Do you speak Russian?

Я говорю по-русски.
*Yah goh-vor-*YOO *poh-*ROOS*-skee.*

I speak Russian.

Говорите ли вы по-русски?
*Goh-voh-*REET*-yeh lee vwee poh-*ROOS*-skee?*
Do you speak Russian?

Я пишу и я читаю по-русски.
*Yah pee-*SHOO *ee yah chee-*TAH*-yoo poh-*ROOS*-skee.*
I write and I read Russian.

Да, говорю немного.
*Dah, goh-vor-*YOO *n'yem-*NOH*-goh.*
Yes, I speak a little.

На каком языке говорит учитель?
*Nah kah-*KOHM *yah-zee-*KEH *goh-voh-*REET *oo-*CHEET*-yel?*
What language does the teacher speak?

Он говорит по-русски.
*Ohn goh-voh-*REET *poh-*ROOS*-skee.*
He speaks Russian.

Говорим ли мы в школе по-английски?
*Goh-voh-*REEM *lee mee v* SHKOHL-*yeh poh-ahn-*GLEE-*skee?*
Do we speak English in school?

Нет, только по-русски.
N'yet, TOHL-*koh poh-*ROOS-*skee.*
No, only Russian.

А, Б, В — это буквы.
*Ah, beh, veh—*EH-*toh* BOOK-*vee.*
A, B, V are letters.

Г — тоже буква.
*Ggeh—*TOH-*zheh* BOOK-*vah.*
G is also a letter.

Я пишу букву Д.
*Yah pee-*SHOO BOOK-*voo deh.*
I am writing the letter D.

Вы пишете другую букву.
Vwee PEE-*shet-yeh droo-*GOO-*yoo* BOOK-*voo.*
You are writing another letter.

NOTE to Student: A letter of the alphabet is **бу́ква** (BOOK-*vah*). A letter in the correspondence sense is **письмо́** (*pees-*MOH).

А — первая буква,
*Ah—p'*YEHR-*vah-yah* BOOK-*vah,*
A is the first letter,

б — вторая буква,
*beh—vtoh-*RAH-*yah* BOOK-*vah,*
b is the second letter,

в — третья,
*veh—*TREHT-*yah,*
v is the third,

г — четвёртая,
*ggeh—chet-v'*YOR-*tah-yah,*
g is the fourth,

д — пятая,
*deh—p'*YAH-*tah-yah,*
d is the fifth,

е — шестая,
*yeh—shes-*TAH-*yah,*
yeh is the sixth,

ё — седьмая,
*yoh—s'yed-*MAH-*yah,*
yoh is the seventh,

ж — восьмая,
*zheh—vos-*MAH-*yah,*
zh is the eighth,

з — девятая,
*zeh—d'yev-*YAH-*tah-yah,*
z is the ninth,

и — десятая,
*ee—d'yes-*YAH-*tah-yah,*
ee is the tenth,

я — последняя.
*yah—posl-*YED-*n'yah-yah.*
yah is the last.

Учитель берёт мел.
*Oo-*CHEET-*yel b'yehr-*YOHT *m'yel.*
The teacher takes the chalk.

Он пишет на доске.
Ohn PEE-*shet nah dos-*KEH.
He writes on the blackboard.

Что он пишет?
Shtoh ohn PEE-*shet?*
What does he write?

Он пишет русскую азбуку.
Ohn PEE-*shet* ROOS-*skoo-yoo* AHZ-*boo-koo.*
He writes the Russian alphabet.

Возьмите перо и бумагу и пишите.
*Voz-*MEET*-yeh p'yeh-*ROH *ee boo-*MAH*-goo ee pee-*SHEET*-yeh.*
Take a pen and paper and write.

Пишите, пожалуйста.
*Pee-*SHEET*-yeh, poh-*ZHAHL*'stah.*
Please, write.

Вы пишете на бумаге, а учитель пишет на доске.
Vwee PEE*-shet-yeh nah boo-*MAHG*-yeh, ah oo-*CHEET*-yel* PEE*-shet nah dos-*KEH.
You are writing on paper and the teacher is writing on the blackboard.

Что пишет учитель?
Shtoh PEE*-shet oo-*CHEET*-yel?*
What does the teacher write?

Он пишет буквы.
Ohn PEE*-shet* BOOK*-vwee.*
He writes letters.

Какая первая буква?
*Kah-*KAH*-yah p'*YEHR*-vah-yah* BOOK*-vah?*
Which is the first letter?

А — первая буква.
*Ah—p'*YEHR*-vah-yah* BOOK*-vah.*
A is the first letter.

Я вас спрашиваю: какая первая буква?
Yah vahs SPRAH*-shee-vah-yoo: kah-*KAH*-yah p'*YEHR*-vah-yah* BOOK*-vah?*
I am asking you: which is the first letter?

Что я делаю?
*Shtoh yah d'*YEH*-lah-yoo?*
What am I doing?

Вы меня спрашиваете.
*Vwee m'yen-*YAH SPRAH*-shee-vah-yet-yeh.*
You are asking me (a question).

Что вы делаете?
*Shtoh vwee d'*YEH*-lah-yet-yeh?*
What are you doing?

Я отвечаю.
*Yah ot-v'yeh-*CHAH*-yoo.*
I am answering.

Ответьте на мой вопрос: кто я?
*Ot-v'*YET*-t'yeh nah moy vop-*ROHS*: ktoh yah?*
Answer my question: who am I?

Вы — учитель.
*Vwee—oo-*CHEET*-yel.*
You are the teacher.

NOTE to Student: Remember in Russian you say **отвечáть на вопрóс,** which literally means "to answer on a question."

Я вам задаю вопрос: сколько букв в русской азбуке?
*Yah vahm zah-dah-*YOO *vop-*ROHS: SKOHL*-koh bookv v* ROOS*-skoy* AHZ*-boo-keh?*
I am asking you the question: how many letters are there in the Russian alphabet?

Тридцать три буквы.
TREED-*tsaht tree* BOOK-*vwee.*
Thirty-three letters.

Это мой ответ.
EH-*toh moy ot-v'*YET.
This is my answer.

Учитель пишет слово "дом".
Oo-CHEET-*yel* PEE-*shet* SLOH-*voh "dohm."*
The teacher writes the word "house."

Дом — это слово.
Dohm—EH-*toh* SLOH-*voh.*
House is a word.

Дом, стена, крыша — слова.
Dohm, st'yeh-NAH, KREE-*shah* —*sloh*-VAH.
House, wall, roof are words.

Напишите слово "город".
Nah-pee-SHEET-*yeh* SLOH-*voh* "GOH-*rod."*
Write the word "town."

В слове "город" пять букв.
V SLOHV-*yeh* "GOH-*rod" p'yaht bookv.*
In the word "gorod" there are five letters.

В слове "дом" три буквы.
V SLOHV-*yeh "dohm" tree* BOOK-*vwee.*
In the word "dom" there are three letters.

"Книга" — русское слово.
*"K'*NEE-*gah"*—ROOS-*skoh-yeh* SLOH-*voh.*
"Kniga" is a Russian word.

"Book" — **слово английское.**
"Book"—SLOH-*voh ahn*-GLEES-*koh-yeh.*
"Book" is an English word.

"Livre" — **французское слово,** "Buch" — **немецкое.**
"Livre"—frahn-TSOOZ-*skoh-yeh* SLOH-*voh, "Buch"—n'yem*-YETS-*koh-yeh.*
"Livre" is a French word, "Buch" is a German one.

Я пишу предложение: "автомобиль на улице".
Yah pee-SHOO *pr'yed-loh*-ZHEH-*nee-yeh*: *"ahv-toh-moh*-BEEL *nah* OO-*lee-tseh."*
I am writing the sentence: "The automobile is in the street."

Сколько слов в этом предложении?
SKOHL-*koh slohv v* EH-*tom pr'yed-loh*-ZHEH-*nee-ee?*
How many words are there in this sentence?

В нём три слова.
V n'yohm tree SLOH-*vah.*
There are three words in it.

Это английские книги?
EH-*toh ahn*-GLEE-*skee-yeh k'*NEE-*ggee?*
Are these English books?

Нет, это не английские книги.
N'yet, EH-*toh n'yeh ahn*-GLEE-*skee-yeh k'*NEE-*ggee.*
No, these are not English books.

Какие это книги?
Kah-KEE-*yeh* EH-*toh k'*NEE-*ggee?*
What kind of books are they?

Это русские книги.
EH-*toh* ROOS-*skee-yeh k'*NEE-*ggee.*
They are Russian books.

Читаете ли вы уже русские газеты?
Chee-TAH-*yet-yeh lee vwee oo*-ZHEH ROOS-*skee-yeh gahz*-YEH-*tee?*
Do you already read Russian newspapers?

Нет, я русских газет ещё не читаю.
N'yet, yah ROOS-*skeekh gahz*-YET *yesh*-CHOH *n'yeh chee*-TAH-*yoo.*
No, I do not yet read Russian newspapers.

REMEMBER: The object of a negative verb is generally in the genitive case rather than in the accusative, although the accusative, too, may be used:

Я не ви́жу зо́нтика I do not see the umbrella.
Я не ем мя́со. I do not eat meat.

However, after **нет**, as contrasted with **есть** ("is") meaning "there is no", "there is not", the genitive must be used: **В ко́мнате нет стола́.** There is no table in the room.

Говорят ли ваши товарищи по-русски?
Goh-vor-YAHT *lee* VAH-*shee toh*-VAH-*reesh-chee poh*-ROOS-*skee?*
Do your comrades speak Russian?

Говорят, но плохо.
Goh-vor-YAHT, *noh* PLOH-*khoh.*
They speak, but badly.

Говорим ли мы тут по-английски?
Goh-voh-REEM *lee mee toot poh-ahn*-GLEE-*skee?*
Do we speak English here?

В школе мы по-английски не говорим.
V SHKOHL-*yeh mee poh-ahn*-GLEE-*skee n'yeh goh-voh*-REEM.
We do not speak English in school.

Знаете ли вы русский алфавит? Знаю.
ZNAH-*yet-yeh lee vwee* ROOS-*skee ahl-fah*-VEET? ZNAH-*yoo.*
Do you know the Russian alphabet? I know it.

Мы изучаем русский язык.
*Mee eez-oo-*CHAH*-yem* ROOS*-skee yah-*ZEEK.
We study the Russian language.

Мы учимся говорить по-русски.
Mee OO*-cheem-sah goh-voh-*REET *poh-*ROOS*-skee.*
We are learning to speak Russian.

Ученики учатся в школе.
*Oo-cheh-nee-*KEE OO*-chaht-sah v* SHKOHL*-yeh.*
The students learn in school.

В школе они читают по-русски.
V SHKOHL*-yeh oh-*NEE *chee-*TAH*-yoot poh-*ROOS*-skee.*
In the school they read Russian.

Чему вы учитесь?
*Cheh-*MOO *vwee* OO*-cheet-yes?*

What do you learn?

Мы учимся русскому языку.
Mee OO*-cheem-sah* ROOS*-skoh-moo yah-zee-*KOO.
We learn the Russian language.

ATTENTION! Notice the peculiar construction with the dative. "To learn a language" is **учи́ться языку́;** "to learn a trade": **учи́ться ремеслу́** (*rem-yes-*LOO).

В Вашингтоне и в Лондоне говорят по-английски.
*V Vah-sheeng-*TOHN*-yeh ee v* LOHN*-don-yeh goh-vor-*YAHT *poh-ahn-*GLEE*-skee.*
In Washington and in London people speak English.

В Москве, в Киеве и во Владивостоке говорят по-русски.
*V Moskv-*YEH, *v* KEE*-yev-yeh ee voh Vlah-dee-vos-*TOH*-keh goh-vor-*YAHT *poh-*ROOS*-skee.*
In Moscow, Kiev, and Vladivostok, Russian is spoken.

Как говорят в Рио де Жанейро?
*Kahk goh-vor-*YAHT *v Ree-yoh-deh-Zhah-*NAY*-roh?*
What do people speak in Rio de Janeiro?

По-португальски.
*Poh-por-too-*GAHL*-skee.*
Portuguese.

NOTE to Student: The literal translation of **говорят** is "they speak" or "they say". The meaning is "people say", "people speak", "one speaks", or "it is said". **Говорят** also means "there is a rumor". Remember that in these instances **говорят** is used without the personal pronoun **они́** ("they").

Пишете ли вы ежедневно русские упражнения?
PEE-*shet-yeh lee vwee yeh-zhedn-*YEV-*noh* ROOS-*skee-yeh oop-rahzh-n'*YEH-*nee-yah?*
Do you write Russian exercises every day?

Да, ежедневно. Вот оно.
*Dah, yeh-zhedn-*YEV-*noh. Voht oh-*NOH.
Yes, every day. Here it is.

Это моё упражнение.
EH-*toh moh-*YOH *oop-rahzh-n'*YEH-*nee-yeh.*
This is my exercise.

Как по-русски thank you?
*Kahk poh-*ROOS-*skee "thank you"?*
How do you say "thank you" in Russian?

Спасибо.
*Spah-*SEE-*boh.*
Spasibo.

Прочитайте это слово.
*Proh-chee-*TIGHT-*yeh* EH-*toh* SLOH-*voh.*
Read this word.

Я читаю: спасибо.
*Yah chee-*TAH-*yoo: spah-*SEE-*boh.*
I am reading: spasibo.

THINKING IN RUSSIAN

(Answers on page 223)

1. Кака́я пе́рвая бу́ква а́збуки?
2. Кака́я тре́тья бу́ква?
3. Что я спра́шиваю?
4. Что де́лаете вы?
5. Отвеча́ете ли вы на вопро́сы учи́теля?
6. Кто э́тот господи́н?
7. Кака́я э́то бу́ква: Г?
8. Что я спра́шиваю?
9. Что вы де́лаете в шко́ле?
10. Что де́лает учи́тель?
11. Чита́ете ли вы ру́сскую а́збуку?
12. Чита́ете ли вы по-ру́сски?
13. Что вы чита́ете?
14. Как вы говори́те в шко́ле?
15. Говори́те ли вы в шко́ле по-англи́йски?
16. Пи́шете ли вы по-ру́сски?
17. Пи́шете ли вы уро́ки?
18. Чита́ете ли вы ру́сские кни́ги?
19. Чита́ете ли вы ру́сскую газе́ту?

УРОК 10

Что мы делаем?
*Shtoh mee d'*YEH*-lah-yem?*
What are we doing?

Возьмите книгу.
*Voz-*MEET*-yeh k'*NEE*-goo.*
Take a book.

Что вы де́лаете?
*Shtoh vwee d'*YEH*-lah-yet-yeh?*
What are you doing?

И я беру книгу.
*Ee yah b'yeh-*ROO *k'*NEE*-goo.*
I am also taking a book.

Вы берёте книгу.
*Vwee b'yehr-*YOHT*-yeh k'*NEE*-goo.*
You are taking a book.

Я беру книгу.
*Yah b'yeh-*ROO *k'*NEE*-goo.*
I take the book.

Мы берём книги.
*Mee b'yehr-*YOHM *k'*NEE*-ggee.*
We are taking books.

Положите вашу книгу на стол.
*Poh-loh-*ZHEET-*yeh* VAH-*shoo k'*NEE-*goo nah stohl.*
Put your book on the table.

И я кладу мою книгу на стол.
*Ee yah klah-*DOO *moh-*YOO *k'*NEE-*goo nah stohl.*
I, too, am putting my book on the table.

Мы кладём наши книги на стол.
*Mee klahd-*YOHM NAH-*shee k'*NEE-*ggee nah stohl.*
We are putting our books on the table.

Книги на столе.
*K'*NEE-*ggee nah stol-*YEH.
The books are on the table.

Откуда мы берём книги?
*Ot-*KOO-*dah mee b'yehr-*YOHM *k'*NEE-*ggee?*
From where do we take the books?

Мы их берём со стола.
*Mee eekh b'yehr-*YOHM *soh stoh-*LAH.
We take them from the table.

Возьмите карандаш со стола и положите его в карман.
*Voz-*MEET-*yeh kah-rahn-*DAHSH *soh stoh-*LAH *ee poh-loh-*ZHEET-*yeh yeh-*VOH *v kahr-*MAHN.
Take the pencil from the table and put it in your pocket.

Где карандаш?
*Gd'*YEH *kah-rahn-*DAHSH*?*
Where is the pencil?

Он в кармане.
*Ohn v kahr-*MAHN-*yeh.*
It is in the pocket.

Откуда вы берёте карандаш?
*Ot-*KOO-*dah vwee b'yehr-*YOHT-*yeh kah-rahn-*DAHSH*?*
From where do you take the pencil?

Из кармана.
*Eez kahr-*MAH-*nah.*
From the pocket.

Откуда вы берёте книгу?
*Ot-*KOO-*dah vwee b'yehr-*YOHT-*yeh k'*NEE-*goo?*
From where do you take the book?

Со стола.
*Soh stoh-*LAH.
From the table.

CLARIFICATION NOTE: There are two ways of expressing "from". If you take a book *up from* the table you say: **я беру́ книгу со стола́**, but if, for example, you take a watch *out* of your pocket, it is: **я беру́ часы́ из карма́на**. However, the word "from where?" is the same **отку́да** for both cases. Ex.: "Where do you come from?" — **Вы отку́да?** As you see, Russian is sometimes shorter, if not simpler than English.

Я бросаю бумагу на пол.
Yah broh-SAH-*yoo boo*-MAH-*goo* NAH-*pol.*
I am throwing the paper to the floor.

Бумага на полу.
Boo-MAH-*gah nah poh*-LOO.
The paper is on the floor.

Откуда я беру бумагу?
Ot-KOO-*dah yah b'yeh*-ROO *boo*-MAH-*goo?*
From where do I take the paper?

Вы её берёте с пола.
Vwee yeh-YOH *b'yehr*-YOHT-*yeh s* POH-*lah.*
You take it from the floor.

Мы вешаем пальто на вешалку.
*Mee v'*YEH-*shah-yem pahl*-TOH *nah v'*YEH-*shahl-koo.*
We hang the overcoat on the rack.

Оно на вешалке.
Oh-NOH *nah v'*YEH-*shahl-keh.*
It is on the rack.

Откуда мы его берём?
Ot-KOO-*dah mee yeh*-VOH *b'yehr*-YOHM*?*
From where do we take it?

Мы его берём с вешалки.
Mee yeh-VOH *b'yehr*-YOHM *s v'*YEH-*shahl-kee.*
We take it from the rack.

Кольцо в коробке.
Kol-TSOH *v koh*-ROHB-*keh.*
The ring is in the box.

Мы берём кольцо из коробки.
Mee b'yehr-YOHM *kol*-TSOH *eez koh*-ROHB-*kee.*
We take the ring from the box.

Я вхожу в класс.
Yah vkhoh-ZHOO *v klahs.*
I enter the class-room.

Ученики входят в класс.
Oo-cheh-nee-KEE VKHOHD-*yaht v klahs.*
The students enter the class-room.

Куда мы входим?
Koo-DAH *mee* VKHOH-*deem?*
Into where do we enter?

Куда они входят?
Koo-DAH *oh*-NEE VKHOHD-*yaht?*
Into where do they enter?

Я выхожу из комнаты.
Yah vwee-khoh-ZHOO *eez* KOHM-*nah-tee.*
I leave the room.

Вы выходите из комнаты.
Vwee vwee-KHOH-*deet-yeh eez* KOHM-*nah-tee.*
You are going out of the room.

Что мы делаем в школе?
*Shtoh mee d'*YEH-*lah-yem v* SHKOHL-*yeh?*
What do we do in school?

Мы читаем, мы пишем, мы учимся.
Mee chee-TAH-*yem, mee* PEE-*shem, me* OO-*cheem-sah.*
We read, we write, we learn.

Что делает учитель?
*Shtoh d'*YEH-*lah-yet oo*-CHEET-*yel?*
What does the teacher do?

Он нас учит.
Ohn nahs OO-*cheet.*
He teaches us.

Что делают ученики?
*Shtoh d'*YEH-*lah-yoot oo-cheh-nee*-KEE*?*
What do the students do?

Они учатся, они читают и пишут.
Oh-NEE OO-*chaht-sah, oh*-NEE *chee*-TAH-*yoot ee* PEE-*shoot.*
They learn, they read and write.

Я сижу за столом.
Yah see-ZHOO *zah stoh*-LOHM.
I am sitting at the table.

Я сажусь за стол.
Yah sah-ZHOOS *zah stohl.*
I sit down at the table.

Что делает Катя?
*Shtoh d'*YEH-*lah-yet* KAHT-*yah?*
What is Kate doing?

Она садится в кресло.
Oh-NAH *sah*-DEET-*sah v* KRES-*loh.*
She sits down in an armchair.

Мы садимся за стол.
Mee sah-DEEM-*sah zah stohl.*
We sit down at the table.

Мы сидим за столом.
Mee see-DEEM *zah stoh*-LOHM.
We are sitting at the table.

Мы обедаем.
Mee ob-YEH-*dah-yem.*
We are having dinner.

Я сажусь на стул.
Yah sah-ZHOOS *nah stool.*
I am sitting down on a chair.

Вы садитесь на диван.
Vwee sah-DEET-*yes nah dee*-VAHN.
You are sitting down on a sofa.

Он встаёт со стула.
On vstah-YOHT *soh* STOO-*lah.*
He is getting up from the chair.

Мы встаём с дивана.
Mee vstah-YOHM *s dee*-VAH-*nah.*
We are getting up from the sofa.

Садитесь, пожалуйста.
Sah-DEET-*yes, poh*-ZHAHL'*stah.*
Sit down, please.

Они садятся.
Oh-NEE *sahd*-YAHT-*sah.*
They sit down.

IMPORTANT NOTE: the unusual verb-forms you have just observed are reflexive forms. For example, "I sit down" is in Russian "I seat myself". — Reflexive verbs are formed by adding **-ся** (after vowels **-сь**) to the respective endings of the verb, e.g.: **одевать** (*od-yeh*-VAHT) "to clothe", **одеваться** (*od-yeh*-VAHT-*sah*) "to clothe oneself"—"to dress", **я одеваюсь** (*yah od-yeh*-VAH-*yoos*)—"I dress (myself)", **вы одеваетесь** (*vwee od-yeh*-VAH-*yet-yes*)—"you dress (yourself)". **-ся** is a shortened form of the reflexive pronoun **себя** (*s'yeb*-YAH) meaning "oneself", "myself", "yourself", etc.

Куда вы идёте?
Koo-DAH *vwee eed*-YOHT-*yeh?*
Where are you going?

Мы идём на вокзал.
Mee eed-YOHM *nah vok*-ZAHL.
We are going to the station.

Ходите ли вы в церковь?
KHOH-*deet-yeh lee vwee v* TSEHR-*kov?*
Do you go to church?

Да, я хожу в церковь.
Dah, yah khoh-ZHOO *v* TSEHR-*kov.*
Yes, I go to church.

Идёте ли вы сегодня в кино?
Eed-YOHT-*yeh lee vwee s'yeh*-VOHD-*n'yah v kee*-NOH?
Are you going to the movies today?

Нет, сегодня я в кино не иду.
N'yet, s'yeh-VOHD-*n'yah yah v kee*-NOH *n'yeh ee*-DOO.
No, today I am not going to the movies.

Ходят ли ваши дети в школу?
KHOHD-*yaht lee* VAH-*shee d'*YEH-*tee v* SHKOH-*loo?*
Do your children go to school?

Идут ли они в школу сегодня?
Ee-DOOT *lee oh*-NEE *v* SHKOH-*loo s'yeh*-VOHD-*n'yah?*
Are they going to school today?

Я иду в город.
Yah ee-DOO *v* GOH-*rod.*
I am going to town.

Мы едем за город.
Mee YED-*yem* ZAH-*gorod.*
We are going out of town.

Мы едем в ресторан.
Mee YED-*yem v res-toh*-RAHN.
We are going to a restaurant.

Поповы едут в Киев?
Poh-POH-*vwee* YEH-*doot v* KEE-*yev?*
Are the Popovs going to Kiev?

Нет, они едут не в Киев, а в Одессу.
N'yet, oh-NEE YEH-*doot n'yeh v* KEE-*yev, ah v Oh*-DES-*soo.*
No, they are not going to Kiev but to Odessa.

NOTE on VEHICLES: Russians use a different word meaning "to go" if the going implies riding in a vehicle: "I go into the room"—**Я иду́ в ко́мнату,** but "I go to Moscow"—**Я е́ду в Москву́.** The implication is that you do not walk to Moscow.

THINKING IN RUSSIAN

(Answers on page 224)

1. Куда́ иду́т ученики́?
2. Что они́ там де́лают?
3. Хо́дите ли вы в шко́лу Бе́рлица?
4. Идёте ли вы в шко́лу?
5. Хо́дите ли вы в кино́?
6. Куда́ мы ве́шаем пальто́?
7. Где виси́т шля́па?
8. Отку́да мы её берём?
9. Где кольцо́?
10. Отку́да мы его́ берём?
11. Вы идёте в го́род?
12. Вы е́дете за́ город?
13. Вы е́дете в рестора́н?
14. Попо́вы е́дут в Москву́?
15. Куда́ они́ е́дут?

УРОК 11

Что мы имеем?
*Shtoh mee eem-*YEH*-yem?*
What have we?

Что у нас?
Shtoh oo nahs?
What have we?

Я имею карандаш.
*Yah eem-*YEH*-yoo kah-rahn-*DAHSH.
I have a pencil.

Возьмите карандаш.
*Voz-*MEET*-yeh kah-rahn-*DAHSH.
Take the pencil.

У меня (есть) карандаш.
*Oo m'yen-*YAH *(yest) kah-rahn-*DAHSH.
I have a pencil.

У вас (есть) карандаш.
*Oo vahs (yest) kah-rahn-*DAHSH.
You have a pencil.

Он имеет часы.
*Ohn eem-*YEH*-yet chah-*SEE.
He has a watch.

У него часы.
*Oo nyeh-*VOH *chah-*SEE.
He has a watch.

Она имеет зонтик.
*Oh-*NAH *eem-*YEH*-yet* ZOHN*-teek.*
She has an umbrella.

У неё зонтик.
*Oo n'yeh-*YOH ZOHN*-teek.*
She has an umbrella.

GRAMMATICAL NOTE: Notice that in Russian you can express "I have" in two ways: First by using the word **иметь** "to have" with the accusative. For example: **Я имею сад** (*yah eem-*YEH*-yoo sahd*)—"I have a garden".

Another and more common way of expressing "have" or "I have" is to say **у меня́** (**есть**) — literally "at me is", **у вас** (**есть**) — "you have", **у него́** (**есть**) "he has", **у неё** (**есть**) — "she has", **у нас** (**есть**) — "we have", **у них** (**есть**) — "they have". The word **есть** usually is omitted. Use it only if you want to stress the word "have".

Мы имеем автомобиль.
*Mee eem-*YEH*-yem ahv-toh-moh-*BEEL.
We have an automobile

У нас автомобиль.
*Oo nahs ahv-toh-moh-*BEEL.
We have an automobile.

Они имеют дом.
*Oh-*NEE *eem-*YEH*-yoot dohm.*
They have a house.

У них дом.
Oo neekh dohm.
They have a house.

Маша имеет на голове шляпу.
MAH*-shah eem-*YEH*-yet nah goh-lov-*YEH *shl'*YAH*-poo.*
Masha has a hat on her head.

У неё на голове шляпа.
*Oo n'yeh-*YOH *nah goh-lov-*YEH *shl'*YAH*-pah.*
She has a hat on her head.

Коля не имеет шляпы.
KOHL*-yah n'yeh eem-*YEH*-yet shl'*YAH*-pee.*
Kolya has no hat.

У него нет шляпы.
*Oo n'yeh-*VOH *n'yet shl'*YAH*-pee.*
He has no hat.

Мужчины имеют короткие волосы.
*Moozh-*CHEE*-nee eem-*YEH*-yoot koh-*ROHT*-kee-yeh* VOH*-loh-see.*
Men have short hair.

У них короткие волосы.
*Oo neekh koh-*ROHT*-kee-yeh* VOH*-loh-see.*
They have short hair.

Женщины имеют длинные волосы.
ZHEN*-shchee-nee eem-*YEH*-yoot* DLEEN*-nee-yeh* VOH*-loh-see.*
Women have long hair.

У них длинные волосы.
Oo neekh DLEEN*-nee-yeh* VOH*-loh-see.*
They have long hair.

У учителя нет волос.
*Oo oo-*CHEET*-yel-yah n'yet voh-*LOHS.
The teacher has no hair.

Какой ужас! Он лысый.
*Kah-*KOY OO*-zhahs! Ohn* LEE*-see.*
What a shame! He is bald.

Есть у вас перо?
*Yest oo vahs p'yeh-*ROH*?*
Do you have a pen?

Да, у меня есть перо.
*Dah, oo m'yen-*YAH *yest p'yeh-*ROH.
Yes, I have a pen.

Перо у вас?
*P'yeh-*ROH *oo vahs?*
Do you have the pen?

Да, перо у меня.
*Dah, p'yeh-*ROH *oo m'yen-*YAH.
Yes, I have the pen.

NOTE on ARTICLE: In Russian there is no special word for the article. The meaning is taken from the circumstances. For instance if you ask: **где кни́га?** it is clear that you are asking for *the* book. However, if there be need to stress the meaning of the article, you do it by changing the relative position of the words in the sentence: **У меня́ часы́** — "I have a watch", **Часы́ у меня́** — "I have the watch".

Что у меня в руке?
*Shtoh oo m'yen-*YAH *v roo-*KEH*?*
What have I in my hand?

У вас в руке цветок.
*Oo vahs v roo-*KEH *tsv'yeh-*TOHK.
You have a flower in your hand.

Что у нас в руках?
*Shtoh oo nahs v roo-*KAHKH*?*
What have we in our hands?

У нас в руках книги.
*Oo nahs v roo-*KAHKH *k'*NEE*-ggee.*
We have books in our hands.

Какой у учителя галстук?
*Kah-*KOY *oo oo-*CHEET*-yel-yah* GAHLS*-took?*
What kind of tie has the teacher?

У него синий галстук.
*Oo n'yeh-*VOH SEE*-nee* GAHLS*-took.*
He has a blue tie.

Какая у учительницы блузка?
*Kah-*KAH*-yah oo oo-*CHEET*-yel-nee-tsee* BLOOZ*-kah?*
What kind of blouse has the teacher (f)?

У неё белая блузка.
*Oo n'yeh-*YOH *b'*YEH*-lah-yah* BLOOZ*-kah.*
She has a white blouse.

У них есть очки?
*Oo neekh yest otch-*KEE*?*
Do they have eyeglasses?

Да, у них очки.
*Dah, oo neekh otch-*KEE.
Yes, they have eyeglasses.

Что у учителя под мышкой?
*Shtoh oo oo-*CHEET*-yel-yah pod* MEESH*-koy?*
What has the teacher under his arm?

У него под мышкой зонтик.
*Oo n'yeh-*VOH *pod* MEESH*-koy* ZOHN*-teek.*
He has an umbrella under his arm.

RUSSIAN is DIFFERENT: Here is an excellent example of the fact that words in one language often have no exact equivalent in another. Russians use the word **рука́** for both "arm" and "hand" although when specific reference is made to the "hand" as such, that part of the arm below the wrist, the word **кисть** is used, but this use is very restricted. For instance, if I say **я даю́ ему́ ру́ку** it is clear that I am giving him not my arm but my hand. On the other hand, to say "under the arm" Russians say **под мы́шкой** meaning literally "under the armpit".

Какие у Ирины волосы?
*Kah-*KEE*-yeh oo Ee-*REE*-nee* VOH*-loh-see?*
What kind of hair has Irene?

У неё русые волосы.
*Oo n'yeh-*YOH ROO*-see-yeh* VOH*-loh-see.*
She has blond hair.

Какие волосы у Коли?
*Kah-*KEE*-yeh* VOH*-loh-see oo* KOH*-lee?*
What kind of hair has Kolya?

У него чёрные волосы.
*Oo n'yeh-*VOH CHOR*-nee-yeh* VOH*-loh-see.*
He has black hair.

Какие у неё глаза?
*Kah-*KEE*-yeh oo n'yeh-*YOH *glah-*ZAH*?*
What kind of eyes does she have?

У неё голубые глаза.
*Oo n'yeh-*YOH *goh-loo-*BEE*-yeh glah-*ZAH.
She has blue eyes.

Какие глаза у Ольги?
*Kah-*KEE*-yeh glah-*ZAH *oo* OHL*-ggee?*
What kind of eyes has Olga?

У неё чёрные глаза.
*Oo n'yeh-*YOH CHOR*-nee-yeh glah-*ZAH.
She has dark (black) eyes.

NOTE on COLORS and EYES: Russians use two words for "blue": **голубо́й** and **си́ний.** The difference is that **голубо́й** refers to "light blue" while **синий** means "blue" in general or medium or dark blue. One usually says in Russian: **голубо́е не́бо** — "light blue sky", **си́нее мо́ре** — "(dark) blue sea".

Remember that, in speaking of eyes, you don't use the word **кори́чневый** for "brown", you say **ка́рий.**

THINKING IN RUSSIAN

(Answers on page 224)

1. Что у учи́теля под мы́шкой?
2. Есть ли у него́ под ле́вой мы́шкой газе́та?
3. В карма́не у учи́теля тру́бка?
4. Где бума́га?
5. Лине́йка под пра́вой ного́й учи́теля?
6. Что у учи́теля в пра́вой руке́?
7. Пе́рья у учи́теля в пра́вой руке́?
8. Есть ли в коро́бке карандаши́?
9. Ключи́ на столе́?
10. Где кни́ги?
11. Есть ли на стена́х карти́ны?
12. Ско́лько книг на столе́?
13. Есть ли у учи́теля де́ньги в карма́не?
14. Есть ли на сту́ле шля́па?

УРОК 12

У кого больше денег?
Oo koh-VOH BOHL-*sheh d'*YEN-*yeg?*
Who has more money?

У меня три рубля.
Oo m'yen-YAH *tree roobl*-YAH.
I have three rubles.

У вас пять рублей.
Oo vahs p'yaht roob-LAY.
You have five rubles.

Сколько у нас денег?
SKOHL-*koh oo nahs d'*YEN-*yeg?*
How much money have we?

У нас восемь рублей.
Oo nahs VOHS-*yem roob*-LAY.
We have eight rubles.

У кого больше денег?
Oo koh-VOH BOHL-*sheh d'*YEN-*yeg?*
Who has more money?

У вас больше денег.
Oo vahs BOHL-*sheh d'*YEN-*yeg.*
You have more money.

У кого меньше денег?
Oo koh-VOH *m'*YEN-*sheh d'*YEN-*yeg?*
Who has less money?

У меня меньше денег.
Oo m'yen-YAH *m'*YEN-*sheh d'*YEN-*yeg.*
I have less money.

У вас больше денег, чем у меня.
Oo vahs BOHL-*sheh d'*YEN-*yeg, chem oo m'yen*-YAH.
You have more money than I.

У меня меньше, чем у вас.
Oo m'yen-YAH *m'*YEN-*sheh, chem oo vahs.*
I have less than you.

У вас много волос.
Oo vahs MNOH-*goh voh*-LOHS.
You have much hair.

У г-на Берлица мало волос.
Oo gos-poh-DEE-*nah Ber-litz-ah* MAH-*loh voh*-LOHS.
Mr. Berlitz has little hair.

В большой книге 500 страниц.
V bol-SHOY *k'*NEE-*ggeh p'yaht*-SOHT *strah*-NEETS.
In the large book there are 500 pages.

В маленькой книге триста.
V MAHL-*yen-koy k'*NEE-*ggeh* TREE-*stah.*
In the small book there are 300.

В какой книге больше страниц, а в какой меньше?
V kah-KOY *k'*NEE-*ggeh* BOHL-*sheh strah*-NEETS, *ah v kah*-KOY *m'*YEN-*sheh?*
In which book are there more pages, and in which fewer?

В большой книге много страниц, а в маленькой мало.
V bol-SHOY *k'*NEE-*ggeh* MNOH-*goh strah*-NEETS, *ah v* MAHL-*yen-koy* MAH-*loh.*
In the large book there are many pages, and in the small one there are few.

В банке много денег.
V BAHN-*keh* MNOH-*goh d'*YEN-*yeg.*
In the bank there is much money.

В моём кармане мало денег.
V moh-YOHM *kahr*-MAHN-*yeh* MAH-*loh d'*YEN-*ycg.*
In my pocket there is little money.

Много ли жителей в этом городе?
MNOH-*goh lee* ZHEET-*yeh-lay v* EH-*tom* GOH-*rod-yeh?*
Are there many inhabitants in this town?

Да, много.
Dah, MNOH-*goh.*
Yes, (there are) many.

Много ли стульев в этой комнате?
MNOH-*goh lee* STOOL-*yev v* EH-*toy* KOHM-*naht-yeh?*
Are there many chairs in this room?

Нет, только два стула.
N'yet, TOHL-*koh dvah* STOO-*lah.*
No, only two chairs.

NOTE on the PREPOSITIONAL CASE: Did you notice above that **э́тот** changed to **э́том** and **э́та** to **э́той,** while **го́род** changed to **го́роде** and **ко́мната** to **ко́мнате. Этом, э́той, го́роде** and **ко́мнате** are in the prepositional case (also called the locative case). The prepositional case is never used without one of the following five prepositions: **в** — "in" (indicating mere position), **на** — "on" (mere position), **по** — "after", "at", "on", etc., **при**—"at, in the presence of", "at the time of", etc. and **о (об, обо)** — "about", "concerning".

See details concerning the prepositional in tables on pages 258-262 (nouns), 267-269 (adjectives), 263-265 (pronouns).

У меня коробка спичек.
*Oo m'yen-*YAH *koh-*ROHB*-kah* SPEE*-chek.*
I have a box of matches.

Сколько в ней спичек?
SKOHL*-koh v n'yay* SPEE*-chek?*
How many matches are there in it?

Много ли в ней спичек или мало?
MNOH*-goh lee v n'yay* SPEE*-chek* EE*-lee* MAH*-loh?*
Are there many matches in it or few?

В ней всего три спички.
*V n'yay vs'yeh-*VOH *tree* SPEECH*-kee.*
There are three matches in it in all.

У меня сто рублей и у вас сто рублей.
*Oo m'yen-*YAH *stoh roobl-*YAY *ee oo vahs stoh roobl-*YAY.
I have a hundred rubles and you have a hundred rubles.

Столько ли у вас денег, сколько у меня?
STOHL*-koh lee oo vahs d'*YEN*-yeg,* SKOHL*-koh oo m'yen-*YAH?
Have you as much money as I?

Да, у меня столько же денег, сколько у вас.
*Dah, oo m'yen-*YAH STOHL*-koh-zheh d'*YEN*-yeg,* SKOHL*-koh oo vahs.*
Yes, I have as much money as you.

ATTENTION! — Notice that "as much as" and "as many as" are expressed by the use of "so much — how much". For example: "I have as many medals as Ivan" — **У меня столько же медалей, сколько у Ивана** — (*Oo m'yen*-YAH STOHL-*koh zheh m'yeh*-DAHL-*yay*, SKOHL-*koh oo Ee*-VAH-*nah*).

У меня три рубля, у вас семь рублей, у него два рубля.
Oo m'yen-YAH *tree roobl*-YAH, *oo vahs s'yem roobl*-YAY, *oo n'yeh*-VOH *dvah roobl*-YAH.
I have three rubles, you have seven rubles, he has two rubles.

У кого больше всех?
Oo koh-VOH BOHL-*sheh vs'*YEKH?
Who has the most of all?

А у кого меньше всех?
Ah oo koh-VOH *m'*YEN-*sheh vs'*YEKH?
And who has the fewest of all?

NOTE on the COMPARATIVE: **Бóльше** and **мéньше** are comparatives. The comparative is formed by cutting off the ending of the adjective and adding **-ее** to the stem e.g.: **дóбрый** ("kind")—**добрée** ("kinder"), **ýмный** ("clever, intelligent"), **умнée** ("more intelligent"), **глýпый** ("stupid") **глупée**— ("more stupid"). **Тáня красúва**—"Tanya is beautiful". **Тамáра красúвее**—"Tamara is more beautiful". Some adjectives have the comparative in **-е.** The comparative ending in **-ее** or **-е** can be used only predicatively. See details on page 270.

THINKING IN RUSSIAN

(Answers on page 224)

1. Ско́лько де́нег у Лёли?
2. Сто́лько ли у неё де́нег, ско́лько у учи́теля?
3. У кого́ бо́льше де́нег, у учи́теля и́ли у тёти Ма́ши?
4. Есть ли у учи́теля за́ ухом каранда́ш?
5. Бо́льше ли у него́ карандаше́й, чем у тёти Ма́ши?
6. У Лёли ме́ньше книг, чем у учи́теля?
7. У кого́ бо́льше всех?
8. У кого́ ме́ньше всех?
9. У Лёли мно́го де́нег?
10. У учи́теля ма́ло книг?
11. Чита́ете ли вы мно́го ру́сских книг?
12. Кто пи́шет бо́льше упражне́ний, вы и́ли учи́тель?
13. В э́той кни́ге мно́го страни́ц?
14. Сто́лько ли страни́ц в Нью Йорк Таймс, ско́лько в э́той кни́ге?
15. Ско́лько у меня́ в карма́не де́нег?
16. Ско́лько у вас де́нег?
17. У неё мно́го шляп?

УРОК 13

Я вам даю книгу
*Yah vahm dah-*YOO *k'*NEE-*goo*
I give you a book

Я вам даю книгу.
*Yah vahm dah-*YOO *k'*NEE-*goo.*

I give you a book.

Вы получаете от меня книгу.
*Vwee poh-loo-*CHAH-*yet-yeh ot m'yen-*YAH *k'*NEE-*goo.*
You receive the book from me.

Что вы получаете от меня?
*Shtoh vwee poh-loo-*CHAH-*yet-yeh ot m'yen-*YAH*?*
What do you receive from me?

Вы её получаете от меня.
*Vwee yeh-*YOH *poh-loo-*CHAH-*yet-yeh ot m'yen-*YAH.
You receive it from me.

Тётя Маша даёт Лёле перчатки.
*T'*YOHT-*yah* MAH-*shah dah-*YOHT *L'*YOHL-*yeh p'yehr-*CHAHT-*kee.*
Aunt Masha gives the gloves to Lola.

Она ей даёт перчатки.
Oh-NAH *yay dah*-YOHT *p'yehr*-CHAHT-*kee.*
She gives her the gloves.

Лёля получает перчатки от тёти Маши.
*L'*YOHL-*yah poh-loo*-CHAH-*yet p'yehr*-CHAHT-*kee ot t'*YOH-*tee* MAH-*shee.*
Lola receives the gloves from Aunt Masha.

Она их получает от неё.
Oh-NAH *eekh poh-loo*-CHAH-*yet ot n'yeh*-YOH.
She receives them from her.

Кто вам даёт книгу?
Ktoh vahm dah-YOHT *k'*NEE-*goo?*
Who gives you the book?

Вы мне даёте книгу.
Vwee mn'yeh dah-YOHT-*yeh k'*NEE-*goo*
You give me the book.

От кого вы получаете книгу?
Ot koh-VOH *vwee poh-loo*-CHAH-*yet-yeh k'*NEE-*goo?*
From whom do you receive the book?

Я её получаю от вас.
Yah yeh-YOH *poh-loo*-CHAH-*yoo ot vahs.*
I receive it from you.

Кому я даю книгу?
Koh-MOO *yah dah*-YOO *k'*NEE-*goo?*
To whom do you give the book?

Вы её даёте мне.
Vwee yeh-YOH *dah*-YOHT-*yeh mn'yeh.*
You give the book to me.

Кто даёт Лёле перчатки?
Ktoh dah-YOHT *L'*YOHL-*yeh p'yehr*-CHAHT-*kee?*
Who gives Lola the gloves?

Тётя Маша даёт ей перчатки.
*T'*YOHT-*yah* MAH-*shah dah*-YOHT *yay p'yehr*-CHAHT-*kee.*
Aunt Masha gives her the gloves.

Кому она даёт перчатки?
Koh-MOO *oh*-NAH *dah*-YOHT *p'yehr*-CHAHT-*kee?*
To whom does she give the gloves?

Она их даёт Лёле.
Oh-NAH *eekh dah*-YOHT *L'*YOHL-*yeh.*
She gives them to Lola.

Кому вы даёте это письмо?
Koh-MOO *vwee dah*-YOHT-*yeh* EH-*toh pees*-MOH?
To whom do you give this letter?

Я его даю г-ну Громову.
Yah yeh-VOH *dah*-YOO *gos-poh*-DEE-*noo* GROH-*moh-voo.*
I give it to Mr. Gromov.

Что он получает от вас?
Shtoh ohn poh-loo-CHAH-*yet ot vahs?*
What does he receive from you?

Он получает от меня письмо.
Ohn poh-loo-CHAH-*yet ot m'yen*-YAH *pees*-MOH.
He receives a letter from me.

Дайте эту шляпу и этот зонтик г-же Марковой.
DIGHT-*yeh* EH-*too shl'*YAH-*poo ee* EH-*tot* ZOHN-*teek gos-poh*-ZHEH MAHR-*koh-voy.*
Give this hat and this umbrella to Mrs. Markov.

Что вы ей даёте?
Shtoh vwee yay dah-YOHT-*yeh?*
What do you give her?

Я ей даю шляпу и зонтик.
Yah yay dah-YOO *shl'*YAH-*poo ee* ZOHN-*teek.*
I give her the hat and the umbrella.

Кому вы даёте шляпу и зонтик?
Koh-MOO *vwee dah*-YOHT-*yeh shl'*YAH-*poo ee* ZOHN-*teek?*
To whom do you give the hat and the umbrella?

Ей, г-же Марковой.
Yay, gos-poh-ZHEH MAHR-*koh-voy.*
To her, to Mrs. Markov.

Что делают учителя?
*Shtoh d'*YEH-*lah-yoot oo-cheet-yel*-YAH?
What are the teachers doing?

Они дают уроки.
Oh-NEE *dah*-YOOT *oo*-ROH-*kee.*
They are giving lessons.

Кому они дают уроки?
Koh-MOO *oh*-NEE *dah*-YOOT *oo*-ROH-*kee?*
To whom are they giving lessons?

Они дают уроки ученикам.
Oh-NEE *dah*-YOOT *oo*-ROH-*kee oo-cheh-nee*-KAHM.
They are giving lessons to the pupils.

Что дают учителя ученикам?
Shtoh dah-YOOT *oo-cheet-yel*-YAH *oo-cheh-nee*-KAHM?
What do the teachers give to the pupils?

Они дают им уроки.
Oh-NEE *dah*-YOOT *eem oo*-ROH-*kee.*
They give them lessons.

Как вас зовут?
Kahk vahs zoh-VOOT?
What is your name?

Меня зовут Алексей.
M'yen-YAH *zoh*-VOOT *Ahl-yek*-SAY.
My name is Alexis.

Скажите мне ваше имя и отчество.
Skah-ZHEET-*yeh mn'yeh* VAH-*sheh* EEM-*yah ee* OHT-*chest-voh.*
Tell me your first and middle name.

Моё имя Алексей,
Moh-YOH EEM-*yah Ahl-yek*-SAY,
My first name is Alexis,

а моё отчество Михайлович.
ah moh-YOH OHT-*chest-voh Mee*-KHIGH-*loh-veech.*
my middle name is Mikhailovich.

Как ваша фамилия?
Kahk VAH-*shah fah*-MEE-*lee-yah?*
What is your family name (surname?)

Моя фамилия Василенко.
Moh-YAH *fah*-MEE-*lee-yah Vah-seel*-YEN-*koh.*
My family name is Vasilenko.

Скажите мне, что лежит на столе.
Skah-ZHEET-*yeh mn'yeh, shtoh l'yeh*-ZHEET *nah stol*-YEH.
Tell me what lies on the table.

На столе ничего нет.
Nah stol-YEH *nee-cheh*-VOH *n'yet.*
There is nothing on the table.

Скажите мне, кто стоит около двери.
Skah-ZHEET-*yeh mn'yeh, ktoh stoh*-EET OH-*koh-loh dv'*YEH-*ree.*
Tell me who is standing near the door.

Там никто не стоит.
Tahm neek-TOH *n'yeh stoh*-EET.
Nobody is standing there.

Скажите мне, как зовут г-на Берлица.
Skah-ZHEET-*yeh mn'yeh kahk zoh*-VOOT *gos-poh*-DEE-*nah* BER-*litz-ah.*
Tell me what is the name and middle name of Mr. Berlitz.

Его зовут Карл Карлович.
Yeh-VOH *zoh*-VOOT *Kahrl* KAHR-*loh-veech.*
His name and middle name is Karl Karlovich.

А как зовут г-жу Берлиц?
Ah kahk zoh-VOOT *gos-poh*-ZHOO *Berlitz?*
And what is the first and middle name of Mrs. Berlitz?

Её зовут Валерия Ивановна.
Yeh-YOH *zoh*-VOOT *Vahl*-YEH-*ree-yah Ee*-VAH-*nov-nah.*
Her name and middle name is Valeria Ivanovna.

AN OLD RUSSIAN CUSTOM: Russians tend to call each other by their first and middle name *instead* of saying Mr., Mrs., etc. The middle name is always the name of the person's father, with the masculine endings **-ович** or **-евич** and the feminine endings **-овна** or **-евна** depending on the name.

Карл Карлович разговаривает с учениками.
Kahrl KAHR-*loh-veech rahz-goh*-VAH-*ree-vah-yet s oo-cheh-nee*-KAH-*mee.*
Karl Karlovich talks with the students.

Он с ними разговаривает.
Ohn s NEE-*mee rahz-goh*-VAH-*ree-vah-yet.*
He talks with them.

Они ему что-то говорят.
Oh-NEE *yeh*-MOO SHTOH-*toh goh-vor*-YAHT.
They are telling him something.

Они с ним о чём-то разговаривают.
Oh-NEE *s neem oh* CHOHM-*toh rahz-goh*-VAH-*ree-vah-yoot.*
They are talking with him about something.

С кем вы говорите?
S k'yem vwee goh-voh-REET-*yeh?*
With whom do you speak?

Я говорю с вами.
Yah goh-vor-YOO *s* VAH-*mee.*
I speak with you.

О чём вы со мной говорите?
Oh chohm vwee soh MNOY *goh-voh*-REET-*yeh?*
About what are you talking with me?

Я говорю с вами о школе.
Yah goh-vor-YOO *s* VAH-*mee oh* SHKOHL-*yeh.*
I am talking with you about the school.

О ком вы говорите с Карлом Карловичем?
Oh kohm vwee goh-voh-REET-*yeh s* KAHR-*lom* KAHR-*loh-vee-chem?*
About whom are you talking with Karl Karlovich?

Об учениках.
Ob oo-cheh-nee-KAHKH.
About the students.

THINKING IN RUSSIAN

(Answers on page 223)

1. Даёт ли учи́тель тёте Ма́ше кни́гу?
2. Что даёт учи́тель Лёле?
3. Что де́лает тётя Ма́ша?
4. Даёт ли тётя Ма́ша учи́телю кни́гу?
5. Кто говори́т с Лёлей?
6. Что ей говори́т учи́тель?
7. Говори́т ли тётя Ма́ша что-нибу́дь соба́чке?
8. Даёт ли она́ ей что-нибу́дь?
9. Что говори́т соба́чка?
10. Говоря́т ли ученики́ с учи́телем?
11. Говоря́т ли они́ ему́ "здра́вствуйте" пе́ред уро́ком?
12. Что им говори́т учи́тель по́сле уро́ка?
13. Скажи́те мне, что у тёти Ма́ши в ле́вой руке́?
14. Что вы мне говори́те?
15. Что говори́т тётя Ма́ша учи́телю?
16. Как вас зову́т?
17. Как зову́т госпожу́ Ма́ркову?
18. Как зову́т ва́шего учи́теля?

УРОК 14

Что на столе?
Shtoh nah stol-YEH?
What is there on the table?

На столе лежит книга.
Nah stol-YEH *l'yeh*-ZHEET *k'*NEE-*gah*.
A book is lying on the table.

На стуле лежит бумага.
Nah STOOL-*yeh l'yeh*-ZHEET *boo*-MAH-*gah*.
A paper is lying on the chair.

В коробке ничего не лежит.
V koh-ROHB-*keh nee-cheh*-VOH *n'yeh l'yeh*-ZHEET.
Nothing is lying in the box.

В ней нет ничего.
V n'yay n'yet nee-cheh-VOH.
Nothing is in it.

Это моя правая рука,
EH-*toh moh*-YAH PRAH-*vah-yah roo*-KAH,
This is my right hand,

а это моя левая рука.
ah EH-*toh moh*-YAH *l'*YEH-*vah-yah roo*-KAH.
and this is my left hand.

В правой руке у меня бумага,
V PRAH-*voy roo*-KEH *oo m'yen*-YAH *boo*-MAH-*gah,*
There is a paper in my right hand,

а в левой нет ничего.
*ah v l'*YEH-*voy n'yet nee-cheh*-VOH.
and there is nothing in my left.

ATTENTION: — **Ничегó** is a very important word in Russian. It is a word with many meanings such as "it does not matter", "don't mention it", "I don't care", or "let's skip it". It even can mean: "don't get upset; eventually everything will be all right". **Нет ничегó** or **ничегó нет**, if translated literally, means "there is not nothing". The real meaning is "there is nothing". Remember that in Russian a double negative does not make an affirmative.

Есть ли что-нибудь на стуле?
Yest lee shtoh-nee-BOOD *nah* STOOL-*yeh?*
Is there anything on the chair?

Да, на стуле есть что-то.
Dah, nah STOOL-*yeh yest* SHTOH-*toh.*
Yes, there is something on the chair.

А есть ли что-нибудь в ящике?
Ah yest lee shtoh-nee-BOOD *v* YAHSH-*chee-keh?*
And is there anything in the drawer?

Нет, в ящике ничего нет.
N'yet, v YAHSH-*chee-keh nee-cheh*-VOH *n'yet.*
No, there is nothing in the drawer.

Лежит ли что-нибудь на столе?
L'yeh-ZHEET *lee shtoh-nee*-BOOD *nah stol*-YEH?
Is anything lying on the table?

Да, на нём лежит книга.
*Dah, nah n'*YOHM *l'yeh*-ZHEET *k'*NEE-*gah.*
Yes, a book is lying on it.

Есть ли что-нибудь в коробке?
Yest lee shtoh-nee-BOOD *v koh*-ROHB-*keh?*
Is there anything in the box?

В ней нет ничего.
V n'yay n'yet nee-cheh-VOH.
There is nothing in it.

Что у меня в правой руке?
Shtoh oo m'yen-YAH *v* PRAH-*voy roo*-KEH?
What have I in my right hand?

А что у меня в левой?
Ah shtoh oo m'yen-YAH *v l'*YEH-*voy?*
And what have I in my left?

В правой руке у вас палка,
V PRAH-*voy roo*-KEH *oo vahs* PAHL-*kah,*
You have a stick in your right hand,

а в левой нет ничего.
*ah v l'*YEH-*voy n'yet nee-cheh*-VOH.
and there is nothing in the left.

На этом стуле сидит Иван.
Nah EH-*tom* STOOL-*yeh see*-DEET *Ee*-VAHN.
On this chair Ivan is sitting.

На том стуле никто не сидит.
Nah tohm STOOL-*yeh neek*-TOH *n'yeh see*-DEET.
No one is sitting on that chair.

Кто стоит у окна?
Ktoh stoh-EET *oo ok*-NAH?
Who is standing near the window?

Там никто не стоит.
Tahm neek-TOH *n'yeh stoh*-EET.
No one is standing there.

Сидит ли кто-нибудь на диване?
See-DEET *lee ktoh-nee*-BOOD *nah dee*-VAHN-*yeh?*
Is anyone sitting on the sofa?

Да, на нём сидит кошка.
*Dah, nah n'*YOHM *see*-DEET KOHSH-*kah.*
Yes, the cat is sitting on it.

Есть ли кто-нибудь в гараже?
Yest lee ktoh-nee-BOOD *v gah-rah*-ZHEH?
Is there anybody in the garage?

Да, там кто-то есть.
Dah, tahm KTOH-*toh yest.*
Yes, there is somebody there.

А сидит ли кто-нибудь в автомобиле?
Ah see-DEET *lee ktoh-nee*-BOOD *v ahv-toh-moh*-BEEL-*yeh?*
And is there anybody sitting in the automobile?

Нет, в нём нет никого.
*N'yet, v n'*YOHM *n'yet nee-koh*-VOH.
No, nobody is in it.

Пётр Петрович в школе?
P'yohtr Peh-TROH-*veech v* SHKOHL-*yeh?*
Is P'yotr Petrovich at the school?

Нет, его в школе нет.
N'yet, yeh-VOH *v* SHKOHL-*yeh n'yet.*
No, he is not at the school.

Кто-то звонит.
KTOH-*toh zvoh*-NEET.
Somebody is ringing (the bell.)

Скажите, что нас дома нет.
Skah-ZHEET-*yeh, shtoh nahs* DOH-*mah n'yet.*
Say that we are not at home.

Никого дома нет, **ни нас, ни вас.**
*Nee-koh-*VOH DOH-*mah n'yet,* *nee nahs, nee vahs.*
Nobody is at home, neither we nor you.

Где Петровы? **В саду?** **Нет, их там нет.**
*Gd'*YEH *Peh-*TROH-*vee?* *V sah-*DOO? *N'yet, eekh tahm n'yet.*
Where are the Petrovs? In the garden? No, they are not there.

Магдалина Васильевна у портнихи?
*Mahg-dah-*LEE-*nah Vah-*SEEL-*yev-nah oo pohrt-*NEE-*khee?*
Is Magdalina Vasilyevna at the dressmaker's?

Нет, её там нет.
*N'yet, yeh-*YOH *tahm n'yet.*
No, she is not there.

THINKING IN RUSSIAN

(Answers on page 225)

1. Есть ли у учи́теля папиро́са в пра́вой руке́?
2. Что у тёти Ма́ши в ле́вой руке́?
3. Име́ет ли Лёля что-нибу́дь в ле́вой руке́?
4. Что у неё в пра́вой руке́?
5. Что во́зле учи́теля?
6. Стои́т ли кто-нибу́дь о́коло него́?
7. Есть ли что-нибу́дь ме́жду учи́телем и Лелей?
8. Де́ржит ли тётя Ма́ша кни́гу в пра́вой руке́?
9. Кто сиди́т на сту́ле?
10. Есть ли что-нибу́дь на столе́?
11. Что у учи́теля под мы́шкой?
12. Стои́т ли кто-нибу́дь напра́во от Лёли?
13. Кто нале́во?
14. Что лежи́т на сту́ле?
15. Лёля стои́т за учи́телем?
16. Есть ли кто-нибу́дь под столо́м?
17. Есть ли у учи́теля шля́па на голове́?
18. Что у учи́теля на голове́?

УРОК 15

Чем мы ходим?
Chem mee KHOH-*deem?*
With what do we walk?

карандаш
kah-rahn-DAHSH
pencil

Мы пишем карандашом.
Mee PEE-*shem kah-rahn-dah*-SHOHM.
We write with the pencil.

рука
roo-KAH
hand

Мы пишем рукой.
Mee PEE-*shem roo*-KOY.
We write with the hand.

руки
ROO-*kee*
hands

Мы работаем руками.
Mee rah-BOH-*tah-yem roo*-KAH-*mee*.
We work with the hands.

ноги
NOH-*ggee*
legs

Мы ходим ногами.
Mee KHOH-*deem noh*-GAH-*mee.*
We walk with the legs.

ключ
kl'yooch
key

Я запираю и отпираю дверь ключом.
Yah zah-pee-RAH-*yoo ee ot-pee*-RAH-*yoo dv'yehr kl'yoo*-CHOHM.
I lock and unlock the door with the key.

нож
nohzh
knife

Мы режем хлеб ножом.
*Mee r'*YEH-*zhem khl'yeb noh*-ZHOHM.
We cut bread with a knife.

Что мы делаем пером?
*Shtoh mee d'*YEH-*lah-yem p'yeh*-ROHM*?*
What do we do with the pen?

Мы пишем.
Mee PEE-*shem.*
We write.

Что мы делаем ключом, ножом, пером?
*Shtoh mee d'*YEH-*lah-yem kl'yoo*-CHOHM, *noh*-ZHOHM, *p'yeh*-ROHM*?*
What do we do with the key, the knife, the pen?

Что мы делаем руками, ногами?
*Shtoh mee d'*YEH-*lah-yem roo*-KAH-*mee, noh*-GAH-*mee?*
What do we do with the hands, the legs?

Чем мы пишем, берём, режем?
Chem mee PEE-*shem, b'yehr*-YOHM, *r'*YEH-*zhem?*
With what do we write, take, cut?

Чем мы ходим?
Chem mee KHOH-*deem?*
With what do we walk?

Чем мы отпираем дверь?
Chem mee ot-pee-RAH-*yem dv'yehr?*
With what do we unlock the door?

Какой рукой я пишу?
Kah-KOY *roo*-KOY *yah pee*-SHOO*?*
With which hand do I write?

Вы пишете правой рукой.
Vwee PEE-*shet-yeh* PRAH-*voy roo*-KOY.
You write with the right hand.

глаз, глаза
glahz, glah-ZAH.
eye, eyes.

Мы видим глазами.
Mee VEE-*deem glah*-ZAH-*mee.*
We see with the eyes.

ухо, уши
OO-*khoh,* OO-*shee.*
ear, ears.

Мы слышим ушами.
Mee SLEE-*sheem oo*-SHAH-*mee.*
We hear with the ears.

Я закрываю глаза; я не вижу.
*Yah zah-kree-*VAH*-yoo glah-*ZAH*;*
yah n'yeh VEE*-zhoo.*
I close the eyes; I don't see.

Я их открываю; я вижу.
*Yah eekh ot-kree-*VAH*-yoo;*
yah VEE*-zhoo.*
I open them; I see.

Вы тут; я вас вижу.
Vwee toot; yah vahs VEE*-zhoo.*
You are here; I see you.

Она там; я её не вижу.
*Oh-*NAH *tahm; yah yeh-*YOH
n'yeh VEE*-zhoo.*
She is there; I don't see her.

Закройте глаза.
*Zah-*KROYT*-yeh glah-*ZAH.
Close your eyes.

Видите ли вы?
VEE*-deet-yeh lee vwee?*
Do you see?

Откройте глаза.
*Ot-*KROYT*-yeh glah-*ZAH.
Open the eyes.

Что вы видите на улице?
Shtoh vwee VEE*-deet-yeh nah* OO*-lee-tseh?*
What do you see in the street?

Кого вы там видите?
*Koh-*VOH *vwee tahm* VEE*-deet-yeh?*
Whom do you see there?

Я там никого не вижу.
*Yah tahm nee-koh-*VOH
n'yeh VEE*-zhoo.*
I do not see anybody there.

Что вы видите в углу?
Shtoh vwee VEE*-deet-yeh*
*v oog-*LOO*?*
What do you see in the corner?

Я там ничего не вижу.
*Yah tahm nee-cheh-*VOH
n'yeh VEE*-zhoo.*
I don't see anything there.

Я говорю; вы меня слышите?
*Yah goh-vor-*YOO*; vwee m'yen-*YAH
SLEE*-sheet-yeh?*
I am talking; do you hear me?

Да, я вас слышу.
Dah, yah vahs SLEE*-shoo.*
Yes, I hear you.

Кого вы слышите?
*Koh-*VOH *vwee* SLEE*-sheet-yeh?*
Whom do you hear?

Я слышу вас.
Yah SLEE*-shoo vahs.*
I hear you.

Я стучу.
*Yah stoo-*CHOO.
I knock.

Слышите ли вы, что я делаю?
SLEE*-sheet-yeh lee vwee, shtoh yah*
*d'*YEH*-lah-yoo?*
Do you hear what I am doing?

Видите ли вы, что я делаю?
VEE*-deet-yeh lee vwee, shtoh yah d'*YEH*-lah-yoo?*
Do you see what I am doing?

Да, я вижу и слышу, что вы делаете.
Dah, yah VEE-*zhoo ee* SLEE-*shoo, shtoh vwee d'*YEH-*lah-yet-yeh.*
Yes, I see and I hear what you are doing.

нос
nohs
nose

Мы нюхаем носом.
*Mee n'*YOO-*khah-yem* NOH-*som.*
We smell with the nose.

Я нюхаю розу.
*Yah n'*YOO-*khah-yoo* ROH-*zoo.*
I smell the rose.

Роза пахнет хорошо.
ROH-*zah* PAKH-*n'yet khoh-roh-*SHOH.
The rose smells good.

Понюхайте сыр.
*Pon-*YOO-*khight-yeh seer.*
Smell the cheese.

Он пахнет плохо.
Ohn PAHKH-*n'yet* PLOH-*khoh.*
It smells bad.

Чем мы нюхаем?
*Chem mee n'*YOO-*khah-yem?*
With what do we smell?

Как пахнет гвоздика, хорошо или плохо?
Kahk PAHKH-*n'yet gvoz-*DEE-*kah, khoh-roh-*SHOH EE-*lee* PLOH-*khoh?*
How does the carnation smell, good or bad?

Мы едим ртом.
*Mee yeh-*DEEM *rtohm.*
We eat with the mouth.

Мы пьём ртом.
Mee p'yohm rtohm.
We drink with the mouth.

Мы едим хлеб, мясо, фрукты, овощи.
*Mee yeh-*DEEM *khl'yeb, m'*YAH-*soh,* FROOK-*tee,* OH-*vosh-chee.*
We eat bread, meat, fruits, vegetables.

Мы пьём воду, молоко, кофе, чай и другие напитки.
Mee p'yohm VOH-*doo, moh-loh-*KOH, KOH-*feh, chigh ee droo-*GGEE-*yeh nah-*PEET-*kee.*
We drink water, milk, coffee, tea, and other beverages.

Едите ли вы хлеб?
*Yeh-*DEET-*yeh lee vwee khl'yeb?*
Do you eat bread?

Да, я ем хлеб ежедневно.
*Dah, yah yem khl'yeb yeh-zheh-dn'*YEV-*noh.*
Yes, I eat bread every day.

Пьёте ли вы кофе?
*P'*YOHT-*yeh lee vwee* KOH-*feh?*
Do you drink coffee?

Нет, я пью чай.
N'yet, yah p'yoo chigh.
No, I drink tea.

Вы пьёте чай с молоком?
*Vwee p'*YOHT-*yeh chigh s moh-loh-*KOHM*?*
Do you drink tea with milk?

Нет, с лимоном.
*Nyet, s lee-*MOH-*nom.*
No, with lemon.

То, что мы едим, называется едой или пищей.
*Toh, shtoh mee yeh-*DEEM, *nah-zee-*VAH-*yet-sah yeh-*DOY EE-*lee* PEESH-*chay.*
What we eat is called food.

То, что мы пьём, называется напитком.
*Toh, shtoh mee p'yohm, nah-zee-*VAH-*yet-sah nah-*PEET-*kom.*
What we drink is called beverage.

Скажите, пожалуйста, что мы едим.
*Skah-*ZHEET-*yeh, poh-*ZHAH-*looy-stah, shtoh mee yeh-*DEEM.
Please, tell me what we eat.

Назовите мне напитки.
*Nah-zoh-*VEET-*yeh mn'yeh nah-*PEET-*kee.*
Tell me the names of (some) beverages.

Лимонад — напиток?
*Lee-moh-*NAHD—*nah-*PEE-*tok?*
Is lemonade a beverage?

Из чего делают вино?
*Eez cheh-*VOH *d'*YEH-*lah-yoot vee-*NOH*?*
What is wine made from?

Его делают из винограда.
*Yeh-*VOH *d'*YEH-*lah-yoot eez vee-noh-*GRAH-*dah.*
It is made from grapes.

Фрукты:	**яблоко,**	**груша,**	**черешня,**	**виноград,**
FROOK-*tee*:	YAHB-*loh-koh,*	GROO-*shah,*	*cheh-*RESH-*n'yah,*	*vee-noh-*GRAHD*,*
Fruits:	apple,	pear,	cherry,	grapes,

апельсин,	**вишня,**	**персик,**	**абрикос.**
*ahp-yel-*SEEN*,*	VEESH-*n'yah,*	*p'*YEHR-*seek,*	*ahb-ree-*KOHS.
orange,	sour cherry,	peach,	apricot.

Ягоды:	**клубника,**	**земляника,**	**малина,**	**черника.**
YAH-*goh-dee*:	*kloob-*NEE-*kah,*	*z'yem-l'yah-*NEE-*kah,*	*mah-*LEE-*nah,*	*chehr-*NEE-*kah.*
Berries:	strawberry,	wild strawberry,	raspberry,	blueberry.

Овощи (зелень):	**картофель,**	**капуста,**	**горох,**
OH-*vosh-chee* (*z'*YEL-*yen*):	*kahr-*TOHF-*yel,*	*kah-*POOS-*tah,*	*goh-*ROHKH*,*
Vegetables (greens):	potato(es),	cabbage,	peas,

морковка,	**фасоль,**	**грибы,**	**салат,**	**редиска,**
mor-KOHV-*kah,*	*fah*-SOHL,	*gree*-BEE,	*sah*-LAHT,	*reh*-DEES-*kah,*
carrot(s),	beans,	mushrooms,	lettuce,	radish(es),

помидор,	**свёкла,**	**арбуз,**	**дыня,**	**тыква.**
poh-mee-DOR,	*sv'*YOHK-*lah,*	*ahr*-BOOZ,	DEEN-*yah,*	TEEK-*vah.*
tomato,	beets,	water melon,	cantaloupe,	pumpkin.

Мясные блюда:	**говядина,**	**телятина,**
M'yahs-NEE-*yeh bl'*YOO-*dah*:	*gov*-YAH-*dee-nah,*	*t'yel*-YAH-*tee-nah,*
Meat dishes:	beef,	veal,

свинина,	**баранина,**	**бифштекс,**	**котлета,**
svee-NEE-*nah,*	*bah*-RAH-*nee-nah,*	*beef*-SHTEKS,	*kotl*-YEH-*tah,*
pork,	lamb (mutton),	beefsteak,	cutlet,

жаркое,	**ветчина,**	**колбаса.**	**Птица:**
zhahr-KOH-*yeh,*	*v'yet-chee*-NAH,	*kol-bah*-SAH.	PTEE-*tsah*:
roast,	ham,	sausage.	Fowl:

курица,	**утка,**	**гусь,**	**индейка,**	**фазан.**
KOO-*ree-tsah,*	OOT-*kah,*	*goos,*	*eend*-YAY-*kah,*	*fah*-ZAHN.
chicken,	duck,	goose,	turkey,	pheasant.

THINKING IN RUSSIAN

(Answers on page 225)

1. Чем учи́тель ню́хает лук?
2. Хорошо́ ли па́хнет лук?
3. Хорошо́ ли па́хнет ро́за?
4. Что ню́хает тётя Ма́ша, ро́зу и́ли лук?
5. Ви́дите ли вы предме́ты, кото́рые за ва́ми?
6. Ви́дим ли мы предме́ты, кото́рые пе́ред на́ми?
7. Стуча́т в дверь. Вы слы́шите?
8. Слы́шите ли вы меня́?
9. Еди́м ли мы хлеб?
10. Ви́дим ли мы карти́ну (в кинемато́графе)?
11. Кладём ли мы са́хар в чай?
12. Едя́т ли америка́нцы бе́лый хлеб?
13. Ру́сские пьют мно́го ча́ю?
14. Еди́м ли мы карто́фель с са́харом?
15. Вы пьёте чай с молоко́м?
16. Чем мы ре́жем мя́со?
17. Еди́м ли мы горо́х ножо́м?
18. Чем мы ре́жем бума́гу?

УРОК 16

Чем мы едим?
*Chem mee yeh-*DEEM*?*
With what do we eat?

ложка	**вилка**	**нож**	**блюдо**	**блюдечко**
LOHZH-*kah*	VEEL-*kah*	*nohzh*	*bl'*YOO-*doh*	*bl'*YOOD-*yech-koh*
spoon	fork	knife	platter, dish	saucer

тарелка	**стакан**	**рюмка**	**чашка**	**бутылка**
*tahr-*YEL-*kah*	*stah-*KAHN	*r'*YOOM-*kah*	CHAHSH-*kah*	*boo-*TEEL-*kah*
plate	glass	wine glass	cup	bottle

скатерть	**салфетка**	**сахарница**	**поднос**
SKAHT-*yehrt*	*sahl-f'*YET-*kah*	SAH-*khar-nee-tsah*	*pod-*NOHS
table cloth	napkin	sugar bowl	tray

Мы едим суп ложкой, а мясо вилкой.
*Mee yeh-*DEEM *soop* LOHZH-*koy, ah m'*YAH-*soh* VEEL-*koy.*
We eat soup with a spoon, and meat with a fork.

Мы пьём воду из стакана,
Mee p'yohm VOH-*doo eez stah-*KAH-*nah,*
We drink water from a glass,

а кофе из чашки.
ah KOH-*feh eez* CHAHSH-*kee.*
and coffee from a cup.

Чем мы едим суп?
*Chem mee yeh-*DEEM *soop?*
With what do we eat soup?

Ложкой.
LOHZH-*koy.*
With a spoon.

DID YOU NOTICE that sometimes the Russian language leaves out the preposition "with" using solely the instrumental case? This occurs when the noun is the *instrument* with which we are doing something. Therefore you say:

Я хожу ногами "I walk with my legs."

but

Я иду с Иваном "I am going with Ivan."

Из чего мы пьём вино?
*Eez cheh-*VOH *mee p'yohm vee-*NOH?
From what do we drink wine?

Из рюмки.
*Eez r'*YOOM-*kee.*
From a wine glass.

Пьём ли мы водку из бутылки?
P'yohm lee mee VOHD-*koo eez boo-*TEEL-*kee?*
Do we drink vodka from a bottle?

Нет, мы наливаем водку из бутылки в рюмку.
*N'yet, mee nah-lee-*VAH-*yem* VOHD-*koo eez boo-*TEEL-*kee v r'*YOOM-*koo.*
No, we pour the vodka from the bottle into the glass.

Из чего пьют кофе?
*Eez cheh-*VOH *p'yoot* KOH-*feh?*
From what do we drink coffee?

Из чашки.
Eez CHAHSH-*kee.*
From a cup.

Сахар на вкус сладкий.
SAH-*khar nah vkoos* SLAHD-*kee.*
Sugar has a sweet taste.

Лимон на вкус кислый.
*Lee-*MOHN *nah vkoos* KEES-*lee.*
Lemon has a sour taste.

Языком мы пробуем еду и напитки.
*Yah-zee-*KOHM *mee* PROH-*boo-yem yeh-*DOO *ee nah-*PEET-*kee.*
With the tongue we taste food and drinks.

Хлеб — еда, чай — напиток.
*Khl'yeb — yeh-*DAH, *chigh — nah-*PEE-*tok.*
Bread is food, tea is a beverage.

В кофе мы кладём сахар.
V KOH-*feh mee klahd-*YOHM SAH-*khar.*
We put sugar into coffee.

Кофе с сахаром вкусный.
KOH-*feh s* SAH-*khah-rom* VKOOS-*nee.*
Coffee with sugar has a pleasant taste.

Кофе без сахара на вкус горький.
KOH-*feh b'yez* SAH-*khah-rah na vkoos* GOR-*kee.*
Coffee without sugar has a bitter taste.

AN IDIOM TO REMEMBER: **на вкус** — "as to the taste". "Chocolate has a sweet taste" — **Шокола́д сла́дкий на вкус.**

Чем мы пробуем пищу?
Chem mee PROH-*boo-yem* PEESH-*choo?*
With what do we taste the food?

Языком.
*Yah-zee-*KOHM.
With the tongue.

Вкусный ли кофе без сахара?
VKOOS-*nee lee* KOH-*feh b'yez* SAH-*khah-rah?*
Is coffee without sugar tasty?

Нет, не вкусный.
N'yet, n'yeh VKOOS-*nee.*
No, it is not tasty.

Какой на вкус сахар?
*Kah-*KOY *nah vkoos* SAH-*khahr?*
What taste has sugar?

Сладкий.
SLAHD-*kee.*
Sweet.

Какой на вкус лимон?
*Kah-*KOY *nah vkoos lee-*MOHN?
What taste has lemon?

Кислый.
KEES-*lee.*
Sour.

Роза пахнет хорошо;
ROH-*zah* PAHKH-*n'yet khoh-roh-*SHOH;
The rose smells good;

она имеет приятный запах.
*oh-*NAH *eem-*YEH-*yet pree-*YAHT-*nee* ZAH-*pahkh.*
it has a pleasant smell.

Запах розы приятный.
ZAH-*pahkh* ROH-*zee* *pree*-YAHT-*nee.*
The odor of the rose is pleasant.

Слышите ли вы, как пахнут розы?
SLEE-*sheet-yeh lee vwee, kahk* PAHKH-*noot* ROH-*zee?*
Do you notice how the roses smell?

NOTE: The primary meaning of the word **слышать** is "to hear" but it is also used to mean "smell," "notice," "perceive" an odor.

Газ пахнет плохо; его запах неприятный.
Gahz PAHKH-*n'yet* PLOH-*khoh; yeh*-VOH ZAH-*pahkh n'yeh-pree*-YAHT-*nee.*
Gas smells bad; its odor is unpleasant.

Земляника вкусная; она имеет хороший вкус.
Z'yeml-yah-NEE-*kah* VKOOS-*nah-yah; oh*-NAH *eem*-YEH-*yet khoh*-ROH-*shee vkoos.*
The strawberry is tasty, it has a good taste.

Вкус земляники приятный.
Vkoos z'yeml-yah-NEE-*kee pree*-YAHT-*nee.*
The taste of the strawberry is pleasant.

Вкус лимона неприятный.
Vkoos lee-MOH-*nah n'yeh-pree*-YAHT-*nee.*
The taste of the lemon is unpleasant.

Имеет ли роза приятный запах?
Eem-YEH-*yet lee* ROH-*zah pree*-YAHT-*nee* ZAH-*pahkh?*
Has the rose a pleasant small?

Имеет ли сыр приятный запах?
Eem-YEH-*yet lee seer pree*-YAHT-*nee* ZAH-*pahkh?*
Has cheese a pleasant smell?

Статуя Венеры красивая.
STAH-*too-yah Vehn*-YEH-*ree krah*-SEE-*vah-yah.*
The statue of Venus is beautiful.

Кавказские горы красивые.
Kavh-KAHZ-*skee-yeh* GOH-*ree krah*-SEE-*vee-yeh.*
The Caucasus mountains are beautiful.

В музее красивые статуи и красивые картины.
V moo-ZEH-*yeh krah*-SEE-*vee-yeh* STAH-*too-yee ee krah*-SEE-*vee-yeh kahr*-TEE-*nee.*
In the museum there are beautiful statues and beautiful pictures.

То, на что нам неприятно смотреть, некрасиво.
*Toh, nah shtoh nahm n'yep-ree-*YAHT*-noh smotr-*YET*, n'yeh-krah-*SEE*-voh.*
What we don't like to look at is ugly.

NOTE to the Student: In Russian if you like something, you say: **мне нрáвится** — "it pleases me". If you do not like it, you say: **мне не нрáвится.** — "it does not please me".

Паук некрасивый.
*Pah-*OOK *n'yeh-krah-*SEE*-vee.*
The spider is ugly.

Обезьяна некрасивая.
*Ob-yez-*YAH*-nah n'yeh-krah-*SEE*-vah-yah.*
The monkey is ugly.

Мы любим приятные запахи.
*Mee l'*YOO*-beem pree-*YAHT*-nee-yeh* ZAH*-pah-khee.*
We like pleasant odors.

Мы любим есть то, что нам нравится.
*Mee l'*YOO*-beem yest toh, shtoh nahm* NRAH*-veet-sah.*
We like to eat what we are fond of.

То, что мы любим есть, мы называем вкусным.
*Toh, shtoh mee l'*YOO*-beem yest, mee nah-zee-*VAH*-yem* VKOOS*-neem.*
What we like to eat we call tasty.

Я ем мясо.
*Yah yem m'*YAH*-soh.*
I eat meat.

Анна Ивановна мяса не ест.
AHN*-nah Ee-*VAH*-nov-nah m'*YAH*-sah n'yeh yest.*
Anna Ivanovna doesn't eat meat.

Она кушает овощи.
*Oh-*NAH KOO*-shah-yet* OH*-vosh-chee.*
She eats vegetables.

Николай Павлович не кушает овощей.
*Nee-koh-*LIGH PAHV*-loh-veech n'yeh* KOO*-shah-yet oh-vosh-*CHAY.
Ivan Pavlovich doesn't eat vegetables.

NOTE on POLITENESS: Although it is grammatically correct to express "I eat" by **я ем** and **я кýшаю,** the verb **кýшать** should never be used in the first person. This is because **кýшать** implies "to eat just a little" or "to taste something". With "he", "she", "you", or "they", this distinction is not observed. Either verb is permissible.

Мы кладём в суп соль.
Mee klahd-YOHM *v soop sohl.*
We put salt in soup.

Мы не кладём соль в кофе.
Mee n'yeh klahd-YOHM *sohl v* KOH-*feh.*
We don't put salt in coffee.

Вы едите фрукты.
Vwee yeh-DEET-*yeh* FROOK-*tee.*
You eat fruit.

Вы не едите фруктов.
Vwee n'yeh yeh-DEET-*yeh* FROOK-*tov.*
You don't eat fruit.

Мы идём в ресторан завтракать.
Mee eed-YOHM *v res-toh*-RAHN ZAHV-*trah-kaht.*
We go into a restaurant for lunch.

Мы садимся за стол.
Mee sah-DEEM-*sah zah stohl.*
We seat ourselves at a table.

К нам подходит официант и подаёт нам меню.
K nahm pod-KHOH-*deet oh-fee-tsee*-AHNT *ee poh-dah*-YOHT *nahm men*-YOO.
A waiter comes to us and gives us the menu.

Мы заказываем борщ, битки с горошком, кисель и чай.
Mee zah-KAH-*zee-vah-yem borshch, beet*-KEE *s goh*-ROHSH-*kom, kees*-YEL *ee chigh.*
We order borshch, (chopped) beef cutlets with (green) peas, jello, and tea.

После завтрака официант подаёт нам счёт.
POHS-*l'yeh* ZAHV-*trah-kah oh-fee-tsee*-YAHNT *poh-dah*-YOHT *nahm shchoht.*
After lunch the waiter gives us the check.

Мы платим и уходим. В Советском Союзе на чай не дают.
Mee PLAH-*teem ee oo*-KHOH-*deem. V Sov*-YET-*skom Soh*-YOOZ-*yeh nah* CHIGH *n'yeh dah*-YOOT.
We pay and leave. One doesn't give tips in the Soviet Union.

THINKING IN RUSSIAN

(Answers on page 226)

1. Прия́тный ли за́пах у ро́зы?
2. Прия́тный ли за́пах име́ет сыр?
3. Прия́тен ли на вкус суп с са́харом?
4. Нра́вится ли вам за́пах капу́сты?
5. Нра́вится ли вам вкус мали́ны?
6. Лю́бите ли вы зелёные я́блоки?
7. Лю́бите ли вы сыр?
8. Де́ти лю́бят конфе́ты?
9. Лю́бите ли вы говори́ть по-ру́сски?
10. Краси́ва ли ста́туя Вене́ры?
11. Она́ вам нра́вится?
12. Как вам нра́вится му́зыка Чайко́вского?
13. Нра́вится ли вам его́ му́зыка?
14. Из чего́ мы пьём во́ду?
15. Из чего́ мы пьём чай?
16. Из чего́ мы пьём вино́?
17. Сова́ краси́ва и́ли некраси́ва?
18. Краси́в ли ру́сский язы́к?
19. Прия́тно ли его́ слу́шать?
20. Ку́шаете ли вы мя́со?
21. Еди́те ли вы ры́бу?

УРОК 17

Я не могу видеть
Yah n'yeh moh-goo VEED-*yet*
I cannot see

Я закрываю дверь.
*Yah zah-kree-*VAH-*you dv'yehr.*
I close the door.

Я не могу выйти.
*Yah n'yeh moh-*GOO VWEE-*tee.*
I cannot go out.

Дверь открыта.
*Dv'yehr ot-*KREE-*tah.*
The door is open.

У меня есть карандаш.
*Oo m'yen-*YAH *yest kah-rahn-*DAHSH.
I have a pencil.

Дверь закрыта.
*Dv'yehr zah-*KREE-*tah.*
The door is closed.

Я открываю дверь.
*Yah oht-kree-*VAH-*you dv'yehr.*
I open the door.

Я могу выйти.
*Yah moh-*GOO VWEE-*tee.*
I can go out.

Я могу писать.
*Yah moh-*GOO *pee-*SAHT.
I can write.

У вас нет карандаша.
*Oo vahs n'yet kah-rahn-dah-*SHAH.
You haven't a pencil.

Вы не можете писать.
Vwee n'yeh MOH-*zhet-yeh pee-*SAHT.
You cannot write.

У Ивана есть нож.
*Oo Ee-*VAH-*nah yest nohzh.*
Ivan has a knife.

Он может резать бумагу.
Ohn MOH-*zhet r'*YEH-*zaht boo-*MAH-*goo.*
He can cut the paper.

У меня нет ножа.
*Oo m'yen-*YAH *n'yet noh-*ZHAH.
I haven't a knife.

Я не могу резать бумагу.
*Yah n'yeh moh-*GOO *r'*YEH-*zaht boo-*MAH-*goo.*
I cannot cut the paper.

REMEMBER:

у меня́ есть	"I have"
у меня́ нет (+ genitive)	"I have not"
у меня́ нет стола́	"I have no table"
у вас нет сту́ла	"you have no chair"
у него́ нет па́лки	"he has no stick"
у неё нет шля́пы	"she has no hat"
у нас нет соба́ки	"we have no dog"
у них нет до́ма	"they have no house"

Я трогаю стол.
Yah TROH-*gah-yoo stohl.*
I touch the table.

Вы трогаете стул.
Vwee TROH-*gah-yet-yeh stool.*
You touch the chair.

Троньте потолок.
TROHNT-*yeh poh-toh-*LOHK.
Touch the ceiling.

Потолок высокий.
*Poh-toh-*LOHK *vwee-*SOH-*kee.*
The ceiling is high.

Вы не можете тронуть потолок.
Vwee n'yeh MOH-*zhet-yeh* TROH-*noot poh-toh-*LOHK.
You cannot touch the ceiling.

Лампа низкая.
LAHM-*pah* NEEZ-*kah-yah.*
The lamp is low.

Я могу её тронуть.
*Yah moh-*GOO *yeh-*YOH TROH-*noot.*
I can touch it.

Я её трогаю.
*Yah yeh-*YOH TROH-*gah-yoo.*
I am touching it.

Я закрываю глаза.
*Yah zah-kree-*VAH-*yoo glah-*ZAH.
I close my eyes.

Я вас не вижу.
Yah vahs n'yeh VEE-*zhoo.*
I don't see you.

Я не могу видеть.
*Yah n'yeh moh-*GOO VEED-*yet.*
I cannot see.

Я открываю глаза.
*Yah ot-kree-*VAH-*yoo glah-*ZAH.
I open my eyes.

Я могу видеть.
*Yah moh-*GOO VEED-*yet.*
I can see.

Я вас вижу.
Yah vahs VEE-*zhoo.*
I see you.

Можем ли мы есть суп вилкой?
MOH-*zhem lee mee yest soop* VEEL-*koy?*
Can we eat soup with a fork?

Нет, не можем.
N'yet, n'yeh MOH-*zhem.*
No, we cannot.

Мы ходим ногами.
Mee KHOH-*deem noh-*GAH-*mee.*
We walk with our legs.

Можем ли мы ходить без ног?
MOH-*zhem lee mee khoh-*DEET *b'yez nohg?*
Can we walk without legs?

Мы видим глазами.
Mee VEE-*deem glah-*ZAH-*mee.*
We see with our eyes.

Можем ли мы видеть без глаз?
MOH-*zhem lee mee* VEED-*yet b'yez glahz?*
Can we see without eyes?

NOTE ON GENITIVE: The regular genitive plural of masculine nouns ends in **-ов**. Ex.: **дом** — "house", **домóв** — "of the houses." But there are a few nouns of which the genitive plural is like the nominative singular: **чулóк** — "stocking", **две пáры чулóк** — "two pairs of stockings"; **пáра сапóг** — "a pair of boots"; **мнóго солдáт** — "many soldiers"; **дéсять человéк** — "ten people"; **пáра глаз** —"a pair of eyes".

У меня нет ножа.
*Oo m'yen-*YAH *n'yet noh-*ZHAH.
I don't have a knife.

Я не могу резать хлеб.
*Yah n'yeh moh-*GOO *r'*YEH-*zaht khl'*YEB.
I cannot cut the bread.

Почему вы не можете?
*Poh-cheh-*MOO *vwee n'yeh* MOH-*zhet-yeh?*
Why can't you?

Потому что у меня нет ножа.
*Poh-toh-*MOO *shtoh oo m'yen-*YAH *n'yet noh-*ZHAH.
Because I have no knife.

Дверь закрыта.
*Dv'yehr zah-*KREE-*tah.*
The door is closed.

Пётр не может выйти.
P'yohtr n'yeh MOH-*zhet* VWEE-*tee.*
Peter cannot go out.

Почему он не может выйти?
Poh-cheh-MOO *ohn n'yeh* MOH-*zhet* VWEE-*tee?*
Why can't he go out?

Потому что дверь закрыта.
Poh-toh-MOO *shtoh dv'yehr zah*-KREE-*tah.*
Because the door is closed.

Сумка маленькая, а книга большая.
SOOM-*kah* MAHL-*yen-kah-yah, a k'*NEE-*gah bol*-SHAH-*yah.*
The hand-bag is small, and the book is large.

Почему мы не можем положить книгу в сумку?
Poh-cheh-MOO *mee n'yeh* MOH-*zhem poh-loh*-ZHEET *k'*NEE-*goo v* SOOM-*koo?*
Why can't we put the book into the hand-bag?

Потому что книга большая, а сумка маленькая.
Poh-toh-MOO *shtoh k'*NEE-*gah bol*-SHAH-*yah, ah* SOOM-*kah* MAHL-*yen-kah-yah.*
Because the book is large and the hand-bag is small.

У господина Берлица очки.
Oo gos-poh-DEE-*nah* BAIR-*litz-ah och*-KEE.
Mr. Berlitz has eye-glasses.

С очками он может читать.
S och-KAH-*mee ohn* MOH-*zhet chee*-TAHT.
With eye-glasses he is able to read.

Можете ли вы читать без очков?
MOH-*zhet-yeh lee vwee chee*-TAHT *b'yez och*-KOHV*?*
Can you read without eye-glasses?

Могу.
Moh-GOO.
I can.

Не могу.
N'yeh moh-GOO.
I cannot.

Я считаю книги.
Yah shchee-TAH-*yoo k'*NEE-*ggee.*
I count the books.

Можете ли вы их сосчитать?
MOH-*zhet-yeh lee vwee eekh sos-chee*-TAHT*?*
Can you count them?

Могу.
Moh-GOO.
I can.

А можете ли вы сосчитать звёзды на небе?
Ah MOH-*zhet-yeh lee vwee sos-chee*-TAHT *zv'*YOHZ-*dee nah n'*YEB-*yeh?*
And can you count the stars in the sky?

Не могу.
N'yeh moh-GOO.
I cannot.

IMPORTANT NOTE: Don't mix them up!

читáть means "to read".
считáть means to "count".
сосчитáть gives the added meaning of a completed action "to count them to the last one." This is the perfective aspect of the verb. You will meet it constantly as we go along.

Вы ломаете спичку.
*Vwee loh-*MAH*-yet-yeh* SPEECH*-koo.*
You break a match.

А можете ли вы сломать ключ?
Ah MOH*-zhet-yeh lee vwee sloh-*MAHT *kl'yooch?*
But can you break a key?

Закройте глаза.
*Zah-*KROYT*-yeh glah-*ZAH.
Close your eyes.

Вы не можете видеть.
Vwee n'yeh MOH*-zhet-yeh* VEED*-yet.*
You cannot see.

Почему вы не можете?
*Poh-cheh-*MOO *vwee n'yeh* MOH*-zhet-yeh?*
Why can't you?

Потому что мои глаза закрыты.
*Poh-toh-*MOO *shtoh* MOH*-ee glah-*ZAH *zah-*KREE*-tee.*
Because my eyes are closed.

Где г. Берлиц?
*Gd'yeh gos-poh-*DEEN *Berlitz?*
Where is Mr. Berlitz?

Его тут нет.
*Yeh-*VOH *toot n'yet.*
He is not here.

Могут ли ученики его видеть?
MOH*-goot lee oo-cheh-nee-*KEE *yeh-*VOH VEED*-yet?*
Can the students see him?

Нет, не могут.
N'yet, n'yeh MOH*-goot.*
No, they cannot.

Почему они не могут его видеть?
*Poh-cheh-*MOO *oh-*NEE *n'yeh* MOH*-goot yeh-*VOH VEED*-yet?*
Why can't they see him?

Потому что его здесь нет.
*Poh-toh-*MOO *shtoh yeh-*VOH *zd'yes n'yet.*
Because he is not here.

NOTE on Grammar: Notice the peculiar use of the genitive in the sentences above. **Его́** is the genitive of **он** "he". You already know that **нет** (in the sense of "there is no", "there is not") always requires the genitive. Accordingly you have to say in Russian:

меня́ здесь нет	I am not here
его́ " "	he is not here
её " "	she is not here
нас " "	we are not here
вас " "	you are not here
их " "	they are not here

Его́ нет до́ма — "He is not at home".

THINKING IN RUSSIAN

(Answers on page 226)

1. Тро́гает ли Лёля соба́чку?
2. Мо́жет ли она́ тро́нуть пра́вую ру́ку учи́теля?
3. Мо́жет ли учи́тель тро́нуть её шля́пу?
4. Тро́гает ли он её?
5. Ла́мпа ни́зкая?
6. Мо́жет ли учи́тель её тро́нуть?
7. Что тро́гает учи́тель?
8. Есть ли у учи́теля очки́?
9. Мо́жет ли он ви́деть без очко́в?
10. Дверь откры́та; мо́жете ли вы вы́йти из ко́мнаты?
11. У меня́ нет ни пера́, ни карандаша́; могу́ ли я писа́ть?
12. Мо́жем ли мы ви́деть предме́ты, кото́рые за на́ми?
13. Мо́гут ли ученики́ тро́нуть потоло́к?
14. Мо́жете ли вы слома́ть спи́чку?
15. Мо́жете ли вы сосчита́ть звёзды на не́бе?
16. Мо́жете ли вы есть суп ви́лкой?

УРОК 18

Что я должен сделать, чтобы выйти из комнаты?
Shtoh yah DOHL-*zhen sd'*YEH-*laht*
SHTOH-*bee* VWEE-*tee eez* KOHM-*nah-tee?*
What must I do to go out of the room?

Дверь открыта.
Dv'yehr ot-KREE-*tah.*
The door is open.

Можете ли вы выйти из комнаты?
MOH-*zhet-yeh lee vwee* VWEE-*tee eez* KOHM-*nah-tee?*
Can you go out of the room?

Да, могу.
Da, moh-GOO.
Yes, I can.

Почему вы не выходите?
Poh-cheh-MOO *vwee n'yeh vwee*-KHOH-*deet-yeh?*
Why don't you go out?

Потому что я не хочу.
Poh-toh-MOO *shtoh yah n'yeh khoh*-CHOO.
Because I do not want to.

Можете ли вы разорвать вашу книгу? — **Да, могу.**
*MOH-zhet-yeh lee vwee rah-zor-*VAHT VAH-*shoo k'*NEE-*goo?* — *Dah, moh-*GOO.
Can you tear apart your book? — Yes, I can.

Почему вы не рвёте вашей книги?
*Poh-cheh-*MOO *vwee n'yeh rv'*YOHT-*yeh* VAH-*shay k'*NEE-*ggee?*
Why don't you tear your book?

Потому что я не хочу.
*Poh-toh-*MOO *shtoh yah n'yeh khoh-*CHOO.
Because I do not want to.

Если вы хотите выйти, вы должны открыть дверь.
YES-*lee vwee khoh-*TEET-*yeh* VWEE-*tee, vwee dolzh-*NEE *ot-*KREET *dv'yehr.*
If you want to go out, you must open the door.

Я должен открыть глаза, если я хочу видеть.
Yah DOHL-*zhen ot-*KREET *glah-*ZAH, YES-*lee yah khoh-*CHOO VEED-*yet.*
I must open my eyes, if I want to see.

Если мы хотим есть суп, мы должны иметь ложку.
YES-*lee mee khoh-*TEEM *yest soop, mee dolzh-*NEE *eem-*YET LOHZH-*koo.*
If we wish to eat soup, we must have a spoon.

Если вы хотите резать мясо, вы должны иметь нож.
YES-*lee vwee khoh-*TEET-*yeh r'*YEH-*zaht m'*YAH-*soh, vwee dolzh-*NEE *eem-*YET *nohzh.*
If you wish to cut meat, you must have a knife.

EXPLANATORY NOTE: **мочь** and **хотéть** are verbs used directly with the infinitive and are conjugated as verbs. EX. — "I want to see". — **Я хочý вúдеть.** "She can speak English". — **Онá мóжет говорúть по-английски,** etc. **Дóлжен** ("must", "be obliged to") is not properly a verb, and only changes its form as an adjective. EX. — "She must do it". — **Онá должнá э́то сдéлать. Должнá** is the feminine form of the adjective.

Я могу сломать мои часы, но я не хочу.
*Yah moh-*GOO *sloh-*MAHT *moh-*EE *chah-*SEE, *noh yah n'yeh khoh-*CHOO.
I can break my watch, but I do not want to.

Я могу разорвать мой платок, но я не хочу.
Yah moh-GOO *rah-zor*-VAHT *moy plah*-TOHK, *noh yah n'yeh khoh*-CHOO.
I can tear my handkerchief apart, but I do not want to.

DON'T FORGET: **хоте́ть** takes the infinitive when a verb follows it, just as **мочь** in the preceding lesson. Example: **Я хочу́ есть** — "I want to eat". **Он не хо́чет пить во́дку** — "He doesn't want to drink vodka".

Можете ли вы говорить по-русски? — **Да, могу.**
MOH-*zhet-yeh lee vwee goh-voh*-REET *poh*-ROOS-*skee?* — *Dah, moh*-GOO.
Can you speak Russian? — Yes, I can.

Хотите ли вы говорить по-русски? — **Да, хочу.**
Khoh-TEET-*yeh lee vwee goh-voh*-REET *poh*-ROOS-*skee?* — *Dah, khoh*-CHOO.
Do you want to speak Russian? — Yes, I want to.

Что вы хотите читать, книгу или газету?
Shtoh vwee khoh-TEET-*yeh chee*-TAHT, *k'*NEE-*goo* EE-*lee gah*-ZEH-*too?*
What do you want to read, the book or the newspaper?

Что вы хотите пить, чай или кофе?
Shtoh vwee khoh-TEET-*yeh peet, chigh* EE-*lee* KOH-*feh?*
What you want to drink, tea or coffee?

Могут ли ученики писать по-русски? — **Да, могут.**
MOH-*goot lee oo-cheh-nee*-KEE *pee*-SAHT *poh*-ROOS-*skee?* — *Dah,* MOH-*goot.*
Can the pupils write Russian? — Yes, they can.

Если дверь закрыта, мы не можем выйти.
YES-*lee dv'yehr zah*-KREE-*tah, mee n'yeh* MOH-*zhem* VWEE-*tee.*
If the door is closed, we cannot go out.

Если мы закрываем глаза, мы не можем видеть.
YES-*lee mee zah-kree*-VAH-*yem glah*-ZAH, *mee n'yeh* MOH-*zhem* VEED-*yet.*
If we close our eyes, we cannot see.

Если у меня нет ни пера, ни карандаша,
YES-*lee oo m'yen*-YAH *n'yet nee p'yeh*-RAH, *nee kah-rahn-dah*-SHAH,
If I have neither pencil nor pen,

я не могу писать на бумаге.
*yah n'yeh moh-*GOO *pee-*SAHT *nah boo-*MAHG*-yeh.*
I cannot write on the paper.

Можем ли мы выйти, если дверь закрыта?
MOH*-zhem lee mee* VWEE*-tee,* YES*-lee dv'yehr zah-*KREE*-tah?*
Can we go out if the door is closed?

Нет, не можем.
N'yet, n'yeh MOH*-zhem.*
No, we cannot.

Можете ли вы резать хлеб, если у вас нет ножа?
MOH*-zhet-yeh lee vwee r'*YEH*-zaht khl'yeb,* YES*-lee oo vahs n'yet noh-*ZHAH*?*
Can you cut bread if you have no knife?

Нет, не могу.
*N'yet, n'yeh moh-*GOO.
No, I cannot.

Что должна иметь Анна Ивановна,
*Shtoh dolzh-*NAH *eem-*YET AHN*-nah Ee-*VAH*-nov-nah.*
What must Anna Ivanovna have,

если она хочет пойти в кино?
YES*-lee oh-*NAH KHOH*-chet poy-*TEE *v kee-*NOH*?*
if she wants to go to the cinema?

Она должна иметь деньги.
*Oh-*NAH *dolzh-*NAH *eem-*YET *d'*YEN*-ggee.*
She must have money.

Что вы должны иметь, чтобы есть суп?
*Shtoh vwee dolzh-*NEE *eem-*YET*,* SHTOH*-bee yest soop?*
What must you have to eat soup?

Что вы должны иметь, чтобы резать мясо?
*Shtoh vwee dolzh-*NEE *eem-*YET*,* STOH*-bee r'*YEH*-zaht m'*YAH*-soh?*
What must you have to cut meat?

Может ли господин Смис поехать в Россию без паспорта?
MOH*-zhet lee gos-poh-*DEEN *Smith poh-*YEH*-khaht v Ros-*SEE*-you b'yez* PAHS*-portah?*
Can Mr. Smith go to Russia without a passport?

Что он должен иметь для того, чтобы поехать в Россию?
Shtoh ohn DOHL-*zhen eem*-YET *dl'yah toh*-VOH, SHTOH-*bee poh*-YEH-*khaht v Ros*-SEE-*you?*
What must he have in order to go to Russia?

Он должен иметь паспорт, визу и деньги.
Ohn DOHL-*zhen eem*-YET PAHS-*port,* VEE-*zoo ee d'*YEN-*ggee.*
He must have a passport, a visa, and money.

Может ли гражданин Голопупенко поехать из Советского Союза в Америку?
MOH-*zhet lee grahzh-dah*-NEEN *Goh-loh*-POO-*pen-koh poh*-YEH-*khaht eez Sov*-YET-*skoh-voh Soh*-YOO-*zah v Ah*-MEH-*ree-koo?*
Can citizen Golopupenko go from the Soviet Union to America?

Нет, не может.
N'yet, n'yeh MOH-*zhet.*
No, he cannot.

Это безнадёжно.
EH-*toh b'yez-nahd*-YOHZH-*noh.*
That's hopeless.

THINKING IN RUSSIAN

(Answers on page 226)

1. Хóчет ли Лёля есть я́блоко?
2. Мóжет ли онá егó достáть?
3. Даёт ли учи́тель я́блоко Лёле?
4. Почемý он егó не даёт Лёле?
5. Хóчет ли он дать егó ей?
6. Должны́ ли мы откры́ть дверь, чтóбы вы́йти?
7. Если мы хоти́м ви́деть, должны́ ли мы откры́ть глазá?
8. Должны́ ли мы имéть дéньги, чтóбы путешéствовать?
9. Что мы должны́ имéть, чтóбы писáть?
10. Что вы должны́ сдéлать, éсли дверь закры́та и éсли вы хоти́те вы́йти?
11. Мóжет ли господи́н Бéрлиц читáть без очкóв?
12. Что он дóлжен имéть, чтóбы читáть?
13. Что мы должны́ имéть, чтóбы пойти́ в óперу?
14. Мóжете ли вы есть суп ножóм?
15. Что вы должны́ имéть, чтóбы есть суп?
16. Должны́ ли вы имéть ви́лку, чтóбы есть суп?
17. Должны́ ли вы сломáть вáши часы́?
18. Дóлжен ли я пойти́ в кинематóграф?

УРОК 19

Который час?
Koh-TOH-*ree chahs?*
What time is it?

Вот карманные часы.
Voht kahr-MAHN-*nee-yeh chah*-SEE.
Here is a pocket watch.

Там, на стене, стенные часы.
Tahm, nah st'yen-YEH, *st'yen*-NEE-*yeh chah*-SEE.
There, on the wall, is a wall clock.

Карманные часы мы носим в кармане,
Kahr-MAHN-*nee-yeh chah*-SEE *mee* NOH-*seem v kahr*-MAHN-*yeh,*
We carry the pocket watch in the pocket,

а стенные висят на стене.
ah st'yen-NEE-*yeh vees*-YAHT *nah st'yen*-YEH.
and the wall clock hangs on the wall.

Карманные часы сделаны из золота, серебра, никеля или стали.
Kahr-MAHN-*nee-yeh chah*-SEE *sd'*YEH-*lah-nee eez* ZOH-*loh-tah, sehr-yeb*-RAH, NEE-*kel-yah* EE-*lee* STAH-*lee.*
A pocket watch is made of gold, silver, nickel or steel.

Они золотые, серебряные, никелевые или стальные.
Oh-NEE *zoh-loh*-TEE-*yeh, sehr*-YEB-*r'yah-nee-yeh,* NEE-*kel-yeh-vee-yeh* EE-*lee stahl*-NEE-*yeh.*
They are of gold, silver, nickel or steel.

NOTE to Student: — **Золотые, серебряные** etc. are adjectives. In Russian you can form an adjective from almost every noun just as you form the adjective "golden" from the noun "gold" in English.

На часах две или три стрелки.
Nah chah-SAKH *dv'yeh* EE-*lee tree str'*YEL-*kee.*
On a watch there are two or three hands (arrows).

Большая стрелка показывает минуты.
Bol-SHAH-*yah str'*YEL-*kah poh*-KAH-*zee-vah-yet mee*-NOO-*tee*
The big hand shows the minutes.

Маленькая стрелка показывает часы, а третья стрелка — секунды.
MAHL-*yen-kah-yah str'*YEL-*kah poh*-KAH-*zee-vah-yet chah*-SEE, *ah* TREHT-*yah str'*YEL-*kah—seh*-KOON-*dee.*
The small hand shows the hours, and the third one—the seconds.

Который час?	**Час.**	**Два часа.**	**Три часа.**
Koh-TOH-*ree chahs?*	*Chahs.*	*Dvah chah*-SAH.	*Tree chah*-SAH.
What time is it?	It is one o'clock.	Two o'clock.	Three o'clock.

NOTE to Student: **Час** is an entire sentence in itself. It means "it is one o'clock". **Два часа** means "it is two o'clock". **Час дня** means "it is 1 P.M.", **час нóчи** — "one A.M.", **два часа дня** — "two P.M." etc.

Пять часов.	**Шесть часов.**	**Четыре часа.**	**Семь часов.**
P'yaht chah-SOHV.	*Shest chah*-SOHV.	*Cheh*-TEE-*reh chah*-SAH.	*S'yem chah*-SOHV.
(It is:) 5 o'clock.	Six o'clock.	Four o'clock.	Seven o'clock.

Четверть первого.
CHET-*v'yehrt p'*YEHR-*voh-voh.*
(It is:) a quarter past twelve.

Половина второго.
*Poh-loh-*VEE-*nah vtoh-*ROH-*voh.*
Half past one.

Три четверти третьего.
Tree CHET-*v'yehr-tee* TREHT-*yeh-voh.*
A quarter to three.

Десять минут четвёртого.
*D'*YES-*yaht mee-*NOOT *chet-v'*YOR-*toh-voh.*
(It is:) ten minutes past three.

Двадцать пять минут восьмого.
DVAHD-*tsaht p'yaht mee-*NOOT *vos-*MOH-*voh.*
Twenty-five minutes past seven.

Без двадцати пяти минут девять.
*B'yez dvahd-tsah-*TEE *p'yah-*TEE *mee-*NOOT *d'*YEV-*yaht.*
(It is:) 25 minutes to nine.

Без семи десять.
*B'yez s'yeh-*MEE *d'*YES-*yaht.*
7 minutes to ten.

Поезд отходит в два тридцать.
POH-*yezd ot-*KHOH-*deet v dvah* TREED-*tsaht.*
The train leaves at 2.30.

Поезд приходит в три десять.
POH-*yezd pree-*KHOH-*deet v tree d'*YES-*yaht.*
The train arrives at 3.10.

в полдень
v POHL-*d'yen*
at noon

в двенадцать часов дня
*v dv'yeh-*NAHD-*tsaht chah-*SOHV *dn'yah*
at twelve o'clock noon

в полночь
v POHL-*noch*
at midnight

в 12 часов ночи
*v dv'yeh-*NAHD-*tsaht chah-*SOHV NOH-*chee*
at twelve o'clock midnight

час ночи
chahs NOH-*chee*
(It is) 1 AM

час дня
chahs dn'yah
1 PM

два часа ночи
*dvah chah-*SAH NOH-*chee*
2 AM

два часа дня
*dvah chah-*SAH *dn'*YAH
2 PM

пять часов утра
*p'yaht chah-*SOHV *oo-*TRAH
(It is) 5 AM

одиннадцать часов утра
*oh-*DEEN-*nahd-tsaht chah-*SOHV *oo-*TRAH
11 AM

семь часов вечера
*s'yem chah-*SOHV *v'*YEH-*cheh-rah.*
7 PM

в два часа пополудни
*v dvah chah-*SAH *poh-poh-*LOOD-*nee*
at two o'clock in the afternoon

в три часа пополудни
*v tree-chah-*SAH *poh-poh-*LOOD-*nee*
at three o'clock in the afternoon

в семь часов утра
*v s'yem chah-*SOHV *oo-*TRAH
at seven in the morning

Который теперь час?
Koh-TOH-*ree t'yep*-YEHR *chahs?*
What time is it now?

Ровно час.
ROHV-*noh chahs.*
It is exactly one o'clock.

Уже третий час.
Oo-ZHEH TREH-*tee chahs.*
It is already past two.

Час состоит из шестидесяти минут.
Chahs soh-stoh-EET *eez sheh*-STEE-*d'yeh-sah-tee mee*-NOOT.
An hour consists of sixty minutes.

Шестьдесят минут составляют час.
Shest-d'yes-YAHT *mee*-NOOT *sos-tavl*-YAH-*yoot chahs.*
Sixty minutes make one hour.

Вы приходите на урок в два часа и вы уходите в пять часов.
Vwee pree-KHOH-*deet-yeh nah oo*-ROHK *v dvah chah*-SAH *ee vwee oo*-KHOH-*deet-yeh v p'yaht chah*-SOHV.
You come to the lesson at two o'clock and you leave at five o'clock.

Сколько часов вы остаётесь здесь?
SKOHL-*koh chah*-SOHV *vwee os-tah*-YOHT-*yes zd'yes?*
How many hours do you remain here?

Я остаюсь тут три часа.
Yah os-tah-YOOS *toot tree chah*-SAH.
I remain here three hours.

REMEMBER:

приходи́ть (я прихожу́) "to come"
уходи́ть to leave, to go away
входи́ть (в ко́мнату) to enter (a room)
выходи́ть (из ко́мнаты) to go, to walk out (of a room)

В котором часу вы сюда приходите?
V koh-TOH-*rom chah*-SOO *vwee s'yoo*-DAH *pree*-KHOH-*deet-yeh?*
At what time do you come here?

В котором часу вы отсюда уходите?
V koh-TOH-*rom chah*-SOO *vwee ot-s'*YOO-*dah oo*-KHOH-*deet-yeh?*
At what time do you leave (from here)?

В котором часу вы обедаете?
V koh-TOH-*rom chah*-SOO *vwee ob*-YEH-*dah-yet-yeh?*
At what time do you have dinner?

Мы садимся обедать в час.
Mee sah-DEEM-*sah ob*-YEH-*daht v chahs.*
We sit down for dinner at one o'clock.

В котором часу вы ужинаете?
V koh-TOH-*rom chah*-SOO *vwee* OO-*zhee-nah-yet-yeh?*
At what time do you have supper?

Мы ужинаем в семь часов.
Mee OO-*zhee-nah-yem v s'yem chah*-SOHV.
We have supper at seven o'clock.

У меня в спальне будильник, который не идёт.
*Oo m'yen-*YAH *v* SPAHL-*n'yeh boo-*DEEL-*neek, koh-*TOH-*ree n'yeh eed-*YOHT.
I have an alarm-clock in my bedroom which doesn't run.

Часы стоят.
*Chah-*SEE *stoh-*YAHT.
The watch is stopped.

Надо их завести.
NAH-*doh eekh zah-v'yes-*TEE.
One must wind it.

Я завожу часы.
*Yah zah-voh-*ZHOO *chah-*SEE.
I wind the watch.

Мои часы не отстают и не спешат.
*Moh-*EE *chah-*SEE *n'yeh ot-stah-*YOOT *ee n'yeh sp'yeh-*SHAHT.
My watch is not slow and not fast.

Они идут правильно.
*Oh-*NEE *ee-*DOOT PRAH-*veel-noh.*
It runs accurately.

Ваши часы спешат на пять минут.
VAH-*shee chah-*SEE *sp'yeh-*SHAHT *nah p'yaht mee-*NOOT.
Your watch is five minutes fast.

Его часы опаздывают на три минуты.
*Yeh-*VOH *chah-*SEE *oh-*PAHZ-*dee-vah-yoot nah tree mee-*NOO-*tee.*
His watch is three minutes slow.

Позвольте вас спросить: который час?
*Poz-*VOHLT-*yeh vahs sproh-*SEET: *koh-*TOH-*ree chahs?*
May I ask you what time it is?
(Literally: Allow me to ask you . . .)

Спасибо.
*Spah-*SEE-*boh.*
Thank you.

Представление в Большом театре начинается в восемь часов.
*Prehd-stahv-l'*YEH-*nee-yeh v Bol-*SHOHM *t'yeh-*AHTR-*yeh nah-chee-*NAH-*yet-sah v* VOHS-*yem chah-*SOHV.
The show at the Bolshoi theatre starts at eight o'clock.

Оно кончается в одиннадцать.
*Oh-*NOH *kon-*CHAH-*yet-sah v oh-*DEEN-*nahd-tsaht.*
It ends at eleven.

Оно продолжается три часа.
*Oh-*NOH *proh-dol-*ZHAH-*yet-sah tree chah-*SAH.
It lasts three hours.

Как называются часы, которые у вас на руке?
*Kahk nah-zee-*VAH-*yoot-sah chah-*SEE, *koh-*TOH-*ree-yeh oo vahs nah roo-*KEH?
What do you call the watch which you have on your hand?

Это часы-браслет.
EH-*toh chah-*SEE—*brahs-l'*YET.
It is a wrist-watch.

Саша умнее, чем Гриша.
SAH-*shah oom-n'*YEH-*yeh, chem* GREE-*shah.*
Sasha is cleverer than Grisha.

Иванов храбрее, чем Павлов.
*Ee-vah-*NOHV *khrahbr-*YEH-*yeh, chem* PAHV-*lov.*
Ivanov is braver than Pavlov.

Пётр умнее Павла.
*P'yohtr oom-n'*YEH*-yeh* PAHV*-lah.*
Peter is more intelligent than Paul.

Орёл смелее курицы.
*Or-*YOHL *sm'yel-*YEH*-yeh* KOO*-ree-tsee.*
The eagle is more daring than the hen.

Роза пахнет хорошо.
ROH*-zah* PAKH*-n'yet khoh-roh-*SHOH.
The rose smells good.

Она пахнет лучше чем тюльпан.
*Oh-*NAH PAHKH*-n'yet* LOOCH*-sheh chem t'yool-*PAHN.
It smells better than the tulip.

Сыр пахнет плохо, и газ пахнет плохо.
Seer PAHKH*-n'yet* PLOH*-khoh, ee gahz* PAHKH*-n'yet* PLOH*-khoh.*
Cheese smells bad and gas smells bad.

Что пахнет хуже?
Shtoh PAHKH*-n'yet* KHOO*-zheh?*
What smells worse?

Пахнет ли гвоздика так же хорошо как роза?
PAKH*-n'yet lee gvoz-*DEE*-kah tahk zheh khoh-roh-*SHOH *kahk* ROH*-zah?*
Does the carnation smell as good as the rose?

Гвоздика, роза и сирень пахнут одинаково хорошо.
*Gvoz-*DEE*-kah,* ROH*-zah ee see-*REN PAHKH*-noot oh-dee-*NAH*-koh-voh khoh-roh-*SHOH.
The carnation, the rose, and the lilac smell equally good.

Что лучше: чай с сахаром или без сахара?
Shtoh LOOCH*-sheh: chigh s* SAH*-khah-rom* EE*-lee b'yez* SAH*-khah-rah?*
What is better: tea with sugar or without sugar?

Я предпочитаю чай с сахаром, а вы предпочитаете чай без сахара.
*Yah prehd-poh-chee-*TAH*-yoo chigh s* SAH*-khah-rom, ah vwee prehd-poh-chee-*TAH*-yet-yeh chigh b'yez* SAH*-khah-rah.*
I prefer tea with sugar, and you prefer tea without sugar.

Вы говорите хорошо по-русски, но вы говорите лучше по-английски.
*Vwee goh-voh-*REET*-yeh khoh-roh-*SHOH *poh-*ROOS*-skee, noh vwee goh-voh-*REET*-yeh* LOOCH*-sheh po-ahn-*GLEE*-skee.*
You speak Russian well, but you speak English better.

Ваше английское произношение лучше моего.
VAH*-sheh ahn-*GLEE*-skoh-yeh proh-eez-noh-*SHEH*-nee-yeh* LOOCH*-sheh moh-yeh-*VOH.
Your English pronunciation is better than mine.

Слово "здравствуйте" часто произносят "здрасьте".
SLOH-*voh* "ZDRAHV-*stvooy-t'yeh*" CHAHS-*toh* *proh-eez*-NOHS-*yaht* "ZDRAHST-*yeh*".
The word "zdravstvuytye" is often pronounced "zdrastye".

Говорите ли вы так же хорошо по-французски как по-русски?
Goh-voh-REET-*yeh lee vwee tahk zheh khoh-roh*-SHOH *poh-frahn*-TSOOZ-*kee kahk poh*-ROOS-*skee?*
Do you speak French as well as Russian?

У господина Берлица очки.
Oo gos-poh-DEE-*nah* BEHR-*lee-tsah och*-KEE.
Mr. Berlitz has eye-glasses.

У вас нет очков.
Oo vahs n'yet och-KOHV.
You have no eye-glasses.

Видите ли вы лучше, чем г. Берлиц?
VEE-*deet-yeh lee vwee* LOOCH-*sheh, chem gos-poh*-DEEN *Berlitz?*
Do you see better than Mr. Berlitz?

Да, я вижу лучше.
Dah, yah VEE-*zhoo* LOOCH-*sheh.*
Yes, I see better.

NOTE ON THE COMPARATIVE WITH THE GENITIVE: If you mention the object of comparison, the comparative form of the adjective is followed by **чем** or **не́жели:**

Це́рковь вы́ше, чем дом. "The church is taller than the house."

Рокфе́ллер бога́че не́жели я. "Rockefeller is wealthier than I."

Another way is simply to have the comparative followed by the object of comparison in the genitive:

Де́рево вы́ше до́ма. "The tree is taller than the house."
Ко́шка ме́ньше соба́ки. "The cat is smaller than the dog."
Сестра́ умне́е бра́та. "The sister is cleverer than the brother."

THINKING IN RUSSIAN

(Answers on page 227)

1. Есть ли часы́ в э́той ко́мнате?
2. Где они́?
3. Есть ли у вас часы́?
4. Они́ у вас в карма́не?
5. Куда́ мы ве́шаем стенны́е часы́?
6. Пока́зывают ли ва́ши часы́ секу́нды?
7. Кото́рый час?
8. Когда́ вы сюда́ прихо́дите?
9. Когда́ вы ухо́дите?
10. Ско́лько мину́т составля́ют час?
11. Из скольки́х часо́в состоя́т су́тки?
12. Ско́лько секу́нд в одно́й мину́те?
13. Ва́ши часы́ иду́т?
14. Что на́до сде́лать, е́сли часы́ не иду́т?
15. Ва́ши часы́ спеша́т?

16. Они́ отстаю́т?
17. Стенны́е часы́ бо́льше, чем карма́нные?
18. Стол бо́льше сту́ла?
19. Стена́ длинне́е, чем карти́на?
20. Пиджа́к коро́че, чем пальто́?
21. Дверь ши́ре, чем окно́?
22. Жиле́т длинне́е руба́шки?
23. Да́мские шля́пы краси́вее, чем мужски́е?
24. Вода́ лу́чше, чем ча́й?
25. Фиа́лка па́хнет лу́чше, чем тюльпа́н?
26. Сыр па́хнет ху́же, чем газ?
27. Ва́ше англи́йское произноше́ние лу́чше, чем ва́ше ру́сское?
28. Ва́ше ру́сское произноше́ние пра́вильное?
29. У ва́шего учи́теля произноше́ние лу́чше и́ли ху́же?
30. Вы пи́шете лу́чше меня́?
31. У вас хоро́шие глаза́?
32. Вы ви́дите хорошо́?
33. Ваш учи́тель ви́дит хорошо́ без очко́в?
34. Ви́дит ли он лу́чше с очка́ми?

УРОК 20

Какое теперь время года?
Kah-KOH-*yeh tyep*-YEHR VREHM-*yah* GOH-*dah?*
What season is it now?

День состоит из двадцати четырёх часов.
D'yen sos-toh-EET *eez dvahd-tsah*-TEE *cheh-teer*-YOHKH *chah*-SOHV.
A day consists of 24 hours.

Неделя состоит из семи дней.
N'yed-YEL-*yah sos-toh*-EET *eez s'yeh*-MEE *dn'yay.*
A week consists of 7 days.

Они называются:
Oh-NEE *nah-zee*-VAH-*yoot-sah*:
They are called:

понедельник	**вторник**	**среда**	**четверг**
pon-yed-YEL-*neek*	VTOHR-*neek*	*sreh*-DAH	*chet-v'*YEHRG
Monday	Tuesday	Wednesday	Thursday

пятница	**суббота**	**и**	**воскресенье,**
*p'*YAHT*-nee-tsah*	*soob-*BOH*-tah*	*ee*	*vos-kr'yes-*YEN*-yeh.*
Friday	Saturday	and	Sunday.

Пять или шесть дней в неделю мы работаем.
P'yaht EE*-lee shest dn'yay v n'yed-*YEL*-yoo mee rah-*BOH*-tah-yem.*
We work five or six days a week.

На седьмой день, в воскресенье, мы отдыхаем.
*Nah s'yed-*MOY *d'yen, v vos-kr'yes-*YEN*-yeh, mee ot-dee-*KHAH*-yem.*
On the seventh day, on Sunday, we rest.

KEEP in MIND: в, во and the accusative is used to indicate "on" a specific day, or "within" a specific period. E. g.: **в суббóту** — "on Saturday", **во втóрник** — "on Tuesday", **в два часа** — "at 2 o'clock", **раз в недéлю** — "once a week", **два рáза в мéсяц** — "twice a month", **пять раз в год** — "five times a year".

Двадцать четыре часа составляют сутки.
DVAHD*-tsaht cheh-*TEE*-reh chah-*SAH *sos-tahv-l'*YAH*-yoot* SOOT*-kee.*
Twenty four hours form a (complete) day.

Вы едите три раза в сутки.
*Vwee yeh-*DEE*-teh tree* RAH*-zah v* SOOT*-kee.*
You eat three times in 24 hours.

NOTE to Student: Russian is sometimes more exact than English. Besides having a word for "day" it has another for a twenty-four hour period: **сутки.**

Тридцать или тридцать один день составляют месяц.
TREED*-tsaht* EE*-lee* TREED*-tsaht oh-*DEEN *d'yen sos-tahv-l'*YAH*-yoot m'*YES*-yahts.*
Thirty or thirty-one days constitute a month.

Год делится на 12 месяцев или на пятьдесят две недели.
*Gohd d'*YEH*-leet-sah nah dv'yeh-*NAHD*-tsaht m'*YEH*-sah-tsev* EE*-lee nah p'yaht-d'yes-*YAHT *dv'yeh n'yed-*YEH*-lee.*
The year is divided into twelve months or into fifty-two weeks.

IMPORTANT NOTICE: You already met reflexive verbs which are formed by adding the ending **ся** (after vowels **сь**) to the verb. For example: **бриться** (BREET-*sah*)—"to shave" (oneself), **мыться** (MEET-*sah*) — "to wash" (oneself). In the above sentence the reflexive ending (**делится**) gives the verb a passive meaning. Other examples:

дом строится	"the house is being built"
город называется . . .	"the town is called" . . .

Год состоит из двенадцати месяцев, которые называются:
*Gohd sos-toh-*EET *eez dv'yeh-*NAHD*-tsah-tee m'*YES*-yah-tsev,*
*koh-*TOH*-ree-yeh nah-zee-*VAH*-yoot-sah*:
A year consists of twelve months which are called:

январь, *yahn-*VAHR, January,	**февраль,** *f'yev-*RAHL, February,	**март,** *mahrt,* March,	**апрель,** *ah-*PRAIL, April,
май, *migh,* May,	**июнь,** *ee-*YOON, June,	**июль,** *ee-*YOOL, July,	**август,** AHV-*goost,* August,
сентябрь, *s'yent-*YAHBR, September,	**октябрь,** *okt-*YAHBR, October,	**ноябрь,** *noh-*YAHBR, November,	**декабрь.** *d'yeh-*KAHBR. December.

Какой теперь месяц?
*Kah-*KOY *t'yep-*YEHR *m'*YES*-yahts?*
What month is it now?

Теперь май месяц.
*T'yep-*YEHR *migh m'*YES*-yahts.*
Now it is the month of May.

Какое сегодня число?
*Kah-*KOH*-yeh s'yeh-*VOH*-dn'yah chees-*LOH*?*
What date is it today?

Второе мая.
*Vtoh-*ROH*-yeh* MAH*-yah.*
The second of May.

Какой сегодня день?
*Kah-*KOY *s'yeh-*VOH*-dn'yah d'yen?*
What day is it today?

Сегодня вторник.
*S'yeh-*VOH*-dn'yah* VTOHR*-neek.*
Today is Tuesday.

Этот месяц — сентябрь.
EH*-tot m'*YES*-yahts—s'yent-*YAHBR.
This month is September.

Прошлый месяц был август.
PROHSH*-lee m'*YES*-yahts beel* AHV*-goost.*
Last month was August.

Следующий будет октябрь, а потом ноябрь.
*Sl'*YEH-*doo-yoosh-chee* BOOD-*yet okt*-YAHBR, *a poh*-TOHM *noh*-YAHBR.
The next will be October and then November.

WATCH OUT! — Notice the use of the past and the future of "to be" in the two preceding sentences. A full explanation will come within the next four lessons.

Сегодня седьмое.
S'yeh-VOH-*dn'yah s'yed*-MOH-*yeh.*
Today is the seventh.

Завтра восьмое.
ZAHV-*trah vos*-MOH-*yeh.*
Tomorrow is the eighth.

Вчера было шестое.
Vcheh-RAH BEE-*loh shes*-TOH-*yeh.*
Yesterday was the sixth.

Март, апрель и май — весенние месяцы.
Mahrt, ah-PRAIL *ee migh—v'yes*-YEN-*nee-yeh m'*YES-*yah-tsee.*
March, April and May are the spring months.

Июнь, июль и август — летние месяцы.
Ee-YOON, *ee*-YOOL *ee* AHV-*goost—l'*YET-*nee-yeh m'*YES-*yah-tsee.*
June, July, and August are the summer months.

Сентябрь, октябрь и ноябрь — осенние месяцы.
S'yent-YAHBR, *okt*-YAHBR *ee noh*-YAHBR—*os*-YEN-*nee'yeh m'*YES-*yah-tsee.*
September, October, and November are the autumn months.

Декабрь, январь и февраль — зимние месяцы.
D'yeh-KAHBR, *yahn*-VAHR *ee f'yev*-RAHL—ZEEM-*nee-yeh m'*YES-*yah-tsee.*
December, January, and February are the winter months.

ATTENTION! — You already know that in Russian adjectives can be derived from almost every Russian noun. This is necessary because, in Russian, you cannot simply join two nouns in order to form a composite word as in English. One of the nouns must be transformed into an adjective. Thus:

"a silk dress"—**шёлковое пла́тье** (**шёлк**—"silk")

"a steel knife"—**стально́й нож** (**сталь**—"steel")

Если мы хотим знать число, мы смотрим в календарь.
YES-*lee mee khoh*-TEEM *znaht chees*-LOH, *mee* SMOH-*treem v kahl-yen*-DAHR.
If we want to know the date we look at the calendar.

Посмотрите: в прошлом, тысяча девятьсот пятидесятом году,
*Pos-mot-*REET*-yeh: v* PROHSH*-lom,* TEES*-yah-chah d'yev-yaht-*SOHT *p'yah-tee-d'yes-*YAH*-tom goh-*DOO*,*
Look: last year, in 1950,

Рождество было в понедельник, а в будущем, пятьдесят втором году,
*Rozh-d'yest-*VOH BEE*-loh v pon-yed-*YEL*-neek, ah v* BOO*-doosh-chem, p'yaht-d'yes-*YAHT *vtoh-*ROHM *goh-*DOO*,*
Christmas was on Monday, and in the next year, fifty-two,

оно будет в среду.
*oh-*NOH BOOD*-yet v* SREH*-doo.*
it will be on Wednesday.

В году четыре времени года:
*V goh-*DOO *cheh-*TEE*-reh* VREH*-m'yeh-nee* GOH*-dah:*
There are four seasons in the year:

весна,	**лето,**	**осень**	**и**	**зима.**
*v'yes-*NAH*,*	*l'*YEH*-toh,*	OHS*-yen,*	*ee*	*zee-*MAH.
spring,	summer,	autumn,	and	winter.

Зимой часто бывает ненастная погода.
*Zee-*MOY CHAHS*-toh bee-*VAH*-yet n'yeh-*NAHST*-nah-yah poh-*GOH*-dah.*
In winter the weather is often murky.

Весной деревья зеленеют и появляются цветы.
*V'yes-*NOY *d'yeh-r'*YEV*-yah zehl-yen-*YEH*-yoot ee poh-yahv-l'*YAH*-yoot-sah tsv'yeh-*TEE.
In spring the trees become green and flowers appear.

Осенью листья желтеют и падают с деревьев.
OHS*-yen-yoo* LEEST*-yah zhelt-*YEH*-yoot ee* PAH*-dah-yoot s d'yehr-*YEV*-yev.*
In autumn the leaves turn yellow and fall from the trees.

NOTICE how verbs are derived from adjectives. **Зеленéют, желтéют** are derived from the adjectives **зелёный, жёлтый.** Other examples:
стáрый—"old", **он старéет**—"he is getting old"
молодóй—"young", **она молодéет**—"she is getting younger"
грýстный—"sad", **грусти́ть**—"to be sad"
весёлый—"gay", **повеселéть**—"to become gay"

Летом приятно жить на севере России, под Ленинградом,
*L'*YEH*-tom pree-*YAHT*-noh zheet nah s'*YEV*-yehr-yeh Ros-*SEE*-ee, pod L'yeh-neen-*GRAH*-dom,*
In summer it is pleasant to live in northern Russia, near Leningrad,

под Москвой, на Ладожском озере или на берегу Балтийского моря.
pod Mosk-VOY, *nah* LAH-*dozh-skom* OHZ-*yehr-yeh* EE-*lee nah b'yehr-yeh*-GOO *Bahl*-TEES-*koh-voh* MOHR-*yah.*
near Moscow, on the Lake Ladoga or on the shore of the Baltic sea.

Летом мы гуляем, ездим верхом, купаемся и катаемся на лодке.
*L'*YEH-*tom mee gool*-YAH-*yem,* YEHZ-*deem v'yehr*-KHOM, *koo*-PAH-*yem-sah ee kah*-TAH-*yem-sah nah* LOHD-*keh.*
In summer we go for a walk, we ride on horseback, we bathe, and we boat.

REMEMBER: If you want to say "near a town" or in the suburbs of a town, you use **под** (literally "under"). Thus: **под Москвой**—"near Moscow", "in the environs of Moscow"; **битва под Полта́вой**—"the battle of Poltava".

Зимой приятнее жить на юге, в Крыму или на Кавказе.
Z*ee*-MOY *pree*-YAHT-*n'yeh-yeh zheet nah* YOOG-*yeh, v Kree*-MOO EE-*lee nah Kahv*-KAHZ-*yeh.*
In winter it is more pleasant to live in the south, in the Crimea or in the Caucasus.

Многие любят северную зиму, ибо зимой можно
MNOH-*ggee-yeh l'*YOOB-*yaht s'*YEV-*yehr-noo-yoo zee*-MOO, EE-*boh zee*-MOY MOHZH-*noh*
Many people like the northern winter because in winter one can

ездить на санях, кататься на коньках и ходить на лыжах.
YEZ-*deet nah sahn*-YAHKH, *kah*-TAHT-*sah nah kon*-KAHKH *ee khoh*-DEET *nah* LEE-*zhahkh.*
drive in a sleigh, ice-skate, and ski.

Любите ли вы кататься на коньках, ездить верхом?
*L'*YOO-*beet-yeh lee vwee kah*-TAHT-*sah nah kon*-KAHKH, YEZ-*deet v'yehr*-KHOHM*?*
Do you like to ice-skate, to ride on horseback?

Умеете ли вы ходить на лыжах?
Oom-YEH-*yet-yeh lee vwee khoh*-DEET *nah* LEE-*zhahkh?*
Do you know how to ski?

THINKING IN RUSSIAN

(Answers on page 227)

1. Ско́лько дней в году́?
2. Из скольки́х дней состои́т неде́ля?
3. Когда́ начина́ется год?
4. Когда́ он конча́ется?
5. Како́й пе́рвый, тре́тий, пя́тый, восьмо́й ме́сяц в году́?
6. Как называ́ются семь дней неде́ли?
7. Как называ́ется после́дний день неде́ли?
8. Како́й сего́дня день неде́ли?
9. Вчера́ бы́ло воскресе́нье?
10. В како́й день вы идёте в це́рковь?
11. В пя́тницу бу́дет пятна́дцатое число́?
12. Како́е сего́дня число́?
13. Како́е число́ бу́дет в бу́дущий понеде́льник?
14. Како́е число́ бы́ло в про́шлый четве́рг?
15. Бу́дет ли за́втра коне́ц ме́сяца?
16. Кото́рый тепе́рь час?
17. В каки́е дни мы рабо́таем?
18. Рабо́таете ли вы в воскресе́нье?
19. Даю́т ли учителя́ уро́ки по воскресе́ньям?
20. Где́ прия́тнее жить зимо́й, на се́вере и́ли на ю́ге?
21. Хо́лодно ли зимо́й в Крыму́?
22. Прия́тно ли ле́том под Москво́й?

УРОК 21

День и ночь
D'yen ee nohch
Day and night

Солнце на небе.
SOHLN-*tseh nah n'*YEHB-*yeh.*
The sun is in the sky.

Мы видим солнце днём.
Mee VEE-*deem* SOHLN-*tseh dn'*YOHM.
We see the sun in the daytime.

SAY IT IN RUSSIAN: Remember to say **на нéбе**—literally "on the sky". **Днём** means in the daytime. This is the instrumental case which you have encountered before. Similarly, you say **нóчью**—"at night", **вéчером**—"in the evening", **ýтром**—"in the morning".

Мы видим луну и звёзды ночью.
Mee VEE-*deem loo-*NOO *ee zv'*YOHZ-*dee* NOH-*ch'yoo.*
We see the moon and the stars at night.

Мы не можем видеть солнце ночью.
Mee n'yeh MOH-*zhem* VEED-*yet* SOHLN-*tseh* NOH-*ch'yoo.*
We cannot see the sun at night.

Оно находится по ту сторону мира.
Oh-NOH *nah*-KHOH-*deet-sah poh too* STOH-*roh-noo* MEE-*rah.*
It is on the other side of the world.

AN INTERESTING COINCIDENCE: **мир** means "world", and it also means "peace". **Наш мир** — "our world"; **заключить мир** (*zah-kl'yoo*-CHEET *meer*)—"to make peace". The context will make the meaning clear.

Днём мы видим хорошо, потому что светло.
Dn'yohm mee VEE-*deem khoh-roh*-SHOH, *poh-toh*-MOO *shtoh sv'yet*-LOH.
During the day we see well because it is light.

Ночью мы видим плохо, потому что темно.
NOH-*ch'yoo mee* VEE-*deem* PLOH-*khoh, poh-toh*-MOO *shtoh t'yem*-NOH.
At night we see badly because it is dark.

В этой комнате светло, потому что в ней большое окно.
V EH-*toy* KOHM-*naht-yeh sv'yet*-LOH, *poh-toh*-MOO *shtoh v n'yay bol*-SHOH-*yeh ok*-NOH.
It is light in this room because there is a big window in it.

Вечером темно.
*v'*YEH-*cheh-rom t'yem*-NOH.
It is dark in the evening.

Мы зажигаем электричество.
Mee zah-zhee-GAH-*yem el-yek*-TREE-*chest-voh.*
We turn on the electric light.

Электричество освещает комнату.
El-yek-TREE-*chest-voh osv-yesh*-CHAH-*yet* KOHM-*nah-too.*
The electric light illuminates the room.

Я зажигаю свет.
Yah zah-zhee-GAH-*yoo sv'yet.*
I turn on the light.

Я тушу свет.
Yah too-SHOO *sv'yet.*
I turn off the light.

Зажгите свет, пожалуйста.
Zazh-GGEET-*yeh sv'yet, poh*-ZHAH-*looy-stah.*
Turn on the light, please.

Спасибо.
Spah-SEE-*boh.*
Thank you.

Светло.
Sv'yet-LOH.
It is light.

Темно.
T'yem-NOH.
It is dark.

ECONOMY NOTE: In Russian sometimes one single word expresses an entire sentence; in this case it is the neuter gender of an adjective. **Хóлодно** (KHOH-*lod-noh*)—"It is cold". **Жáрко** (ZHAHR-*koh*)—"It is hot".

Мы зажигаем папиросу спичкой или зажигалкой.
Mee zah-zhee-GAH-*yem pah-pee*-ROH-*soo* SPEECH-*koy* EE-*lee zah-zhee*-GAHL-*koy.*
We light a cigarette with a match or with a lighter.

Дайте мне, пожалуйста, спичку.
DIGHT-*yeh mn'yeh, poh*-ZHAH-*looy-stah,* SPEECH-*koo.*
Give me a match, please.

Большое спасибо.
Bol-SHOH-*yeh spah*-SEE-*boh.*
Thank you very much.

Начало дня называется утром, а его конец — вечером.
Nah-CHAH-*loh dn'yah nah-zee*-VAH-*yet-sah* OOT-*rom, ah yeh*-VOH *kon*-YETS—VEH-*cheh-rom.*
The beginning of the day is called the morning and its end (is called) the evening.

IMPORTANT NOTE: After **называ́ться**—"to be called" the instrumental case is used; also after **звать**—"to call": **Его́ зову́т Михайлом**—"His name is Michael" (literally: "They call him Michael").

Утром солнце всходит.
OOT-*rom* SOHLN-*tseh vs'*KHOH-*deet.*
The sun rises in the morning.

Вечером оно заходит.
V'YEH-*cheh-rom oh*-NOH *zah*-KHOH-*deet.*
It sets in the evening.

Солнце всходит на востоке.
SOHLN-*tseh vs'*KHOH-*deet nah vos*-TOHK-*yeh.*
The sun rises in the east.

Оно заходит на западе.
Oh-NOH *zah*-KHOH-*deet nah* ZAH-*pahd-yeh.*
It sets in the west.

В полдень солнце на юге.
V POHLD-*yen* SOHLN-*tseh nah* YOOG-*yeh.*
At noon the sun is in the south.

Север напротив юга.
S'YEH-*v'yehr nah*-PROH-*teev* YOO-*gah.*
North is opposite to south.

SPECIAL WORD: напро́тив (with the genitive) means "opposite'" e.g.:
напро́тив на́шего до́ма—"opposite our house"
Он живёт напро́тив меня́—"He lives opposite me."

Летом солнце всходит очень рано,
L'YEH-*tom* SOHLN-*tseh vs'*KHOH-*deet* OH-*chen* RAH-*noh,*
In summer the sun rises very early,

в три или четыре часа утра,
v tree EE-*lee cheh*-TEE-*reh chah*-SAH *oot*-RAH,
at 3 or 4 in the morning,

и дни очень долгие, а ночи короткие.
ee dnee OH-*chen* DOHL-*ggee-yeh, ah* NOH-*chee koh*-ROHT-*kee-yeh.*
and the days are very long, and the nights short.

WATCH OUT! In Russian there are two words for "long", one for *size* and one for *time*: **Дли́нная па́лка**—"a long stick", **до́лгий день**—"a long day".

Но зимой оно всходит поздно,
Noh zee-MOY *oh*-NOH *vs'*KHOH-*deet* POHZD-*noh,*
But in winter it rises late,

в семь часов или ещё позже.
v s'yem chah-SOHV EE-*lee yesh*-CHOH POHZ-*zheh.*
at seven o'clock or still later.

Тогда дни короткие.
Tog-DAH *dnee koh*-ROHT-*kee-yeh.*
Then the days are short.

Днём мы работаем.
*Dn'*YOHM *mee rah*-BOH-*tah-yem.*
During the day we work.

Вечером мы идём спать.
V'YEH-*cheh-rom mee eed*-YOHM *spaht.*
In the evening we go to sleep.

Утром мы встаём.
OOT-*rom mee vstah*-YOHM.
In the morning we get up.

Мы умываемся.
Mee oo-mee-VAH-*yem-sah.*
We wash our face.

Мы бреемся.
Mee BREH-*yem-sah.*
We shave.

Мы причёсываемся.
Mee pree-CHOH-*see-vah-yem-sah.*
We comb our hair.

Мы одеваемся,
Mee od-yeh-VAH-*yem-sah,*
We dress,

мы завтракаем.
mee ZAHV-*trah-kah-yem.*
we have breakfast.

AN OLD RUSSIAN CUSTOM: Пить чай — While this expression literally means "to drink tea", it is generally used in the sense of having breakfast. It can also mean to gather at any time around the samovar for a light snack.

Потом мы надеваем пальто.
Poh-TOHM *mee nahd-yeh*-VAH-*yem pahl*-TOH.
Then we put on our coat.

Мы выходим на улицу,
Mee vwee-KHOH-*deem nah* OO-*lee-tsoo,*
We go out into the street,

и мы идём на работу или в школу.
ee mee eed-YOHM *nah rah*-BOH-*too* EE-*lee v* SHKOH-*loo.*
and we go to work or to school.

HELPFUL HINT: На can denote "on", "in", "to", or "at":

на почте — "at the post office"

на заводе — "at the factory"

на вокзале — "at the station"

я иду на вокзал — "I am going to the station"

на улице — "in the street"

сидеть на солнце — "to sit in the sun"

я иду на работу — "I am going to work"

идти на охоту — "to go hunting".

THINKING IN RUSSIAN

(Answers on page 228)

1. Когда́ светло́?
2. Темно́ ли сейча́с?
3. Отку́да прихо́дит дневно́й свет?
4. Где со́лнце?
5. Ви́дно ли со́лнце но́чью?
6. Как освеща́ется э́та ко́мната ве́чером?
7. Что мы де́лаем для того́, что́бы ви́деть, когда́ темно́?
8. Что вы ви́дите но́чью на не́бе?
9. Как называ́ются четы́ре страны́ све́та?
10. Когда́ всхо́дит со́лнце?
11. В кото́ром часу́ оно́ всхо́дит в ма́рте ме́сяце?
12. Ра́но ли захо́дит со́лнце ле́том?
13. В кото́ром вре́мени го́да дни до́лгие?
14. Мо́жете ли вы ви́деть, когда́ не светло́?
15. Когда́ вы ложи́тесь спать?
16. В кото́ром часу́ вы за́втракаете?
17. Лю́бите ли вы рабо́тать?
18. Свет луны́ сильне́е све́та со́лнца?
19. Когда́ луна́ освеща́ет мир?
20. Мо́жно ли сосчита́ть звёзды?
21. Где всхо́дит со́лнце?
22. Где оно́ захо́дит?
23. В кото́ром часу́ вы ложи́тесь?
24. По́зже ли вы ложи́тесь спать ле́том, чем зимо́й?

УРОК 22

Какая сегодня погода?
Kah-KAH-*yah s'yeh*-VOHDN-*yah poh*-GOH-*dah?*
How is the weather today?

Небо пасмурное.
N'YEH-*boh* PAHS-*moor-noh-yeh.*

The sky is overcast.

Оно покрыто облаками.
Oh-NOH *poh*-KREE-*toh ob-lah*-KAH-*mee.*
It is covered with clouds.

Какого цвета небо?
Kah-KOH-*voh tsv*'YEH-*tah n*'YEH-*boh?*
What color is the sky?

Оно серое.
Oh-NOH *s*'YEH-*roh-yeh.*
It is gray.

Чем оно покрыто?
CHEM *oh*-NOH *poh*-KREE-*toh?*
What is it covered with?

Облаками.
Ob-lah-KAH-*mee.*
With clouds.

Какого цвета облака?
Kah-KOH-*voh tsv*'YEH-*tah ob-lah*-KAH?
What color are the clouds?

Они серые.
Oh-NEE *s*'YEH-*ree-yeh.*
They are gray.

Когда небо покрыто облаками, идёт дождь.
Kog-DAH *n'*YEH-*boh poh*-KREE-*toh ob-lah*-KAH-*mee, eed*-YOHT *dohzhd.*
When the sky is covered with clouds, it rains.

Зимой идёт снег.
Zee-MOY *eed*-YOHT *sn'yeg.*
In winter it snows.

Зимой в Москве погода плохая.
Zee-MOY *v Mosk-v'*YEH *poh*-GOH-*dah ploh*-KHAH-*yah.*
In winter the weather is bad in Moscow.

Но в Крыму светит солнце.
Noh v Kree-MOO *sv'*YEH-*teet* SOHLN-*tseh.*
But in the Crimea the sun shines.

Там хорошая погода.
Tahm khoh-ROH-*shah-yah poh*-GOH-*dah.*
There the weather is fair.

NOTE on the WEATHER: There is no single word in Russian meaning "to rain" or "to snow". You have to say **идёт дождь** or **идёт снег** literally: "the rain goes", "the snow goes".

Вот зонтик.
Voht ZOHN-*teek.*
Here is an umbrella.

Когда идёт дождь, мы открываем зонтик.
Kog-DAH *eed*-YOHT *dohzhd, mee ot-kree*-VAH-*yem* ZOHN-*teek.*
When it rains we open an umbrella.

Много ли дождя в апреле?
MNOH-*goh lee dozhd*-YAH *v ah*-PRAIL-*yeh?*
Is there much rain in April?

Да, в апреле часто идёт дождь.
Dah, v ah-PRAIL-*yeh* CHAHS-*toh eed*-YOHT *dohzhd.*
Yes, in April it frequently rains.

Идёт ли снег летом?
Eed-YOHT *lee sn'yeg l'*YEH-*tom?*
Does it snow in summer?

Нет, летом снег не идёт.
*N'yet, l'*YEH-*tom sn'yeg n'yeh eed*-YOHT.
No, in summer it doesn't snow.

Идёт ли снег зимой?
Eed-YOHT *lee sn'yeg zee*-MOY*?*
Does snow fall in winter?

Да, зимой часто идёт снег.
Dah, zee-MOY CHAHS-*toh eed*-YOHT *sn'yeg.*
Yes, in winter snow often falls.

Чем покрыты дома и улицы зимой в Москве? Снегом.
CHEM *poh*-KREE-*tee doh*-MAH *ee* OO-*lee-tsee zee*-MOY *v mosk-v'*YEH*? Sn'*YEH-*gom.*
What are the houses and streets covered with in winter in Moscow? With snow.

Когда мы выходим на улицу в дождь без зонтика,
*Kog-*DAH *mee vwee-*KHOH*-deem nah* OO*-lee-tsoo v dohzhd b'yez* ZOHN*-tee-kah,*
When we go out in the street in rainy weather without an umbrella,

мы промокаем.
*mee pro-moh-*KAH*-yem.*
we get wet.

Какая буря!
*Kah-*KAH*-yah* BOOR*-yah!*
What a rain-storm!

Я весь мокрый.
Yah v'yes MOHK*-ree.*
I am wet through.

Надо снять мокрую одежду и надеть сухую,
NAH*-doh sn'*YAHT MOH*-kroo-yoo od-*YEZH*-doo ee nahd-*YET *soo-*KHOO*-yoo.*
You must take off your wet clothes and put on dry ones,

чтобы не простудиться.
SHTOH*-bee n'yeh proh-stoo-*DEET*-sah.*
so as not to catch cold.

Летом мы надеваем лёгкую одежду.
L'YEH*-tom mee nahd-yeh-*VAH*-yem l'*YOKH*-koo-yoo od-*YEZH*-doo.*
In summer we put on light clothing.

Зимой мы надеваем пальто?
*Zee-*MOY *mee nahd-yeh-*VAH*-yem pahl-*TOH*?*
Do we put on an overcoat in winter?

Да, мы надеваем пальто или шубу.
*Dah, mee nahd-yeh-*VAH*-yem pahl-*TOH EE*-lee* SHOO*-boo.*
Yes, we put on an overcoat or a shuba (fur-lined coat).

SARTORIAL NOTE:
надеть, надевать means "to put on".

Я надеваю пиджак, шляпу, башмаки, перчатки. "I put on a coat, a hat, shoes, gloves".

одеваться means "to dress". It is a reflexive verb (formed by adding **ся** or **сь** meaning "oneself, myself, yourself" etc.)

Я одеваюсь — "I dress (myself)".

мы одеваемся — "We dress (ourselves)".

Летом жарко.
L'YEH-*tom* ZHAHR-*koh.*
In summer it is hot.

Зимой холодно.
Zee-MOY KHOH-*lod-noh.*
In winter it is cold.

Жарко ли в августе?
ZHAHR-*koh lee v* AHV-*goost-yeh?*
Is it hot in August?

Да, очень жарко.
Dah, OH-*chen* ZHAHR-*koh.*
Yes, very hot.

Жарко ли в январе?
ZHAHR-*koh lee v yahn-vahr*-YEH?
Is it hot in January?

Нет, в Москве в январе не жарко.
*N'yet, v Mosk-v'*YEH *v yahn-vahr*-YEH *n'yeh* ZHAHR-*koh.*
No, in Moscow it is not hot in January.

Напротив, там обыкновенно очень холодно.
Nah-PROH-*teev, tahm oh-beek-nov*-YEN-*noh* OH-*chen* KHOH-*lod-noh.*
On the contrary, it is usually very cold there.

Жарко ли в центральной Африке?
ZHAHR-*koh lee v tsen*-TRAHL-*noy* AH-*free-keh?*
Is it hot in Central Africa?

Ещё бы!
Yesh-CHOH-*bee!*
Naturally!

Если вы ходите летом на солнце, вам жарко.
YES-*lee vwee* KHOH-*deet-yeh l'*YEH-*tom nah* SOHLN-*tseh, vahm* ZHAHR-*koh.*
If you walk in the sun in summer you are hot.

Если вы выходите зимой без пальто, вам холодно.
YES-*lee vwee vwee*-KHOH-*deet-yeh zee*-MOY *b'yes pahl*-TOH, *vahm* KHOH-*lod-noh.*
In winter, if you go out without an overcoat, you are cold.

В доме тепло, а на улице холодно.
v DOHM-*yeh t'yep*-LOH, *ah nah* OO-*lee-tseh* KHOH-*lod-noh.*
It is warm in the house, but it is cold in the street.

TEMPERATURE NOTE: Note the following expressions:

мне холодно—"I am cold" **нам холодно**—"we are cold"
вам тепло—"you are warm"
ему жарко—"he is hot" **им жарко**—"they are hot"

The pronoun is in the dative case. What you are really saying is "it is cold to me" etc.

Чай горячий.
Chigh gor-YAH-*chee.*
The tea is hot.

Молоко холодное.
Moh-loh-KOH *khoh*-LOHD-*noh-yeh.*
The milk is cold.

Если кофе слишком горячий,
YES-*lee* KOH-*feh* SLEESH-*kom* *gor*-YAH-*chee,*
If the coffee is too hot,

вы не можете его пить.
vwee n'yeh MOH-*zhet-yeh yeh*-VOH *peet.*
you cannot drink it.

WATCH OUT! There are two words in Russian meaning "hot"; which cannot be used indiscriminately. You say:

"the weather is hot" **пого́да жа́ркая**
"I am hot" **мне жа́рко**
but you must use **горячий** when you want to say
"the tea is hot" **чай горя́чий**
"a fiery love" **горя́чая любо́вь**

Троньте радиатор; горячий ли он или холодный?
TROHNT-*yeh rah-dee*-AH-*tohr; gor*-YAH-*chee lee ohn* EE-*lce khoh*-LOHD-*nee?*
Touch the radiator; is it hot or cold?

На Кавказе климат тёплый,
Nah Kahv-KAHZ-*yeh* KLEE-*maht* *t'*YOHP-*lee,*
In the Caucasus the climate is warm,

в центральной Америке — жаркий.
v tsen-TRAHL-*noy Ah*-MEH-*ree-keh* ZHAHR-*kee.*
in Central America, hot.

Холодно ли вам или жарко?
KHOH-*lod-noh lee vahm* EE-*lee* ZHAHR-*koh?*
Are you cold or hot?

Мне ни холодно, ни жарко, мне приятно.
Mn'yeh nee KHOH-*lod-noh nee* ZHAHR-*koh, mn'yeh pree*-YAHT-*noh.*
I am neither cold nor hot, I am comfortable.

На северном полюсе холодно и зимой и летом.
*Nah s'*YEH-*vehr-nom* POHL-*yoos-yeh* KHOH-*lod-noh ee zee*-MOY *ee l'*YEH-*tom.*
At the North Pole it is cold summer and winter.

Там всегда холодно.
Tahm vs'yeg-DAH KHOH-*lod-noh.*
It is always cold there.

В Нью-Йорке иногда холодно, а иногда жарко.
V New YOR-*keh ee-nog*-DAH KHOH-*lod-noh, ah ee-nog*-DAH ZHAHR-*koh.*
In New York it is sometimes cold and sometimes hot.

В Одессе зимой иногда идёт снег.
V Oh-DESS-*yeh zee*-MOY *ee-nog*-DAH *eed*-YOHT *sn'yeg.*
In Odessa it sometimes snows in winter.

Летом в Киеве никогда не идёт снег.
L'YEH-*tom v* KEE-*yev-yeh nee-kog*-DAH *n'yeh eed*-YOHT *sn'yeg.*
In Kiev snow never falls in summer.

Идёт ли иногда снег в марте?
Eed-YOHT *lee ee-nog*-DAH *sn'yeg v* MAHRT-*yeh?*
Does it snow sometimes in March?

Да, иногда.
Dah, ee-nog-DAH.
Yes, sometimes.

Идёт ли иногда снег в августе?
Eed-YOHT *lee ee-nog*-DAH *sn'yeg v* AHV-*goost-yeh?*
Does it sometimes snow in August?

Нет, никогда.
N'yet, nee-kog-DAH.
No, never.

В Батуме часто идёт дождь.
V Bah-TOOM-*yeh* CHAH-*stoh eed*-YOHT *dohzhd.*
In Batum it rains frequently.

В Туркестане редко идёт дождь.
V Toor-kes-TAHN-*yeh r'*YED-*koh eed*-YOHT *dohzhd.*
In Turkestan it rains seldom.

Там, в общем, всегда ясная погода.
Tahm, v OHBSH-*chem vs'yeg*-DAH YAHS-*nah-yah poh*-GOH-*dah.*
There, generally, the weather is always fair.

USEFUL THOUGH LACONIC expressions about the weather.

Пасмурно.
PAHS-*moor-noh.*
The weather is gloomy.

Холодно.
KHOH-*lod-noh.*
It is cold.

Тепло.
T'yep-LOH.
It is warm.

Жарко.
ZHAHR-*koh.*
It is hot.

Ветрено.
V'YET-*reh-noh.*
It is windy.

THINKING IN RUSSIAN

(Answers on page 228)

1. Како́го цве́та не́бо, когда́ плоха́я пого́да?
2. Чем покры́то не́бо?
3. Идёт ли тепе́рь дождь?
4. Что па́дает с не́ба зимо́й?
5. Прия́тно ли ходи́ть по у́лицам, когда́ они́ покры́ты водо́й?
6. Что у вас в рука́х, когда́ идёт дождь?
7. Кака́я сего́дня пого́да?
8. Выхо́дите ли вы, когда́ пого́да плоха́я?
9. Сли́шком ли жа́рко в э́той ко́мнате?
10. Хо́лодно ли на се́верном по́люсе?
11. В каки́е ме́сяцы идёт снег?
12. Ча́сто ли па́дает снег в феврале́?
13. Ча́сто ли идёт снег в апре́ле?
14. А идёт ли иногда́ снег в а́вгусте?
15. В ма́рте ча́сто ду́ет ве́тер?
16. Лю́бите ли вы грозу́?

УРОК 23

На Кавказе

Nah Kahv-KAHZ-*yeh*

In the Caucasus

Нина: Вы бывали на черноморском побережье?
NEE-*nah*: *Vwee bee*-VAH-*lee nah chehr-noh*-MOR-*skom poh-b'yeh*-REHZH-*yeh?*
Nina: Have you been on the shore of the Black Sea?

Таня: Да, бывала.
TAHN-*yah*: *Dah, bee*-VAH-*lah.*
Tanya: Yes, I have been.

Нина: А были ли вы в Сочи?
Ah BEE-*lee lee vwee v* SOH-*chee?*
And have you been in Sochi?

Таня: Да, я ездила туда много раз.
Dah, yah YEZ-*dee-lah too*-DAH MNOH-*goh rahz.*
Yes, I have gone there many times.

IMPORTANT NOTE: Here is something really unusual! Russian is easier than most languages . . . at least in one respect: it has but one past tense. The past tense is formed by dropping off the ending **ть** of the infinitive, and replacing it by **л.**

де́лать	"to do"	**я делал**	"I did"
ви́деть	"to see"	**я ви́дел**	"I saw"
ходи́ть	"to walk"	**я ходи́л**	"I walked"

If the subject is feminine add **а:**
"She drank tea" — **Она́ пила́ чай.**

If the subject is neuter add **о:**
" My ring fell on the floor". — **Моё кольцо́ упа́ло на пол.**

If the subject is plural add **и** for all genders:
"The ladies drank chocolate". — **Да́мы пи́ли шокола́д.**

That's practically all there is to it!

Нина: Расскажите мне, пожалуйста, про Сочи.
*Ras-skah-*ZHEET-*yeh mn'yeh, poh-*ZHAH-*looy-stah, proh* SOH-*chee.*
Tell me, please, about Sochi.

Таня: С удовольствием. А что вас особенно интересует?
*S oo-doh-*VOHLST-*vee-yem. Ah shtoh vahs oh-*SOHB-*yen-noh eent-yeh-reh-*SOO-*yet?*
With pleasure. What are you especially interested in?

Нина: Скажите, верно ли, что там зимой цветут розы?
*Skah-*ZHEET-*yeh, v'*YEHR-*noh lee, shtoh tahm zee-*MOY *tsv'yeh-*TOOT ROH-*zee?*
Tell me, is it true that roses bloom there in winter?

Таня: Да, это правда. В прошлом году я съездила туда
Dah, EH-*toh* PRAHV-*dah, v* PROHSH-*lom goh-*DOO *yah s'*YEZ-*dee-lah too-*DAH
That's true. Last year I went there

на Новый Год, и там цвели розы.
nah NOH-*vee Gohd, ee tahm tsv'yeh-*LEE ROH-*zee.*
for New Year, and roses were blooming there.

ATTENTION: Remember encountering the "perfective aspect" of verbs in Lesson 18? **съёздила** above is the perfective aspect of **ездить.** The difference in meaning here is that **съёздить** means "to go once," and **éздить** — "to go a number of times."

Watch out for these perfective aspects, which occur in the future and in the past, but not in the present.

Нина: А где вы там жили, в отеле или в частном доме?
Ah gd'yeh vwee tahm ZHEE-*lee, v ot*-YEL-*yeh* EE-*lee v* CHAHST-*nom* DOHM-*yeh?*
And where did you live there, at a hotel or at a private house?

Таня: В чудной гостинице, на самом берегу моря.
v CHOOD-*noy gos*-TEE-*nee-tseh, nah* SAH-*mom b'yeh-reh*-GOO MOR-*yah.*
In a wonderful hotel right on the seashore.

Нина: Ах, как интересно!
Akh, kahk eent-yeh-RES-*noh!*
Oh, how interesting!

Таня: У меня был балкон, который выходил прямо на пляж.
Oo m'yen-YAH *beel bahl*-KOHN, *koh*-TOH-*ree vwee-khoh*-DEEL *pr'*YAH-*moh nah pl'yahzh.*
I had a balcony, which looked right out on the beach.

Нина: И вы там часто купались или только грелись на солнце?
Ee vwee tahm CHAHS-*toh koo*-PAH-*lees* EE-*lee* TOHL-*koh gr'*YEH-*lees nah* SOHLN-*tseh?*
And did you often go bathing there or (did you) only bask in the sun?

Таня: Конечно, я плавала в море ежедневно.
Kon-YECH-*noh, yah* PLAH-*vah-lah v* MOR-*yeh yeh-zheh-dn'*YEV-*noh.*
Naturally, I swam every day in the sea.

Нина: Вы долго оставались в Сочи?
Vwee DOHL-*goh os-tah*-VAH-*lees v* SOH-*chee?*
Did you stay long in Sochi?

Таня: В прошлом году я прожила в Сочи около трёх недель.
v PROHSH-*lom goh*-DOO *yah proh-zhee*-LAH *v* SOH-*chee* OH-*koh-loh tr'*YOHKH *n'yed*-YEL.
Last year I stayed in Sochi for about three weeks.

Нина: Мои родители рассказывали мне,
Moh-EE *roh*-DEET-*yeh-lee rahs*-SKAH-*zee-vah-lee mn'yeh.*
My parents have told me

что они останавливались в Сочи
shtoh oh-NEE *os-tah*-NAHV-*lee-vah-lees v* SOH-*chee*
that they used to stay at Sochi

в большой гостинице у самого моря.
v bol-SHOY *gos*-TEE-*nee-tseh oo* SAH-*moh-voh* MOHR-*yah.*
in a large hotel right on the shore.

Таня: Как называлась эта гостиница?
Kahk nah-zee-VAH-*lahs* EH-*tah gos*-TEE-*nee-tsah?*
What was the name of that hotel?

Нина: Мне кажется — Кавказская Ривьера.
Mn'yeh KAH-*zhet-sah — Kahv*-KAHZ-*skah-yah Reev*-YEH-*rah.*
It seems to me — The Caucasian Riviera.

Таня: Это та же самая гостиница, в которой жила я в прошлом году.
EH-*toh* TAH-*zheh* SAH-*mah-yah goh*-STEE-*nee tsah, v koh*-TOH-*roy zhee*-LAH *yah v* PROHSH-*lom* GOH-*doo.*
That is the same hotel where I stayed last year.

Перед революцией она принадлежала
*P'*YEH-*red reh-vol*-YOO-*tsee-yay oh*-NAH *pree-nahd-l'yeh*-ZHAH-*lah*
Before the revolution it belonged

богатому московскому купцу,
boh-GAH-*toh-moo mos*-KOHV-*skoh-moo koop*-TSOO,
to a wealthy Moscow merchant,

который её построил. После революции
koh-TOH-*ree yeh*-YOH *poh*-STROH-*eel.* POHSL-*yeh reh-vol*-YOO-*tsee-ee*
who built it. After the revolution

её национализировали.
yeh-YOH *nah-tsee-oh-nah-lee*-ZEE-*roh-vah-lee.*
it was nationalized.

Нина: А были ли вы на Красной Поляне?
Ah BEE-*lee lee vwee nah* KRAHS-*noy Pol*-YAHN-*yeh?*
And have you been to Krasnaya Polyana?

Таня: Я туда ездила несколько раз.
Yah too-DAH YEZ-*dee-lah n'*YES-*kol-koh rahz.*
I went there several times.

TRANSPORTATION NOTE: **éхать** and **éздить** both mean, "to go", (not on foot, but in some other way). **Ехать** means "to go", "to be going". **Я éду в Москвý**—"I am going to Moscow" (by train or car). **Ездить** means "to go often". **Мы éздим в Нью Йорк два рáза в недéлю**—"We use to go to New York twice a week" (by train or car or boat). Here are some related expressions:

приезжáть, приéхать	"to arrive" (by train etc.)
уезжáть, уéхать	"to depart" (by train etc.)
Я уезжáю в Кúев.	"I am leaving for Kiev."
Он приéхал вчерá	"He arrived yesterday."

Нина: Как туда ездят? Поездом или
*Kahk too-*DAH YEZD-*yaht?* POH-*yez-dom* EE-*lee*
How does one go there? By train, or

в автомобиле или на лошадях?
*v ahv-toh-moh-*BEEL-*yeh* EE-*lee nah loh-shahd-*YAHKH*?*
by auto, or by horse cart?

Таня: Я ездила туда в автомобиле и на лошадях.
Yah YEZ-*dee-lah too-*DAH *v ahv-toh-moh-*BEEL-*yeh ee nah loh-shahd-*YAKH.
I went there by car and by horse cart.

Мы ехали по чудному шоссе,
Mee YEH-*khah-lee poh* CHOOD-*noh-moo shos-*SEH,
We drove over a wonderful highway,

сперва вдоль морского берега,
*sp'yehr-*VAH *vdohl mor-*SKOH-*voh b'*YEH-*reh-gah,*
first along the seashore,

а затем мы повернули в горы.
*ah zaht-*YEM *mee poh-v'yehr-*NOO-*lee v* GOH-*ree.*
and then we turned into the mountains.

Нина: А далеко ли туда?
*Ah dahl-yeh-*KOH *lee too-*DAH*?*
Is it far there?

Таня: Около восьмидесяти километров.
OH-*koh-loh vos-*MEED-*yes-yah-tee kee-loh-*MEH-*trov.*
About 80 kilometers.

Справа и слева мелькали дачи и сады.
SPRAH-*vah ee sl'*YEH-*vah m'yel-*KAH-*lee* DAH-*chee ee sah-*DEE.
On the right and left "dachas" and orchards flashed by.

Нина: Чьи эти дачи?
Ch'yee EH-*tee* DAH-*chee?*
Whose are these dachas?

GRAMMATICAL NOTE: Чьи is the plural of **чей** (masc.), **чья** (fem.), **чьё** (neuter) — "whose". This plural is used for all genders:

Чьи э́ти дома́?	Whose houses are these?
Чьи э́ти ло́шади?	Whose horses are these?
Чьи э́ти ко́льца?	Whose rings are these?

Таня: Теперь все они национализированы.
T'yep-YEHR *vs'yeh oh*-NEE *nah-tsee-oh-nah-lee*-ZEE-*roh-vah-nee.*
Now they are all nationalized.

Нина: Прежние владельцы были наверное богачи?
PREHZH-*nee-yeh vlahd*-YEL-*tsee* BEE-*lee nahv*-YEHR-*noh-yeh boh-gah*-CHEE*?*
The former owners were no doubt rich people?

Таня: Нет, далеко не все.
N'yet, dahl-yeh-KOH *n'yeh vs'yeh.*
No, not all by far.

И у моих родителей там была дачка,
Ee oo moh-EEKH *roh*-DEET-*yel-yay tahm bee*-LAH DAHCH-*kah,*
My parents, too, had a small country house there,

а они совсем не были богаты.
ah oh-NEE *sovs*-YEM *n'*YEH *bee-lee boh*-GAH-*tee.*
but they were not rich at all.

A RUSSIAN HABIT: Russians are very fond of using diminutives. **Да́чка** is the diminutive of **да́ча** — "country house". **-ик** and **-ок** are masculine diminutive endings: **стол** — "table", **сто́лик** — "small table"; **сын** — "son", **сыно́к** — "little son". **-ка** and **-ица** are feminine diminutive endings: **дочь** — "daughter", **до́чка** — "small daughter". **-ышко** *and* **-ечко** are neuter diminutive endings: **со́лнце** — "sun", **со́лнышко** — "little sun".

Нина: Неужели и у вас его отобрали?
N'yeh-oo-ZHEH-*lee ee oo vahs yeh*-VOH *ot-oh*-BRAH-*lee?*
Is it possible that they took it away from you, too?

Таня: Да, отобрали.
Dah, ot-oh-BRAH-*lee.*
Yes, they took it away.

Нина: Как жаль!
Kahk zhahl!
What a pity!

Нина: А что вы делали на Красной Поляне?
*Ah shtoh vwee d'*YEH-*lah-lee nah* KRAHS-*noy Pol-*YAHN-*yeh?*
And what did you do at Krasnaya Polyana?

Таня: Мы ходили в лес, собирали ягоды и грибы,
*Mee khoh-*DEE-*lee v l'yes, soh-bee-*RAH-*lee* YAH-*goh-dee ee gree-*BEE,
We used to go walking in the woods, we picked berries and mushrooms,

ловили рыбу и поднимались на горы.
*loh-*VEE-*lee* REE-*boo ee pod-nee-*MAH-*lees* NAH-*goh-ree.*
we went fishing and climbed the mountains.

AVOID CONFUSION—(if you can!)

ходи́ть means "to go" (on foot), "to walk", **идти́** generally means "to be going',, "to go" or "to come" with a definite purpose at a given time. Here are some helpful examples:

Ко́ля идёт в шко́лу	Kolya is going to school (now).
Ко́ля хо́дит в шко́лу	Kolya goes to school, i.e. he attends school.
Не ходи́те по траве́.	Don't walk on the grass.
Иди́те сюда́!	Come here.
Иду́.	I am coming (now).
По́езд идёт.	The train is coming (now).

На Красной Поляне удивительно хорошо!
Nah KRAHS-*noy Pol-*YAHN-*yeh oo-dee-*VEET-*yel-noh khoh-roh-*SHOH!
It is wonderful in Krasnaya Polyana!

Поезжайте туда непременно.
*Poh-yez-*ZHIGHT-*yeh too-*DAH *n'yeh-prem-*YEN-*noh.*
Go there without fail.

Ну, а теперь до свидания. Мне пора домой.
*Noo, a t'yep-*YEHR *doh svee-*DAH-*nee-yah. Mn'yeh poh-*RAH *doh-*MOY.
So, and now goodbye. It is time for me to go home.

THINKING IN RUSSIAN

(Answers on page 229)

1. Бы́ли ли вы на Кавка́зе?
2. Ка́к вы туда́ е́здили, по желе́зной доро́ге и́ли мо́рем?
3. Быва́ли ли вы на черномо́рском побере́жье?
4. Цвели́ ли там зимо́й ро́зы?
5. Где жила́ Та́ня в Со́чи?
6. Как называ́лась гости́ница?
7. Кто её постро́ил?
8. Чья э́та гости́ница тепе́рь?
9. Бы́л ли у Та́ни балко́н?
10. Куда́ выходи́л балко́н?
11. Та́ня купа́лась в мо́ре?
12. Пла́вала ли она́?
13. Куда́ она́ е́здила из Со́чи?
14. Как е́здила Та́ня на Кра́сную Поля́ну?
15. Ездила ли она́ туда́ по́ездом?
16. Ходи́ла ли она́ туда́ пешко́м?
17. А вы́ туда́ е́здили?
18. Что де́лала Та́ня на Кра́сной Поля́не?
19. Ходи́ла ли она́ в лес?
20. Что она́ собира́ла в лесу́?

УРОК 24

Что мы будем делать завтра?
Shtoh mee BOOD-*yem d'*YEH-*laht* ZAHV-*trah?*
What shall we do tomorrow?

Коля: Завтра у меня свободный день.
KOHL-*yah*: ZAHV-*trah oo m'yen*-YAH *svoh*-BOHD-*nee d'yen.*
Kolya: Tomorrow I have a free day.

Если будет хорошая погода, **давай поедем за город.**
YES-*lee* BOOD-*yet khoh*-ROH-*shah-yah poh*-GOH-*dah,* *dah*-VIGH *poh*-YED-*yem* ZAH-*goh-rod.*
If the weather will be good, let's go out of town.

IDIOM TO REMEMBER: To express "let's", use the imperative of "to give" in the second person, singular or plural. Thus:

"Let's go to the museum." — **Дава́йте пойдём в музе́й.**
"Let's speak Russian." — **Дава́й говори́ть по-русски.**

Маша: У меня на завтра другие планы.
MAH-*shah*: *Oo m'yen*-YAH *nah* ZAHV-*trah droo*-GGEE-*yeh* PLAH-*nee*.
Masha: I have other plans for tomorrow.

Я пойду в город и куплю себе тёплое пальто.
Yah poy-DOO *v* GOH-*rod ee koopl*-YOU *seb*-YEH *t'*YOHP-*loh-yeh pahl*-TOH.
I shall go to town and buy myself a warm overcoat.

Коля: Пальто успеешь купить позже . . .
Pahl-TOH *oosp*-YEH-*yesh koo*-PEET POHZ-*zheh* . . .
You will have time later to buy a coat . . .

IMPORTANT NOTE:

THE FUTURE TENSE is formed in two different ways:

1) The future of the verb **быть** — "to be" is combined with the infinitive of the verb in question, e.g.:

Я бу́ду чита́ть кни́гу — "I shall read the book", or "I shall be reading the book."

This, however, does not indicate whether I shall read the book to the end or not. (Imperfective aspect of the verb).
Notice the other forms of **быть** (future tense):

ты бу́дешь идти́	you will go (familiar)
он бу́дет петь	he will sing
мы бу́дем писа́ть	we will write
вы бу́дете ви́деть	you will see
они́ бу́дут игра́ть	they will play

2) By the perfective aspect of the verb with the endings of the present tense.

чита́ть — прочита́ть	
я чита́ю	I am reading
я прочита́ю	I shall read (I shall finish reading).
писа́ть — написа́ть	
я пишу́	I am writing
я напишу́	I shall write (I shall finish writing).

Маша: Когда мне успеть? **Я занята весь день.**
Kog-DAH *mn'yeh oosp*-YET? *Yah zahn-yah*-TAH *v'yes d'yen.*
When do I have time? I am busy all day.

Иногда мне приходится стоять в очередях по целым дням . . .
Ee-nog-DAH *mn'yeh pree*-KHOH-*deet-sah stoh*-YAHT *v oh-cheh-red*-YAKH *poh* TSEH-*leem dn'yahm* . . .
Sometimes I have to stay in line for whole days . . .

Коля: Ну, полно-те, Маша. **Нечего сердиться.**
Noo, POHL-*not-yeh,* MAH-*shah.* *N'*YEH-*cheh-voh s'yehr*-DEET-*sah.*
Well, that's enough, Masha. There is no reason for being angry.

IMPORTANT NOTE: Don't confound **нéчего** with **ничегó**. **Ничегó** means "nothing", while **нéчего** means "there is nothing". **Ничегó** requires a double negation:

Там ничегó нет —"There is nothing there."

while **нéчего** is used without a second negation:

Мне нéчего дéлать —"There is nothing for me to do."

Давай используем последние тёплые дни.
Dah-VIGH *ees*-POHL-*zoo-yem pohsl*-YED-*nee-yeh t'*YOHP-*lee-yeh dnee.*
Let's make the most of the last warm days.

Поедем в деревню. **Завтра рабочий день,**
Poh-YED-*yem v d'yehr*-YEVN-*you.* ZAHV-*trah rah*-BOH-*chee d'yen,*
Let's go to the country. Tomorrow is a working day,

пассажиров будет мало, **ехать будет удобно.**
pas-sah-ZHEE-*rov* BOOD-*yet* MAH-*loh,* YEH-*khaht* BOOD-*yet oo*-DOHB-*noh.*
there will be few passengers, it will be comfortable to travel.

Мы приедем в Колпино **и сразу пойдём в лес.**
Mee pree-YEHD-*yem v* KOHL-*pee-noh* *ee* SRAH-*zoo poyd*-YOHM *v l'yes.*
We shall arrive in Kolpino and go to the woods right away.

Посидим в лесу под нашей берёзкой,
Poh-see-DEEM *v l'yeh*-SOO *pod* NAH-*shay b'yehr*-YOHZ-*koy,*
We shall sit under our little birch tree in the woods.

а потом пойдём к Поповым обедать.
ah poh-TOHM *poyd*-YOHM *k Poh*-POH-*veem ob*-YEH-*daht.*
and then we'll go to the Popovs for lunch.

Маша: Ведь Поповы нас не ждут. **Так нельзя.**
V'yed Poh-POH-*vee nahs n'yeh zhdoot.* *Tahk n'yelz*-YAH.
But the Popovs don't expect us. It is impossible.

A USEFUL WORD: **Нельзя́** means "it is impossible", "it is not allowed", "it cannot be done". The opposite is **нáдо** which means "it is necessary", "one must".

Это нáдо сдéлать. "This has to be done."
Этого нельзя́ сдéлать. "It cannot be done."

Вспомни пословицу: **незваный гость хуже татарина.**
VSPOHM-*nee pos*-LOH-*vee-tsoo*: *n'yeh*-ZVAH-*nee gohst* KHOO-*zheh tah*-TAH-*ree-nah.*
Remember the saying: an uninvited guest is worse than a Tartar.

HISTORICAL NOTE: Masha evokes historical memories of Tartar domination. The Tartars even caused the Russians to abandon their pleasant capital of Kiev and build a new one in the forests of the North. The new city was Moscow.

Коля: Поповы нас пригласили, **и я обещал, что мы приедем.**
Poh-POH-*vee nahs pree-glah*-SEE-*lee,* *ee yah ob-yesh*-CHAHL *shtoh mee pree*-YED-*yem.*
The Popovs have invited us, and I promised that we will come.

Маша: Коли так, ничего не поделаешь.
Koh-LEE *tahk, nee-cheh*-VOH *n'yeh pod*-YEH-*lah-yesh.*
If it is so, there is nothing we will be able to do about it.

Надо ехать. А что будет, **если завтра польёт дождь?**
NAH-*doh* YEH-*khaht. Ah shtoh* BOOD-*yet,* YES-*lee* ZAHV-*trah pol*-YOHT *dohzhd?*
We must go. But what will happen, if it starts pouring tomorrow?

IDIOMS TO REMEMBER:

мóжно — "it is possible"

невозмóжно — "it is impossible"

необходи́мо — "it is necessary".

Коля: В таком случае мы останемся в городе,
V tah-KOHM SLOO-*chah-yeh mee os*-TAHN-*yem-sah v* GOH-*rod-yeh,*
In such case we shall stay in town,

и ты купишь себе пальто.
ee tee KOO-*peesh seb*-YEH *pahl*-TOH.
and you will buy yourself a coat.

Маша: Вот с этим я согласна. **Посмотрим, что будет завтра.**
Voht s EH-*teem yah sog*-LAHS-*nah.* *Pos*-MOHT-*reem shtoh* BOOD-*yet* ZAHV-*trah.*
With this I agree. We shall see what will happen tomorrow.

Коля: Но что мы будем делать в городе
Noh shtoh mee BOOD-*yem d'*YEH-*laht v* GOH-*rod-yeh*
But what shall we do in town

после того, как ты купишь себе пальто?
POHSL-*yeh toh*-VOH, *kahk tee* KOO-*peesh seb*-YEH *pahl*-TOH?
after you will buy yourself a coat?

Маша: Мы погуляем по главным улицам,
Mee poh-gool-YAH-*yem poh* GLAHV-*neem* OO-*lee-tsahm,*
We shall walk along the main streets,

и мы будем смотреть витрины больших магазинов.
ee mee BOOD-*yem smot-r'*YET *veet*-REE-*nee bol*-SHEEKH *mah-gah*-ZEE-*nov.*
and shall look at the windows of the big stores.

Это ничего не стоит
EH-*toh nee-cheh*-VOH *n'yeh* STOH-*eet*
That doesn't cost anything

и доставит мне удовольствие.
ee doh-STAH-*veet mn'yeh oo-doh*-VOHLST-*vee-yeh.*
and will give me pleasure.

Потом мы пообедаем в хорошем ресторане.
Poh-TOHM *mee poh-ob*-YEH-*dah-yem v khoh*-ROH-*shem res-toh*-RAHN-*yeh.*
Afterwards we shall lunch in a good restaurant.

Вечером мы пойдём в театр . . .
VEH-*cheh-rom mee poyd*-YOHM *v t'yeh*-AHTR . . .
In the evening we shall go to the theatre . . .

Коля: Не будет ли всё это стоить слишком дорого?
N'yeh BOOD-*yet lee vs'yoh* EH-*toh* STOH-*eet* SLEESH-*kom* DOH-*roh-goh?*
Won't all that cost too much?

Не забывай, что на твоё зимнее пальто
N'yeh zah-bee-VIGH, *shtoh nah tvoh*-YOH ZEEMN-*yeh-yeh pahl*-TOH
Don't forget that my two months earnings will go

уйдёт мой двухмесячный заработок.
ooeed-YOHT *moy dvookh-m'*YES-*yach-nee* ZAH-*rah-boh-tok.*
for your winter coat.

Маша: Ах, да, об этом я совершенно забыла.
Akh, dah, ob EH-*tom yah soh-vehr*-SHEN-*noh zah*-BEE-*lah.*
Ah, yes! I completely forgot about that.

Как это досадно!
Kahk EH-*toh doh*-SAHD-*noh!*
How annoying this is!

Бедный Коля,
B'YED-*nee* KOHL-*yah,*
Poor Kolya,

в этом году ты не сможешь купить себе пальто.
v EH-*tom goh*-DOO *tee n'yeh* SMOH-*zhesh koo*-PEET *seb*-YEH *pahl*-TOH.
this year you won't be able to buy yourself a coat.

Знаешь что, Коля? Вместо театра,
ZNAH-*yesh shtoh,* KOHL-*yah? Vm'*YES-*toh t'yeh*-AHT-*rah,*
Do you know what, Kolya? Instead of the theatre

мы пойдём в публичную библиотеку.
mee poyd-YOHM *v poob*-LEECH-*noo-you beeb-lee-ot*-YEH-*koo.*
we'll go to the public library.

Коля: В публичную библиотеку ходят зимой,
V poob-LEECH-*noo-you beeb-lee-ot*-YEH-*koo* KHOHD-*yaht zee*-MOY,
One goes to the public library in winter,

когда в квартире холодно и неуютно,
kog-DAH *v kvahr*-TEER-*yeh* KHOH-*lod-noh ee n'yeh-oo*-YOOT-*noh,*
when it is cold and uncomfortable in the apartment,

а в библиотеке тепло . . .
ah v beeb-lee-ot-YEH-*keh t'yep*-LOH . . .
but warm in the library . . .

Да, Коля, ты прав.
Dah, KOHL-*yah, tee prahv.*
Yes, Kolya, you are right.

Завтра вечером мы посидим дома.
ZAHV-*trah* VEH-*cheh-rom mee poh-see*-DEEM DOH-*mah.*
Tomorrow night we shall sit at home.

Коля: И будем мечтать . . .
Ee BOOD-*yem mech*-TAHT . . .
And we'll daydream . . .

Маша: Да, помечтаем. Мы будем мечтать о том,
Dah, poh-mech-TAH-*yem. Mee* BOOD-*yem mech*-TAHT *oh tom,*
Yes let us daydream. We shall daydream about

как мы летом будем отдыхать в Крыму . . .
*kahk mee l'*YEH-*tom* BOOD-*yem ot-dee*-KHAHT *v Kree*-MOO . . .
how we shall rest in the Crimea in summer . . .

Поведут ли меня
вечером в кино?
Когда наконец
подадут обед?
А жаркое-то
пригорит?

THINKING IN RUSSIAN

(Answers on page 229)

1. Поéдут ли Кóля и Мáша в дерéвню?
2. В какóм слýчае онú поéдут?
3. Знáете ли вы, бýдет ли зáвтра я́сная погóда?
4. Хорóшая ли бýдет зáвтра погóда úли плохáя?
5. Если Кóля и Мáша поéдут в Кóлпино, как онú тудá поéдут?
6. Какóй зáвтра бýдет день, воскресéнье úли бýдень?
7. Чтó Кóля и Мáша бýдут дéлать в лесý?
8. Под какúм дéревом онú посидя́т?
9. У когó онú бýдут обéдать?
10. Почемý говоря́т: незвáный гость хýже татáрина?
11. Бýдут ли Попóвы ждать Кóлю и Мáшу?
12. А чтó бýдут дéлать Кóля и Мáша, éсли польёт дождь?
13. Остáнутся ли онú в гóроде?
14. Пойдýт ли онú покупáть пальтó?
15. Где онú кýпят пальтó?
16. Чтó онú бýдут дéлать потóм?
17. Пойдýт ли онú гуля́ть?
18. Чтó онú бýдут смотрéть?
19. Где онú бýдут обéдать?
20. А потóм онú пойдýт в теáтр?
21. Отчегó онú не пойдýт?
22. Идёте ли вы сегóдня в теáтр?
23. Чáсто ли вы хóдите в теáтр?
24. Скóлько бýдет стóить мáшино пальтó?

УРОК 25

Животные

Zhee-VOHT-*nee-yeh*

Animals

На рисунке мы видим лошадь, корову, овцу, свинью, кошку.
Nah ree-SOON-*keh mee* VEE-*deem* LOH-*shahd, koh*-ROH-*voo, ov*-TSOO, *sveen*-YOO, KOHSH-*koo.*
In the drawing we see a horse, a cow, a sheep, a pig, a cat.

Лошадь, корова, кошка, собака — домашние животные.
LOH-*shahd, koh*-ROH-*vah,* KOHSH-*kah, soh*-BAH-*kah* — *doh*-MAHSH-*nee-yeh zhee*-VOHT-*nee-yeh.*
The horse, the cow, the cat, the dog are domestic animals.

Медведь, лев, тигр, слон, волк — это дикие животные.
*M'yed-v'*YED, *l'yev, teegr, slohn, vohlk* — EH-*toh* DEE-*kee-yeh zhee*-VOHT-*nee-yeh.*
The bear, the lion, the tiger, the elephant, the wolf are wild animals.

NOTE on the RUSSIAN BEAR:
The meaning of **медвéдь** is literally "honey eater". In case you meet a bear in Russia, the pet name for all bears is **Ми́шка**—"little Michael".

Домашние животные работают для человека.
Doh-MAHSH-*nee-yeh zhee*-VOHT-*nee-yeh rah*-BOH-*tah-yoot dl'yah cheh-lov*-YEH-*kah.*
The domestic animals work for man.

Собака сторожит дом.
Soh-BAH-*kah stoh-roh*-ZHEET *dohm.*
The dog guards the house.

Кошка ловит мышей.
KOHSH-*kah* LOH-*veet mee*-SHAY.
The cat catches mice.

Лошадь тянет повозку.
LOH-*shahd t'*YAHN-*yet poh*-VOHZ-*koo.*
The horse pulls the cart.

Корова даёт нам молоко.
Koh-ROH-*vah dah*-YOHT *nahm moh-loh*-KOH.
The cow gives us milk.

Дикие звери живут в лесу.
DEE-*kee-yeh zv'*YEH-*ree zhee*-VOOT *v l'yeh*-SOO.
Wild animals live in the forest.

Встретить льва или тигра или волка опасно.
*Vstr'*YEH-*teet lvah* EE-*lee* TEEG-*rah* EE-*lee* VOHL-*kah oh*-PAHS-*noh.*
To meet a lion or a tiger or a wolf is dangerous.

На охоте в сибирских лесах вы можете встретить волка.
Nah oh-KHOHT-*yeh v see*-BEER-*skeekh l'yeh*-SAHKH *vwee* MOH-*zhet-yeh vstr'*YEH-*teet* VOHL-*kah.*
While hunting in Siberian forests you may encounter a wolf.

Ваш приятель вам крикнет:
Vahsh pree-YAHT-*yel vahm* KREEK-*n'yet*:
Your friend will shout:

Берегись! Волк идёт!
Beh-reh-GGEES! *Vohlk eed*-YOHT!
Watch out! A wolf is coming!

IMPORTANT NOTE: Here are some useful expressions for emergencies:

"Look out!"—**Береги́сь!**
"Go away!"—**Убира́йся!**
"Help!"—**Помоги́те!**
"Stop!"—**Стой!**
"Police!"—**Поли́ция!**
"Fire!"—**Пожа́р!**
"I love you!"—**Я вас люблю́!**
"To your health!"—**За ва́ше здоро́вье!**

У лошади четыре ноги,
Oo LOH-*shah-dee cheh*-TEE-*reh noh*-GGEE,
The horse has four legs,

которыми она ходит, бегает и прыгает.
koh-TOH-*ree-mee oh*-NAH KHOH-*deet, b'*YEH-*gah-yet ee* PREE-*gah-yet.*
with which it walks, runs, and jumps.

На картине мы видим петуха.
Nah kahr-TEEN-*yeh mee* VEE-*deem p'yeh-too*-KHAH.
In the picture we see a rooster.

Петух и курица — птицы.
P'yeh-TOOKH *ee* KOO-*ree-tsah* — PTEE-*tsee.*
The rooster and the hen are birds.

Утка, гусь, орёл, воробей, голубь — тоже птицы.
OOT-*kah, goos, or*-YOHL, *voh-roh*-BAY, GOH-*loob*—TOH-*zheh* PTEE-*tsee.*
The duck, the goose, the eagle, the sparrow, the pigeon are also birds.

У птиц две ноги и два крыла.
Oo pteets dv'yeh noh-GGEE *ee dvah kree*-LAH.
Birds have two legs and two wings.

У них крылья для того, чтобы летать.
Oo neekh KREEL-*yah dl'yah toh*-VOH, SHTOH-*bee l'yeh*-TAHT.
They have wings for flying.

REMEMBER! When the specific number 2, 3, or 4 is mentioned with a noun, the noun uses genitive singular endings. This accounts for the difference between **два крылá** "two wings" and **кры́лья** "wings", as seen above.

Птицы летают в воздухе.
PTEE-*tsee l'yeh*-TAH-*yoot v* VOHZ-*doo-kheh.*
Birds fly in the air.

Птицы покрыты перьями.
PTEE-*tsee poh*-KREE-*tee p'*YEHR-*yah-mee.*
Birds are covered with feathers.

Тело животных покрыто шерстью.
*T'*YEH-*loh zhee*-VOHT-*neekh poh*-KREE-*toh* SHEHRST-*yoo.*
The body of animals is covered with hair.

NOTE on FURS: When hair is on the animal it is called **шерсть**, when on a fur coat, it becomes **мех**. Thus:

У нóрки глáдкая шерсть "The mink has smooth fur"
меховóе пальтó "a fur coat"
пальтó на мехý "a fur-lined coat"

Рыбы живут в воде.
REE-*bee zhee*-VOOT *v vod*-YEH.
Fish live in the water.

Они плавают.
Oh-NEE PLAH-*vah-yoot.*
They swim.

У них нет ни ног, ни крыльев.
Oo neekh n'yet nee nohg, nee KREEL-*yev.*

They have neither legs nor wings.

Они двигаются плавая.
Oh-NEE DVEE-*gah-yoot-sah* PLAH-*vah-yah.*
They move by swimming.

GRAMMATICAL NOTE: **пла́вая,** which means "while swimming", "by swimming", is a gerund. It is usually obtained from the root of the present tense by adding the endings **-а,** or **-я.** Gerunds don't change; they are used to denote a secondary action explaining or completing the main action. Ex.: **Она́ шла, напева́я пе́сенку** — "She was walking, and singing a little song." **Зна́я, что Ма́ша там, я зашёл.** — "Knowing (because I knew) that Mary was there, I dropped in." **Он спит сто́я** — "He sleeps standing."

Змея ползёт по земле.
Zm'yeh-YAH *polz*-YOHT *poh z'yeml*-YEH.
The snake crawls on the ground.

Лягушки живут на земле и в воде.
L'yah-GOOSH-*kee zhee*-VOOT *nah z'yeml*-YEH *ee v vod*-YEH.
Frogs live on the land and in the water.

Во Франции их едят.
Voh FRAHN-*tsee-ee eekh yed*-YAHT.

People eat them in France.

В России не едят лягушек.
V Ros-SEE-*ee n'yeh yed*-YAHT *l'yah*-GOO-*shek.*
In Russia people don't eat frogs.

Муха, комар, бабочка — насекомые.
MOO-*khah, koh*-MAHR, BAH-*boch-kah—nahs-yeh*-KOH-*mee-yeh.*
The fly, the mosquito, the butterfly are insects.

WATCH OUT! Don't confuse **ба́бушка** (BAH-*boosh-kah*) and **ба́бочка.** The former means "grandmother", the latter "butterfly".

Пчела, которая делает мёд, полезна.
Pcheh-LAH, *koh*-TOH-*rah-yah d'*YEH-*lah-yet m'yohd, pol*-YEZ-*nah.*
The bee, which makes honey, is useful.

Мухи и комары бесполезны и даже вредны.
MOO-*khee ee koh-mah*-REE *b'yes-pol*-YEZ-*nee ee* DAH-*zheh* VREHD-*nee.*
Flies and mosquitoes are useless and even harmful.

Когда мы их видим, мы стараемся их убить.
Kog-DAH *mee eekh* VEE-*deem, mee stah*-RAH-*yem-sah eekh oo*-BEET.
When we see them, we try to kill them.

Когда они мертвы, они уже не могут нас кусать.
Kog-DAH *oh*-NEE *mehrt*-VEE, *oh*-NEE *oo*-ZHEH *n'yeh* MOH-*goot nahs koo*-SAHT.
When they are dead they cannot bite us any more.

THINKING IN RUSSIAN

(Answers on page 229)

1. Каки́х живо́тных вы ви́дите на рису́нке?
2. Дома́шние ли э́то живо́тные и́ли ди́кие?
3. Поле́зны ли дома́шние живо́тные?
4. Что́ даёт нам коро́ва?
5. Что́ даёт нам пчела́?
6. Что́ де́лает для нас ло́шадь?
7. Что́ де́лает соба́ка?
8. Что́ де́лает ко́шка?
9. Ско́лько ног у ло́шади?
10. Ско́лько лап у ти́гра?
11. Ско́лько кры́льев у орла́?
12. Где́ лета́ют пти́цы?
13. Че́м покры́то те́ло живо́тных?
14. Как дви́гается змея́?
15. Хо́дит ли змея́?
16. Есть ли у змей но́ги?
17. Есть ли но́ги у ры́бы?
18. Как дви́гаются ры́бы?
19. Где́ они́ живу́т?
20. Пла́вают ли лягу́шки?
21. Поле́зны ли му́хи и комары́?
22. Мно́го ли мух в ва́шем до́ме?

УРОК 26

Ощущения и чувства
Osh-choosh-CHEH-*nee-yah ee* CHOOVST-*vah*
Emotions and feelings

Превосходит ли человек животных?
Preh-vos-KHOH-*deet lee cheh-lov*-YEK *zhee*-VOHT-*neekh?*
Is man superior to the animals?

Животные могут делать многое лучше, чем человек.
Zhee-VOHT-*nee-yeh* MOH-*goot d'*YEH-*laht* MNOH-*goh-yeh* LOOCH-*sheh,*
chem cheh-lov-YEK.
Animals can do many things better than man.

Например: у орла зрение острее, чем у человека.
Nah-preem-YEHR: *oo or*-LAH *zr'*YEH-*nee-yeh ostr*-YEH-*yeh,*
chem oo cheh-lov-YEH-*kah.*
For instance: The eagle has sharper vision than man.

Рыба плавает лучше,
REE-*bah* PLAH-*vah-yet* LOOCH-*sheh,*
The fish swims better,

а лошадь бежит быстрее человека.
ah LOH-*shahd b'yeh*-ZHEET *beestr*-YEH-*yeh cheh-lov*-YEH-*kah.*
and the horse runs faster than man.

Слон гораздо сильнее многих людей взятых вместе.
Slohn goh-RAHZ-*doh seeln*-YEH-*yeh* MNOH-*ggeekh l'yood*-YAY *vz'*YAH-*teekh vm'*YEST-*yeh.*
The elephant is much stronger than many men put together.

Все же человек превосходит животных своим мозгом.
*Vs'*YOH-*zheh cheh-lov*-YEK *preh-vos*-KHOH-*deet zhee*-VOHT-*neekh svoh*-EEM MOHZ-*gom.*
Nevertheless man is superior to the animals because of his brain.

NOTE to STUDENT: Remember this use of the instrumental "through his brain", or "because of", "on account of" etc.

Говорят, что лев — царь животных.
Goh-vor-YAHT, *shtoh l'yev — tsahr zhee*-VOHT-*neekh.*
They say that the lion is the king of animals.

Но это неверно.
Noh EH-*toh n'yev*-YEHR-*noh.*
But this is not true.

Человек — царь, потому что у него мозг более развит.
Cheh-lov-YEK — *tsahr, poh-toh*-MOO *shtoh oo n'yeh*-VOH *mohzg* BOHL-*yeh-yeh* RAHZ-*veet.*
Man is the king because his brain is more (highly) developed.

ROYALTY NOTE: "Tsar" is an old word meaning "king" or "emperor". It doesn't exclusively refer to the former Russian emperor.

Мозгом, который находится в голове, мы мыслим.
MOHZ-*gom, koh*-TOH-*ree nah*-KHOH-*deet-sah v goh-lov*-YEH, *mee* MEES-*leem.*
With the brain, which is in the head, we think.

Без того, чтобы мыслить, мы не можем говорить.
B'yez toh-VOH, SHTOH-*bee* MEES-*leet, mee n'yeh* MOH-*zhem goh-voh*-REET.
Without thinking we cannot speak.

WATCH OUT! Note the above construction for "without thinking". You really must say: "without that in order to think". Quite a mouthful!

В мозгу у нас образуются мысли.
*V moz-*GOO *oo nahs ob-rah-*ZOO*-yoot-sah* MEES*-lee.*
Thoughts are formed in our brain.

Мы говорим для того, чтобы сообщать свои мысли другим людям.
*Mee goh-voh-*REEM *dl'yah toh-*VOH, SHTOH*-bee soh-ob-*SHCHAHT *svoh-*EE MEES*-lee droog-*EEM *l'*YOOD*-yahm.*
We speak in order to communicate our thoughts to other people.

Вы думаете сейчас о вашем уроке.
Vwee DOO*-mah-yeht-yeh say-*CHAHS *oh* VAH*-shem oo-*ROH*-keh.*
Now, you are thinking about your lesson.

О чём вы думаете в полдень, когда стол накрыт?
Oh chohm vwee DOO*-mah-yet-yeh v* POHLD*-yen, kog-*DAH *stohl nah-*KREET*?*
What do you think about at noon, when the table is set?

Человека, который думает много и правильно, называют умным.
*Cheh-lov-*YEH*-kah, koh-*TOH*-ree* DOO*-mah-yet* MNOH*-goh ee* PRAH*-veel-noh, nah-zee-*VAH*-yoot* OOM*-neem.*
They call a person who thinks much and well, intelligent.

Умные люди учатся легко, а глупые — туго.
OOM*-nee-yeh l'*YOO*-dee* OO*-chaht-sah l'yekh-*KOH*, ah* GLOO*-pee-yeh*—TOO*-goh.*
Intelligent people learn easily, stupid ones (learn) with difficulty.

Умён ли осёл?
*Oom-*YOHN *lee os-*YOHL*?*
Is the donkey intelligent?

Нет, он глуп.
N'yet, ohn gloop.
No, he is stupid.

GRAMMATICAL NOTE: Умён and **глуп** are the "short" forms of the adjectives **у́мный** and **глу́пый**. Only adjectives denoting quality have short forms. Note the following examples where the short form is used as a predicate adjective.

"a healthy young man"—	**здоро́вый молодо́й челове́к.**
"He is young and healthy."—	**Он мо́лод и здоро́в.**
"a beautiful young woman"—	**краси́вая молода́я же́нщина.**
"She is young and beautiful."—	**Она́ мо́лода и краси́ва.**

If the stem ends in two consonants which are difficult to pronounce, an **"о"** or **"е"** is inserted between them. For example: **у́мный — умён, ни́зкий — ни́зок.** There is one useful adjective which has the short form only: **рад, -а, -о** "glad":

Я ра́да вас ви́деть — "I am glad to see you."

Мы умеем делать то, что мы выучили.
*Mee oom-*YEH*-yem d'*YEH*-laht toh, shtoh mee* VEE*-oo-chee-lee.*
We know how to do what we have learned.

Вы умеете считать по-русски.
*Vwee oom-*YEH*-yet-yeh shchee-*TAHT *poh-*ROOS*-skee.*
You know how to count in Russian.

Но умеете ли вы считать по-китайски?
*Noh oom-*YEH*-yet-yeh lee vwee shchee-*TAHT *poh-kee-*TIGH*-skee?*
But can you count in Chinese?

Я знаю ваше имя.
Yah ZNAH*-you* VAH*-sheh* EEM*-yah.*
I know your name.

Знаете ли вы моё?
ZNAH*-yet-yeh lee vwee moh-*YOH*?*
Do you know mine?

Вы не знаете, что у меня в кармане.
Vwee n'yeh ZNAH*-yet-yeh shtoh oo m'yen-*YAH *v kahr-*MAHN*-yeh.*
You don't know what is in my pocket.

WATCH OUT! Уме́ть and **знать** — both are translated in English by "to know". But in Russian there is difference in the meaning. **Уме́ть** means "to know how" to do something, while **знать** has the connotation of "to be acquainted with". Thus:

Зна́ете ли вы Бе́рлица? "Do you know Mr. Berlitz?"
Уме́ете ли вы игра́ть в ша́хматы? "Do you know how to play chess?"

Некоторые события и факты мы забываем.
*N'*YEH*-koh-toh-ree-yeh soh-*BEE*-tee-yah ee* FAHK*-tee mee zah-bee-*VAH*-yem.*
We forget some events and facts.

Легко ли вы запоминаете имена? И забываете их легко?
*L'yekh-*KOH *lee vwee zah-poh-mee-*NAH*-yet-yeh ee-m'yeh-*NAH*? Ee zah-bee-*VAH*-yet-yeh eekh l'yekh-*KOH*?*
Do you remember names easily? And do you also forget them easily?

У человека ощущения и чувства сильнее, чем у животных.
*Oo cheh-lov-*YEH*-kah osh-choosh-*CHEH*-nee-yah ee* CHOOV*-stvah seeln-*YEH*-yeh, chem oo zhee-*VOHT*-neekh.*
Man has stronger feelings and emotions than animals.

Мы любим нашу семью.
*Mee l'*YOO-*beem* NAH-*shoo s'yem*-YOO.
We love our family.

Мы любим нашу родину.
*Mee l'*YOO-*beem* NAH-*shoo* ROH-*dee-noo.*
We love our native country.

Когда с нами случается что-то приятное, мы радуемся.
Kog-DAH *s* NAH-*mee sloo*-CHAH-*yet-sah* SHTOH-*toh pree*-YAHT-*noh-yeh, mee* RAH-*doo-yem-sah.*
When something pleasant happens to us, we are glad.

Когда случается что-то неприятное, нам грустно.
Kog-DAH *sloo*-CHAH-*yet-sah* SHTOH-*toh n'yeh-pree*-YAHT-*noh-yeh, nahm* GROOST-*noh.*
When something unpleasant happens, we are sad.

Когда учитель вам говорит, что
Kog-DAH *oo*-CHEET-*yel vahm goh-voh*-REET, *shtoh*
When the teacher tells you that you are

вы очень хороший ученик, вы довольны.
vwee OH-*chen khoh*-ROH-*shee oo-cheh*-NEEK, *vwee doh*-VOHL-*nee.*
a very good pupil, you are satisfied.

Дети боятся темноты.
*D'*YEH-*tee boh*-YAHT-*sah t'yem-noh*-TEE.
Children are afraid of the dark.

Некоторые девочки боятся пауков, мышей и змей.
*N'*YEH-*koh-toh-ree-yeh d'*YEH-*voch-kee boh*-YAHT-*sah pah-oo*-KOHV, *mee*-SHAY *ee zmay.*
Some girls are afraid of spiders, mice and snakes.

Человека, который ничего не боится, мы называем храбрым.
Cheh-lov-YEH-*kah, koh*-TOH-*ree nee-cheh*-VOH *n'yeh boh*-EET-*sah, mee nah-zee*-VAH-*yem* KHRAHB-*reem.*
We call a person brave who doesn't fear anything.

Храбры ли казаки?
KHRAHB-*ree lee kah-zah*-KEE?
Are the Cossacks brave?

NOTE on COSSACKS: The Cossacks are not a race. They are Russians and speak Russian. They are descendants of Russian "pioneers" who settled and extended the frontier and formed communities of warlike horsemen from which the Tsars drew their crack regiments. Even today the USSR has not forgotten the value of this policy of the old regime.

Когда мы должны ждать долгое время
Kog-DAH *mee dolzh*-NEE *zhdaht* DOHL-*goh-yeh* VREHM-*yah*
When we must wait a long time

в очереди, чтобы купить хлеб, мы недовольны.
v OH-*cheh-reh-dee,* SHTOH-*bee koo*-PEET *khl'yeb, mee n'yeh-doh*-VOHL-*nee.*
in line to buy bread, we are dissatisfied.

Когда ваш приятель вам говорит,
Kog-DAH *vahsh pree*-YAHT-*yel vahm goh-voh*-REET,
When your friend tells you

что он не может прийти к вам обедать,
shtoh ohn n'yeh MOH-*zhet pree*-TEE *k vahm ob*-YEH-*daht,*
that he cannot come (to you) for dinner,

потому что он болен, вы ему говорите:
poh-toh-MOO *shtoh ohn* BOHL-*yen, vwee yeh*-MOO *goh-voh*-REET-*yeh*:
because he is sick, you say to him:

мне очень жаль; я надеюсь, что завтра вам будет лучше.
mn'yeh OH-*chen zhahl; yah nahd*-YEH-*yoos, shtoh* ZAHV-*trah vahm* BOOD-*yet* LOOCH-*sheh.*
I am very sorry; I hope that you will be better tomorrow.

REMEMBER THESE EXPRESSIONS: In expressing sensations and feelings you usually use reflexive verbs instead of adjectives. Thus:

"I am glad"—	**я ра́дуюсь**
"I am angry"—	**я сержу́сь**
"I am afraid"—	**я бою́сь**
"I am proud"—	**я горжу́сь**

Other expressions are:

"I am happy"—	**я сча́стлив**
"I am unhappy"—	**я несча́стен**
"I am sad"—	**мне гру́стно**
"I am amused"—	**мне смешно́**

Иное чувство — страх.
Ee-NOH-*yeh* CHOOV-*stvoh—strahkh.*
Another feeling is fear.

Маленькие государства иногда боятся больших и более сильных.
MAHL-*yen-kee-yeh goh-soo*-DAHRST-*vah ee-nog*-DAH *boh*-YAHT-*sah bol*-SHEEKH *ee* BOHL-*yeh-yeh* SEEL-*neekh.*
Small countries are sometimes afraid of bigger and stronger ones.

Мы не любим неприятностей.
*Mee n'yeh l'*YOO-*beem n'yeh-pree-*YAHT-*nost-yay.*
We do not like unpleasant things.

Мы ненавидим шум, когда мы хотим спать.
*Mee n'yeh-nah-*VEE-*deem shoom, kog-*DAH *mee khoh-*TEEM *spaht.*
We hate noise when we want to sleep.

Когда человек очень недоволен, он сердит.
*Kog-*DAH *cheh-lov-*YEK OH-*chen n'yeh-doh-*VOHL-*yen, ohn s'yehr-*DEET.
When a person is very annoyed, he is angry.

Когда сталкиваются два автомобиля, шофёры злятся.
*Kog-*DAH STAHL-*kee-vah-yoot-sah dvah ahv-toh-moh-*BEEL-*yah, shof-*YOH-*ree zl'*YAHT-*sah.*
When two automobiles crash, the chauffeurs are angry.

Смешное нас заставляет смеяться.
*Sm'yesh-*NOH-*yeh nahs zah-stahvl-*YAH-*yet sm'yeh-*YAHT-*sah.*
Funny things make us laugh.

Смеётесь ли вы, когда вы видите в кинематографе комика?
*Sm'yeh-*YOHT-*yes lee vwee, kog-*DAH *vwee* VEE-*deet-yeh v keen-yeh-mah-*TOH-*graf-yeh* KOH-*mee-kah?*
Do you laugh when you see a comedian in the movies?

Иногда мы плачем, когда нам грустно.
*Ee-nog-*DAH *mee* PLAH-*chem, kog-*DAH *nahm* GROOST-*noh.*
Sometimes we cry, when we are sad.

Часто ли плачут дети?
CHAHS-*toh lee* PLAH-*choot d'*YEH-*tee?*
Do children often cry?

Что приятнее: ребёнок, который плачет, или ребёнок, который смеётся?
*Shtoh pree-*YAHTN-*yeh-yeh: reb-*YOH-*nok, koh-*TOH-*ree* PLAH-*chet,* EE-*lee reb-*YOH-*nok, koh-*TOH-*ree sm'yeh-*YOHT-*sah?*
Which is more pleasant: a child who cries or a child who laughs?

NOTE to STUDENT: The plural of **ребёнок** is **дéти.** The plural of **человéк** is **лю́ди.** They are actually different words. Remember that with nouns which have no singular, you must use the collective numerals: **двóе, трóе, чéтверо, пя́теро** instead of **два, три, четы́ре, пять.** Thus:

"He has three children". **У негó трóе детéй.**
"We traveled 48 hours". **Мы éхали двóе сýток.**

THINKING IN RUSSIAN

(Answers on page 230)

1. Отчего́ учи́тель дово́лен?
2. Почему́ Лёля пла́чет?
3. Тётя Ма́ша грустит?
4. Чем челове́к превосхо́дит живо́тных?
5. Где́ у нас образу́ются мы́сли?
6. Чем мы мы́слим?
7. Кто бежи́т быстре́е, челове́к и́ли ло́шадь?
8. Кто пла́вает лу́чше?
9. Кто ви́дит лу́чше, орёл и́ли челове́к?
10. Кто царь живо́тных?
11. О чём вы ду́маете сейча́с?
12. О чём вы ду́маете, когда́ вам хо́чется спать?
13. Хоро́шая ли у вас па́мять?
14. Легко́ ли вы запомина́ете ру́сские слова́?
15. По́мните ли вы все ру́сские слова́, кото́рые вы учи́ли?
16. Ча́сто ли вы се́рдитесь?
17. Дово́льны ли вы, когда́ вас хва́лят?
18. Кого́ мы называ́ем хра́брым?
19. Что́ лу́чше, пла́кать и́ли смея́ться?
20. Бои́тесь ли вы пауко́в?
21. Легко́ ли вас мо́жно испуга́ть?

УРОК 27

Едемте в Москву!
YEH-*d'yemt-yeh v Mosk*-VOO!
Let's go to Moscow!

Короленко: Здравствуй, Саша, дружище! Ты откуда?
Koh-rol-YEN-*koh*: ZDRAHVST-*vooy,* SAH-*shah, droo*-ZHEESH-*cheh. Tee ot*-KOO-*dah?*
Korolenko: Hello, Sasha, old fellow, where from do you come?

Панов: Я только-что приехал из Америки . . .
Pah-NOHV: *Yah* TOHL-*koh-shtoh pree*-YEH-*khahl eez Ah*-MEH-*ree-kee.*
Panov: I have just arrived from America.

ANOTHER EXAMPLE of condensed Russian expressions:

Вы куда́?	Where are you going?
Вы отку́да?	Where are you coming from?

Короленко: Как я рад тебя видеть. Вот не ожидал.
*Kahk yah rahd t'yeb-*YAH VEED-*yet. Voht n'yeh oh-zhee-*DAHL.
How glad I am to see you. I really didn't expect it.

Глядя на тебя, я вспоминаю, как ты прилетел в Ростов во время войны...
*Gl'*YAHD-*yah nah t'yeb-*YAH, *yah vspoh-mee-*NAH-*yoo kahk tee pree-l'yet-*YEHL *v Ros-*TOHV *voh* VREHM-*yah voy-*NEE.
Looking at you I remember how you arrived by plane in Rostov during the war. . . .

Ты приехал в Киев по делам?
*Tee pree-*YEH-*khahl v* KEE-*yev poh d'yeh-*LAHM?
Did you come to Kiev on business?

Панов: Нет, я еду в Москву. Но, зная, что ты здесь,
N'yet, yah YEH-*doo v Mosk-*VOO. *Noh,* ZNAH-*yah shtoh tee zd'yes,*
No, I am going to Moscow, but knowing that you were here,

я остановился в Киеве, чтобы повидаться с тобой.
*yah os-tah-noh-*VEEL-*sah v* KEE-*yev-yeh,* SHTOH-*bee poh-vee-*DAHT-*sah s toh-*BOY.
I stopped in Kiev for the purpose of seeing you.

NOTE on the GERUND: Гля́дя and **зна́я** are gerunds. The gerund form never changes.

Гля́дя means "(while) looking", **зна́я** — "(while) knowing". "since knowing", "since I know", "by knowing" are fairly analogous constructions. The gerund is obtained from the 3rd person plural of the present tense by replacing the endings **-ут, -ют, -ат, ят** with the ending **-я** (after certain consonants by the ending **-а**), thus

Он пи́шет стóя —	"He writes while standing".
Они́ сидéли мóлча —	"They were sitting in silence".

Короленко: Надеюсь, что ты останешься в Киеве несколько дней.
*Nahd-*YEH-*yoos, shtoh tee os-*TAHN-*yesh-sah v* KEE-*yev-yeh n'*YES-*kol-koh dn'yay.*
I hope that you will stay in Kiev for a few days.

Панов: Никак не могу. Я должен быть послезавтра в Москве.
*Nee-*KAHK *n'yeh moh-*GOO. *Yah* DOHL-*zhen beet posl-yeh-*ZAHV-*trah v Moskv-*YEH.
I can't by any means. I must be in Moscow the day after tomorrow.

Короленко: Как жаль! У меня как раз отпуск.
*Kahk zhahl! Oo m'yen-*YAH *kahk rahz* OHT-*poosk.*
What a pity! I am just on leave.

Оставаясь лишний день, ты сможешь осмотреть Киев.
*Os-tah-*VAH-*yahs* LEESH-*nee d'yen, tee* SMOH-*zhesh os-motr-*YET KEE-*yev.*
By staying one more day you will be able to have a look around Kiev.

Ты ведь в Киеве никогда не был.
Tee v'yed v KEE-*yev-yeh nee-kog-*DAH *n'*YEH *beel.*
You have really never been in Kiev.

AN IDIOM to REMEMBER: Ведь is not translatable. It means "then", "really", "indeed", or "in fact", according to context.

Панов: Я и Москвы не знаю. А ты в Москве бывал.
*Yah ee Mosk-*VEE *n'yeh* ZNAH-*you. A tee v Moskv-*YEH *bee-*VAHL.
I don't know Moscow either. But you have often been in Moscow.

Ты можешь показать мне Москву.
Tee MOH-*zhesh poh-kah-*ZAHT *mn'yeh Mosk-*VOO.
You can show me Moscow.

Короленко: Ты хочешь, чтобы я поехал с тобой в Москву?
Tee KHOH-*chesh,* SHTOH-*bee yah poh-*YEH-*khahl s toh-*BOY *v Mosk-*VOO?
Do you wish me to go to Moscow with you?

Панов: А почему бы тебе не поехать?
*Ah poh-cheh-*MOO *bee t'yeb-*YEH *n'yeh poh-*YEH-*khaht?*
And why shouldn't you go?

У тебя ведь отпуск.
*Oo t'yeb-*YAH *v'yed* OHT-*poosk.*
You are on leave anyway.

IDIOMATIC NOTE: Тебé means "to you" or "for you". Therefore you are really saying "why not to go for you"? It sounds funny to us but natural to the Russians.

Короленко: Мысль эта мне нравится.
Meesl EH-*tah mn'yeh* NRAH-*veet-sah.*
I like the idea.

У меня есть в Москве дело.
*Oo m'yen-*YAH *yest v Mosku-*YEH *d'*YEH*-loh.*
I have some business in Moscow.

Хорошо, поедем вместе.
*Khoh-roh-*SHOH, *poh-*YED*-yem vm'*YEST*-yeh.*
Good, let's go together.

Панов: Надо узнать, можем ли мы
NAH*-doh ooz-*NAHT, MOH*-zhem lee mee*
We must find out if we can

получить места в самолёте на завтра.
*poh-loo-*CHEET *m'yeh-*STAH *v sah-mol-*YOHT*-yeh nah* ZAHV*-trah.*
get places on tomorrow's plane.

Короленко: Я сейчас позвоню на аэродром и узнаю.
*Yah say-*CHAHS *poz-von-*YOU *nah ah-eh-roh-*DROHM *ee ooz-*NAH*-you.*
I'll phone the airport right away and find out.

Панов: А нет ли у вас тут конторы, где бы можно навести справки?
*Ah n'yet lee oo vahs toot kon-*TOH*-ree gd'yeh bee* MOHZH*-noh nah-ves-*TEE SPRAHV*-kee?*
But don't you have an office here where you can make an inquiry?

Короленко: Я совершенно забыл, конечно есть.
*Yah soh-v'yehr-*SHEN*-noh zah-*BEEL, *kon-*YECH*-noh yest.*
I completely forgot, naturally there is.

Мы там же и купим билеты.
Mee TAHM *zheh ee* KOO*-peem beel-*YEH*-tee.*
We'll also buy the tickets there.

Но сперва нам надо позавтракать.
*Noh sp'yehr-*VAH *nahm* NAH*-doh poh-*ZAHV*-trah-kaht.*
But first we must have lunch.

Позавтракав(ши), мы отправимся в контору.
*Poh-*ZAHV*-trah-kahv-(shee), mee ot-*PRAH*-veem-sah v kon-*TOH*-roo.*
Having had lunch we will go to the office.

Панов: Хорошо, идём завтракать.
*Khoh-roh-*SHOH, *eed-*YOHM ZAHV*-trah-kaht.*
All right, let's go to lunch.

GRAMMATICAL NOTE: **Поза́втракавши** or **поза́втракав** is the past gerund and means "having had lunch". It is obtained from the infinitive by replacing **-ть** by the ending **-в** or **-вши**, e.g.: **Прочита́в письмо́, он положи́л его́ в карма́н** —"Having read the letter, he put it into his pocket".

(В конторе)
(*V kon*-TOHR-*yeh*)
(At the office)

Короленко: Есть ли у вас ещё два места на самолёте в Москву на завтра?
Yest lee oo vahs yesh-CHOH *dvah m'*YES-*tah nah sah-mol*-YOHT-*yeh v Mosk*-VOO *nah* ZAHV-*trah?*
Do you still have two seats on the Moscow plane for tomorrow?

Служащий: Завтра утром у нас два самолёта на Москву:
SLOO-*zhash-chee*: ZAHV-*trah* OOT-*rom oo nahs dvah sah-mol*-YOH-*tah nah Mosk*-VOO.
Employee: Tomorrow morning we have two planes for Moscow:

в 7.30 и в 8.30.
v s'yem TREED-*tsaht ee v* VOHS-*yem* TREED-*tsaht.*
at 7:30 and 8:30.

Короленко: Есть ли у вас ещё два места в 7.30?
Yest lee oo vahs yesh-CHOH *dvah m'*YES-*tah v s'yem* TREED-*tsaht?*
Do you still have two seats for 7:30?

Служащий: Есть.
SLOO-*znash-chee*: *Yest.*
Employee: We have.

Короленко: Сколько стоит билет в Москву?
SKOHL-*koh* STOH-*eet beel*-YET *v Mosk*-VOO?
How much is a ticket to Moscow?

Служащий: 100 рублей в один конец, 150 рублей в оба конца.
Stoh roobl-YAY *v oh*-DEEN *kon*-YETS, *stoh-p'yaht-d'yeh*-SAHT *roobl*-YAY *v* OH-*bah kon*-TSAH.
100 rubles one way, 150 rubles round trip.

Короленко: Пожалуйста, дайте мне билет в один конец.
Poh-ZHAH-*looy-stah*, DIGHT-*yeh mn'yeh beel*-YET *v oh*-DEEN *kon*-YETS.
Please give me a one way ticket.

Служащий: А вам, гражданин?
SLOO-*zhash-chee*: *Ah vahm, grazh-dah*-NEEN?
Employee: And for you, citizen?

Панов: Мне — туда и обратно.
Mn'yeh—too-DAH *ee ob*-RAHT-*noh.*
For me—there and back.

Короленко: Купив билеты, мы теперь поездим по Киеву,
Koo-PEEV *beel*-YEH-*tee, mee t'yep*-YEHR *poh*-YEZ-*deem poh* KEE-*yeh-voo,*
Now that we have bought the tickets, we shall now drive around Kiev a little

и я тебе покажу всё самое интересное.
ee yah t'yeb-YEH *poh-kah*-ZHOO *vs'yoh* SAH-*moh-yeh eent-yeh*-RES-*noh-yeh.*
and I'll show you all the most interesting things.

REMEMBER: Did you notice the above use of the gerund in **купи́в** — "having bought". We have translated it "now that we have bought" which means the same thing.

Панов: Спасибо. Я давно хотел посмотреть Киев.
Spah-SEE-*boh. Yah dahv*-NOH *khot*-YEL *pos-motr*-YET KEE-*yev.*
Thank you. For a long time I have wished to see Kiev,

Ведь это — первая столица русского государства,
V'yed EH-*toh p'*YEHR-*vah-yah stoh*-LEE-*tsah* ROOS-*skoh-voh goh-soo*-DAHRST-*vah,*
as it (was) the first capital of the Russian State,

мать русских городов.
maht ROOS-*skeekh goh-roh*-DOHV.
the mother of Russian cities.

Короленко: Только не забудь сказать в гостинице,
TOHL-*koh n'yeh zah*-BOOD *skah*-ZAHT *v gos*-TEE-*nee-tseh,*
Only don't forget to tell (them) at the hotel,

чтобы тебя завтра разбудили в пять часов утра.
SHTOH-*bee t'yeb*-YAH ZAHV-*trah rahz-boo*-DEE-*lee v p'*YAHT *chah*-SOHV *oot*-RAH.
that they should wake you up at five o'clock in the morning.

Панов: Почему так рано?
Poh-cheh-MOO *tahk* RAH-*noh?*
Why so early?

Короленко: Лучше по-раньше, чтобы не опоздать.
LOOCH-*sheh poh*-RAHN-*sheh,* SHTOH-*bee n'yeh oh-poz*-DAHT.
Better earlier, so as not to be late.

Я за тобой заеду в шесть часов утра.
Yah zah toh-BOY *zah*-YEH-*doo v shest chah*-SOHV *oot*-RAH.
I'll come to get you at six o'clock in the morning.

THINKING IN RUSSIAN

(Answers on page 230)

1. Откýда приéхал Панóв?
2. Как егó зовýт?
3. Что вспоминáет Королéнко, глядя на Сáшу?
4. На дóлго ли приéхал Панóв в Кѝев?
5. Почемý он приéхал в Кѝев?
6. Отчегó Панóв не мóжет остáться в Кѝеве нéсколько дней?
7. Знáет ли Панóв Москвý?
8. Знáете ли вы Одéссу?
9. Бывáли ли вы в Вашингтóне?
10. Почемý Королéнко мóжет показáть Панóву Москвý?
11. У вáс тепéрь óтпуск?
12. Когдá у вáс бýдет óтпуск?
13. Что вы дéлаете, когдá вы в отпускý?
14. Едут ли Королéнко и Панóв пóездом ѝли же онѝ летят в Москвý на самолёте?
15. Где справляются онѝ, есть ли ещё свобóдные местá?
16. Где онѝ зáвтракают?
17. Что онѝ дéлают, позáвтракавши?
18. Берёт ли Королéнко билéт в одѝн конéц или в два концá?
19. Берёт ли Панóв обрáтный билéт?
20. Почемý Панóв давнó ужé хотéл осмотрéть Кѝев?

УРОК 28

Отъезд на аэродром
Ot-YEZD *nah ah-eh-roh*-DROHM
The departure for the Airport

(Звонит телефон.)
(*Zvoh*-NEET *t'yel-yeh*-FOHN.)
(The telephone rings.)

Панов (отвечает): Слушаю. Кто говорит?
Pah-NOHV (*ot-v'yeh*-CHAH-*yet*): SLOO-*shah-yoo. Ktoh goh-voh*-REET?
Panov (answers): I am listening. Who is speaking?

Телефонист: Уже шесть часов.
*T'yel-yeh-foh-*NEEST: *Oo-*ZHEH *shest chah-*SOHV.
Telephone operator: It is already six o'clock.

Мы вас будим уже второй раз.
Mee vahs BOO-*deem oo-*ZHEH *vtoh-*ROY *rahz.*
We are waking you up already for the second time.

Панов: Неужели? Я опаздываю.
*N'yeh-oo-*ZHEH-*lee? Yah oh-*PAHZ-*dee-vah-yoo.*
Is it possible? I am late.

Скажите, пожалуйста, в кассе, чтобы приготовили счёт.
*Skah-*ZHEET-*yeh, poh-*ZHAH-*looy-stah, v* KAHS-*yeh,* SHTOH-*bee pree-goh-*TOH-*vee-lee shchoht.*
Please tell the cashier to prepare the bill.

Телефонист: Хорошо. Я пришлю мальчика за багажом.
*Khoh-roh-*SHOH. *Yeh preeshl-*YOU MAHL-*chee-kah zah bah-gah-*ZHOHM.
Good. Ill send the boy for your luggage.

(В конторе гостиницы:)
(*V kon-*TOHR-*yeh gos-*TEE-*nee-tsee*:)
(At the hotel office:)

Кассир: Вот ваш счёт, гражданин.
*Kahs-*SEER: *Voht vahsh shchoht, grahzh-dah-*NEEN.
Cashier: Here is your bill, citizen.

24 рубля 50 копеек.
DVAHD-*tsaht cheh-*TEE-*reh roobl-*YAH, *p'yaht-d'yes-*YAHT *kop-*YEH-*yek.*
24 rubles, 50 kopecks.

NOTE on SOVIET CUSTOMS: As the hotel employee does not know who Panov is, he does not call him "Comrade" — **тов́арищ** but "citizen" — **граждан́ин** which can be applied to anyone. If he and Panov were both party members he would probably call him **тов́арищ.**

Панов: В это включено всё?
V EH-*toh vkl'yoo-cheh-*NOH *vs'*YOH?
Is everything included in this?

Кассир: Да, всё, — счёт ресторана и телефон.
*Dah, vs'yoh, shchoht res-toh-*RAH-*nah ee t'yel-yeh-*FOHN.
Yes, everything, restaurant checks and telephon calls.

Пожалуйста, не забудьте оставить ключ.
*Poh-*ZHAH-*looy-stah, n'yeh zah-*BOOD-*t'yeh os-*TAH-*veet kl'yooch.*
Please, don't forget to leave the key.

Панов: Вот деньги. Я оставил ключ в комнате.
*Voht d'*YEN*-ggee. Yah os-*TAH*-veel kl'yooch v* KOHM*-naht-yeh.*
Here is the money. I left the key in the room.

Кассир: Спасибо, желаю вам счастливого пути.
*Spah-*SEE*-boh, zheh-*LAH*-yoo vahm shchahst-*LEE*-voh-voh poo-*TEE.
Thank you. I wish you a pleasant trip.

Панов: Спасибо и до свидания.
*Spah-*SEE*-boh ee doh svee-*DAH*-nee-yah.*
Thank you and goodbye.

Кассир: Эй, Федя, возьми багаж и позови такси.
Ay, FEHD*-yah, voz-*MEE *bah-*GAHZH *ee poh-zoh-*VEE *tak-*SEE.
Hey there Fedya! Take the luggage and call a taxi.

NOTE on IMPERATIVE: You have noticed the use of **скажи́те, не забу́дьте**—"say", "don't forget", **возьми́** "take!" **позови́** "call!". These are the imperative forms of the verbs **сказа́ть, забы́ть, взять, позва́ть** respectively. These forms are generally obtained by dropping the endings from the 3rd person plural of the perfective aspect and adding **-и** for the singular, or **-ите** for the plural.

Панов: Такси звать не надо. Вот мой приятель.
*Tak-*SEE *zvaht n'yeh* NAH*-doh. Voht moy pree-*YAHT*-yel.*
It is not necessary to call a taxi. Here is my friend.

Он за мной заехал.
Ohn zah MNOY *zah-*YEH*-khal.*
He came to get me.

Федя: Который ваш багаж?
FEHD*-yah: Koh-*TOH*-ree vahsh bah-*GAHZH*?*
Fedya: Which is your luggage?

Панов: Вот этот чемодан.
Voht EH*-toht cheh-moh-*DAHN.
This suitcase here.

Не берите маленького саквояжа.
*N'yeh b'yeh-*REET*-yeh* MAHL*-yen-koh-voh sak-voh-*YAH*-zhah.*
Don't take the little case.

Я его возьму сам.
*Yah yeh-*VOH *voz-*MOO *sahm.*
I'll take it myself.

FURTHER NOTE on the IMPERATIVE: Did you notice the difference: **Возьми́ бага́ж** — "take the luggage", but **не бери́те ма́ленького саквоя́жа** — "don't take the small case!". The reason for this difference is that negative commands usually are given in the imperfective aspect of the verb.

(В автомобиле).
(*V av-toh-moh*-BEEL-*yeh*)
(In the car.)

Короленко: Отчего ты так опоздал?
Ot-cheh-VOH *tee tahk oh-poz*-DAHL*?*
Why are you so late?

Панов: Меня не разбудили во время.
M'yen-YAH *n'yeh raz-boo*-DEE-*lee* VOH-*vrem-yah.*
They didn't wake me up in time.

Дома я не привык вставать так рано.
DOH-*mah yah n'yeh pree*-VEEK *vstah*-VAHT *tahk* RAH-*noh.*
At home I am not used to getting up so early.

Короленко: Ну, ничего. У нас ещё есть время. До аэродрома недалеко.
Noo, nee-cheh-VOH. *Oo nahs yesh*-CHOH *yest* VREHM-*yah. Doh ah-eh-roh*-DROH-*mah n'yeh-dahl-yeh*-KOH.
Well, never mind. We still have time. It's not far to the airport.

(На аэродроме).
(*Nah ah-eh-roh*-DROHM-*yeh.*)
(At the airport.)

Короленко: У нас два билета в Москву на самолёт, который отлетает
Oo NAHS *dvah beel*-YEH-*tah v Mosk*-VOO *nah sah-mol*-YOHT, *koh*-TOH-*ree otl-yeh*-TAH-*yet*
We have two tickets for Moscow on the plane which takes off

в 7.30. Вот билеты.
v s'yem TREED-*tsaht. Voht beel*-YEH-*tee.*
at 7:30. Here are the tickets.

Фамилии наши Короленко и Панов.
Fah-MEE-*lee-ee* NAH-*shee Koh-rol*-YEN-*koh ee Pah*-NOHV.
Our names are Korolenko and Panov.

ATTENTION! Although the numbers of tickets remain the same, note that when Korolenko says "two" of them, he must say **билéта** which is the dual form. If he simply says "tickets", he uses the plural **билéты.**

Служащий аэродрома: Прекрасно. Фамилии ваши занесены в список.
SLOO-*zhahsh-chee ah-eh-roh*-DROH-*mah*: *Preh*-KRAHS-*noh. Fah*-MEE-*lee-ee* VAH-*shee zahn-yeh-seh*-NEE *v* SPEE-*sok.*
Airport employee: Very well. Your names are entered on the list.

А где ваш багаж? Сколько у вас мест?
Ah gd'yeh vahsh bah-GAHZH? SKOHL-*koh oo* VAHS *m'yest?*
And where is your luggage? How many pieces have you?

A WORD to REMEMBER: Ме́сто also means, "space" or "place". For example: **За́нято ли э́то ме́сто?** — "Is this space occupied?"

Короленко: Вот они. Всего два чемодана и маленький саквояж. Всего три места.
Voht oh-NEE. *Vs'yeh*-VOH *dvah cheh-moh*-DAH-*nah ee* MAHL-*yen-kee sak-voh*-YAHZH. *Vs'yeh*-VOH *tree m'*YEH-*stah.*
Here it is. In all, two suitcases and a small bag. Three in all.

Надо взвесить?
NAH-*doh vzv'*YEH-*seet?*
Is it necessary to weigh them?

Служащий: Нет, не надо. Сойдёт и так. Все в порядке.
SLOO-*zhahsh-chee*: *N'yet, n'yeh* NAH-*doh. Soyd*-YOHT *ee tahk. Vs'yoh v por*-YAHD-*keh.*
Employee: No, it is not necessary. It will do. Everything is all right.

До отлёта осталось ещё сорок минут.
Doh otl-YOH-*tah os*-TAH-*los yesh*-CHOH SOH-*rok mee*-NOOT.
There are still forty minutes left before take-off.

Панов: Идём пока в ресторан.
Eed-YOHM *poh*-KAH *v res-toh*-RAHN.
Let's go to the restaurant in the meantime.

Я голоден. Я ещё не завтракал.
Yah GOH-*lod-yen. Yah yesh*-CHOH *n'yeh* ZAHV-*trah-kahl.*
I am hungry. I haven't had breakfast yet.

Короленко: Идём. У нас достаточно времени.
Eed-YOHM. *Oo* NAHS *dos*-TAH-*toch-noh* VREHM-*yeh-nee.*
Let's go. We have enough time.

(В ресторане).
(*V res-toh*-RAHN-*yeh.*)
(At the restaurant.)

Официант: Что прикажете?
Oh-fee-tsee-YAHNT: *Shtoh pree*-KAH-*zhet-yeh?*
Waiter: What do you order? (What do you desire?)

Панов: Стакан чаю, два яйца всмятку, хлеба, масла и стакан воды.
Stah-KAHN CHAH-*yoo, dvah yigh*-TSAH *v sm'*YAHT-*koo, khl'*YEH-*bah,* MAHS-*lah ee stah*-KAHN *voh*-DEE.
A glass of tea, two soft-boiled eggs, bread, butter, and a glass of water.

Только по-скорее, у нас мало времени.
TOHL-*koh pos-kor*-YEH-*yeh, oo nahs* MAH-*loh* VREHM-*yeh-nee.*
Only (make it) as soon as possible. We have little time.

Официант: Сию минуту.
See-YOO *mee*-NOO-*too.*
This minute.

Короленко: Вот уже зовут пассажиров на Москву.
Voht oo-ZHEH *zoh*-VOOT *pas-sah*-ZHEE-*rov nah Mosk*-VOO.
There! They are already calling the passengers for Moscow.

Панов: Официант! Не надо ничего. У нас нет времени.
Oh-fee-tsee-YAHNT! *N'yeh* NAH-*doh nee-cheh*-VOH. *Oo* NAHS *n'yet* VREHM-*yeh-nee.*
Waiter! We don't need anything. We haven't time.

Официант: Слушаюсь!
SLOO-*shah-yoos!*
All right!

A USEFUL WORD: The expression **слу́шаюсь** really means "I obey" but it has come to mean "very well" etc. It is also what the soldier replies to an officer when given an order.

Панов: Какая досада! Придётся помирать с голоду.
Kah-KAH-*yah doh*-SAH-*dah! Preed*-YOHT-*sah poh-mee*-RAHT *s* GOH-*loh-doo.*
How annoying! I will have to die of hunger.

THINKING IN RUSSIAN

(Answers on page 230)

1. Вста́л ли Пано́в во́ время?
2. Почему́ он опозда́л?
3. Ско́лько раз его́ буди́ли?
4. Кто взял его́ бага́ж из ко́мнаты?
5. Ско́лько у него́ было чемода́нов?
6. Как зва́ли ма́льчика, кото́рый нёс его́ чемода́ны?
7. Где оста́вил Пано́в ключ от ко́мнаты?
8. Кто ему́ пожела́л счастли́вого пути́?
9. Что сказа́л Пано́в ма́льчику?
10. Почему́ он не хоте́л, что́бы ма́льчик взял ма́ленький саквоя́ж?
11. Далеко́ ли от гости́ницы до аэродро́ма?
12. Кто зае́хал за Пано́вым?
13. Что сказа́л Короле́нко?
14. Ско́лько оста́лось вре́мени до отлёта аэропла́на?
15. Мно́го ли бы́ло багажа́ у Пано́ва и Короле́нко?
16. Ско́лько у ни́х бы́ло мест?
17. Успе́ли ли они́ поза́втракать пе́ред отлётом в Москву́?
18. Почему́ Пано́ву хоте́лось есть?
19. Лю́бите ли вы лета́ть?
20. Лета́ли ли вы уже́?

УРОК 29

Приезд
Pree-YEZD
The Arrival

Панов: Послушай, Саша, далеко ли ещё до Москвы?
Pah-NOHV: *Poh*-SLOO-*shigh,* SAH-*shah, dahl-yeh*-KOH *lee yesh*-CHOH *doh Mosk*-VEE*?*
Panov: Listen, Sasha, is it still far to Moscow?

Короленко: Нет, уже недалеко.
Koh-rol-YEN-*koh*: *N'yet, oo*-ZHEH *n'yeh dahl-yeh*-KOH.
Korolenko: No, it is not far any more,

Всего ещё минут двадцать.
Vs'yeh-VOH *yesh*-CHOH *mee*-NOOT DVAHD-*tsaht.*
about twenty minutes more in all.

HELPFUL HINT: If the numeral is placed after the word to which it belongs, the meaning is "about". For example:

"He is thirty years old."	**Ему́ три́дцать лет.**
"He is about thirty."	**Ему́ лет три́дцать.**
"Come at three o'clock."	**Приходи́те в три часа́.**
"Come at about three o'clock."	**Приходи́те часа́ в три.**

Панов: Отчего это у вас не кормят голодающих в аэропланах?
Ot-cheh-VOH EH-*toh oo* VAHS *n'yeh* KORM-*yaht goh-loh*-DAH-*yoosh-cheekh v ah-eh-roh*-PLAH-*nakh?*
Why don't they feed the starving people on the planes in your country?

GRAMMATICAL NOTE: Голода́ющие is the present participle of **голода́ть** — "to starve". The participle of the present tense is obtained from the present tense by dropping the **т** of the third person plural **(-ут, -ют, -ат -ят)** and adding **-щий, -щая, -щее, -щие** according to gender and number: **ма́льчик, бегу́щий по у́лице** — "the boy who is running in the street"; **же́нщина, стоя́щая у окна́** — "the woman who is standing at the window". Participles change their endings, according to number and gender and are declined like adjectives.

У нас, в Америке, можно позавтракать в самолёте.
Oo NAHS, *v Ah*-MEH-*ree-keh,* MOHZH-*noh poh*-ZAHV-*trah-kaht v sah-mol*-YOHT-*yeh.*
With us, in America, you can have breakfast on the plane.

Короленко: Это тебе не Америка. Забудь об этом.
EH-*toh t'yeb*-YEH *n'yeh Ah*-MEH-*ree-kah. Zah*-BOOD *ob* EH-*tom.*
This is not America. Forget about it.

Панов: Сытый голодного не понимает.
SEE-*tee goh*-LOHD-*noh-voh n'yeh poh-nee*-MAH-*yet.*
The well-fed man doesn't understand the man who is hungry.

Короленко: Надо тебе было встать по-раньше, как я тебе говорил.
NAH-*doh t'yeb*-YEH BEE-*loh vstaht poh*-RAHN-*sheh, kahk yah t'yeb*-YEH *goh-voh*-REEL.
You should have risen earlier, as I told you.

Ты мог позавтракать в Киеве.
Tee mohg poh-ZAHV-*trah-kaht v* KEE-*yev-yeh.*
You could have had breakfast in Kiev.

Но, ничего. Как говорит пословица:
Noh, nee-cheh-VOH. *Kahk goh-voh*-REET *pos*-LOH-*vee-tsah*:
But never mind. As the proverb says:

Терпи, казак, атаманом будешь.
T'yehr-PEE, *kah*-ZAHK, *ah-tah*-MAH-*nom* BOOD-*yesh.*
Cossack, suffer, you will become the Ataman (chief).

Вот уже видна Москва.
Voht oo-ZHEH *veed*-NAH *Mosk*-VAH.
There is Moscow already in sight.

Панов: А где Воробьёвы горы, откуда
Ah gd'yeh Voh-rob-YOH-*vee* GOH-*ree, ot*-KOO-*dah*
And where are the Hills of the Sparrows, from which

Наполеон впервые увидел Москву?
Nah-pol-yeh-OHN *vp'yehr*-VEE-*yeh oo*-VEED-*yel Mosk*-VOO?
Napoleon first saw Moscow?

Короленко: Вот они! Только они теперь
VOHT *oh*-NEE! TOHL-*koh oh*-NEE *t'yep*-YEHR
There they are! But now

называются Ленинскими горами.
nah-zee-VAH-*yoot-sah L'*YEH-*neen-skee-mee goh*-RAH-*mee.*
they are called the Hills of Lenin.

DON'T FORGET: After **называ́ться**—"to be called", the instrumental case is used as seen in the above example. "This town is called Kiev" — **Этот го́род называ́ется Ки́евом.**

Панов: А где канал, соединяющий Москва-реку с Волгой?
Ah gd'yeh kah-NAHL, *soh-yeh-deen*-YAH-*yoosh-chee Mosk*-VAH-*r'yeh*-KOO *s* VOHL-*goy?*
And where is the canal which connects the Moskva river with the Volga?

Короленко: Там, налево.
Tahm, nahl-YEH-*voh.*
There, to the left.

Панов: Кажется, мы уже снижаемся.
KAH-*zhet-sah, mee oo*-ZHEH *snee*-ZHAH-*yem-sah.*
It seems that we are already descending.

Короленко: Да, снижаемся. Пора собираться.
Dah, snee-ZHAH-*yem-sah. Poh*-RAH *soh-bee*-RAHT-*sah.*
Yes, we are. It is time to get ready.

Панов: Эх, красива Москва!
Ekh, krah-SEE-*vah Mosk*-VAH!
Oh, Moscow is beautiful!

Сколько церквей и золотых куполов!
SKOHL-*koh tserk*-VAY *ee zoh-loh*-TEEKH KOO-*poh-lov!*
How many churches and golden cupolas!

Неужели их сорок сороков, как говорили встарь?
*N'yeh-oo-*ZHEH-*lee eekh* SOH-*rok soh-roh-*KOHV, *kahk goh-voh-*REE-*lee vstahr?*
Is it true that there are 40 times 40 of them, as they used to say in olden times?

Короленко: Это только так кажется. Их не так много.
EH-*toh* TOHL-*koh tahk* KAH-*zhet-sah. Eekh n'yeh tahk* MNOH-*goh.*
It only seems that way. There are not so many of them.

Теперь держись! Самолёт приземляется.
*T'yep-*YEHR *d'yehr-*ZHEES! *Sah-mol-*YOHT *pree-zeml-*YAH-*yet-sah.*
Now hold on! The airplane is landing.

Панов: Кто эти люди на аэродроме, бегущие нам на встречу?
Ktoh EH-*tee l'*YOO-*dee nah ah-eh-roh-*DROHM-*yeh, b'yeh-*GOOSH-*chee-yeh nahm nah vstr'*YEH-*choo?*
Who are those people at the airfield, who are running towards us?

Короленко: Это, должно быть, всякого рода
EH-*toh dolzh-*NOH *beet, vs'*YAH-*koh-voh* ROH-*dah*
They must be various

служащие аэродрома, носильщики . . .
SLOO-*zhahsh-chee-yeh ah-eh-roh-*DROH-*mah, noh-*SEELSH-*chee-kee . . .*
airport employees, porters . . .

USEFUL WORDS TO REMEMBER:

вся́кого ро́да	all kinds of
пора́	it is time to
ка́жется	it seems
мне ка́жется	it seems to me

Носильщик! Возьмите эти три чемодана.
*Noh-*SEELSH-*cheek! Voz-*MEET-*yeh* EH-*tee tree cheh-moh-*DAH-*nah.*
Porter! Take these three bags.

Носильщик: На такси или в автобус?
*Noh-*SEELSH-*cheek: Nah tak-*SEE EE-*lee v av-*TOH-*boos?*
Porter: To the taxi or to the bus?

Короленко: На такси.
*Nah tahk-*SEE.
To the taxi.

(В гостинице).
*(V gos-*TEE-*nee-tseh.)*
(At the hotel.)

Короленко: Есть ли у вас свободные комнаты?
Yest lee oo VAHS *svoh-*BOHD-*nee-yeh* KOHM-*nah-tee?*
Have you any rooms free?

Служащий гостиницы: Да, есть. Вам две комнаты?
SLOO-*zhahsh-chee gos*-TEE-*nee-tsee*: *Dah, yest. Vahm dv'yeh* KOHM-*nah-tee?*
Hotel employee: Yes, there are. Two rooms for you?

Короленко: Да, две, по возможности в верхних этажах.
Dah, dv'yeh, poh voz-MOHZH-*nos-tee v* VEHRKH-*neekh eh-tah*-ZHAKH.
Yes, two, if possible in the upper floors.

Служащий: Заполните, пожалуйста, эти бланки
Zah-POHL-*neet-yeh, poh*-ZHAH-*looy-stah,* EH-*tee* BLAHN-*kee*
Please fill out these blanks

и дайте мне ваши паспорты.
ee DIGHT-*yeh mn'yeh* VAH-*shee* PAHS-*por-tee.*
and give me your passports.

Короленко: Вот мой паспорт.
VOHT *moy* PAHS-*port.*
Here is my passport.

Панов: А вот мой.
Ah VOHT *moy.*
And here is mine.

Служащий: Эй, Петя, покажи этим гражданам
Ay, PEHT-*yah, poh-kah*-ZHEE EH-*teem* GRAHZH-*dah-nahm*
Hey there, Peter, show these citizens

комнаты номер 134 и 135.
KOHM-*nah-tee* NOM-*yehr stoh* TREED-*tsaht cheh*-TEE-*reh ee stoh* TREED-*tsaht p'yaht.*
to rooms 134 and 135.

Петя: Пожалуйте в лифт.
PEHT-*yah*: *Poh*-ZHAH-*looyt-yeh v leeft.*
Petya: Please enter the elevator.

Петя: Как вам нравятся эти комнаты?
Kahk vahm NRAHV-*yaht-sah* EH-*tee* KOHM-*nah-tee?*
How do you like these rooms?

Короленко (Панову): Как по-твоему?
Koh-rol-YEN-*koh* (*Pah*-NOH-*voo*): *Kahk poh*-TVOH-*yeh-moo?*
Korolenko (to Panov): What's your opinion?

USEFUL PHRASE:

"according to my opinion"—**по мóему**
"according to our opinion"—**по нáшему**
"according to your opinion"—**по вáшему**

Above, Korolenko says **по твóему** to Panov because, being his friend, he uses the familiar form to him.

Панов: Ничего, сойдёт.
Nee-cheh-VOH, *soyd*-YOHT.
All right, it will do.

А где здесь ванная комната?
Ah gd'yeh zd'yes VAHN-*nah-yah* KOHM-*nah-tah?*
And where is the bathroom here?

Петя: В коридоре направо.
V koh-ree-DOHR-*yeh nah*-PRAH-*voh.*
In the corridor to the right.

Короленко: Хорошо. Мы берём эти комнаты.
Khoh-roh-SHOH. *Mee b'yehr*-YOHM EH-*tee* KOHM-*nah-tee.*
Very well. We take these rooms.

Принесите, пожалуйста, наши чемоданы.
Preen-yeh-SEET-*yeh, poh*-ZHAH-*looy-stah,* NAH-*shee cheh-moh*-DAH-*nee.*
Please bring our bags.

Петя: Слушаюсь. Сейчас принесу.
SLOO-*shah-yoos. Say*-CHAHS *preen-yeh*-SOO.
Very well. I'll bring them right away.

Панов: Скажи-ка, Саша, почему у тебя спросили паспорт?
Skah-ZHEE-*kah,* SAH-*shah, poh-cheh*-MOO *oo t'yeb*-YAH *sproh*-SEE-*lee* PAHS-*port?*
Tell me, Sasha, why did they ask a passport from you?

Ты ведь советский гражданин.
Tee v'yed sov-YET-*skee grahzh-dah*-NEEN.
You're certainly a Soviet citizen.

Короленко: Да, советский. Но каждый советский
Dah, sov-YET-*skee. Noh* KAHZH-*dee sov*-YET-*skee*
Yes, I am a Soviet citizen. But every Soviet

гражданин обязан иметь при себе паспорт.
grahzh-dah-NEEN *ob*-YAH-*zahn eem*-YET *pree seb*-YEH PAHS-*port.*
citizen is obliged to carry his passport with him.

Панов: Странно . . .
STRAHN-*noh* . . .
Strange . . .

Короленко: Ничего тут странного нет.
Nee-cheh-VOH *toot* STRAHN-*noh-voh n'yet.*
There is nothing strange about it.

Ты ничего не понимаешь. Ты — американец.
*Tee nee-cheh-*VOH *n'yeh poh-nee-*MAH*-yesh. Tee— ah-meh-ree-*KAHN*-yets.*
You don't understand anything. You are an American.

Ты не знаешь, что человек состоит из тела, души и паспорта.
Tee n'yeh ZNAH*-yesh, shtoh cheh-lov-*YEK *soh-stoh-*EET *eez t'*YEH*-lah, doo-*SHEE *ee* PAHS*-por-tah.*
You don't know that a man is made up of his body, his soul, and his passport.

THINKING IN RUSSIAN

(Answers on page 231)

1. Поза́втракал ли Пано́в на аэродро́ме?
2. Почему́ ему́ не удало́сь поза́втракать?
3. Поза́втракал ли он на самолёте?
4. Что он говори́т по э́тому по́воду Короле́нко?
5. Что отвеча́ет Короле́нко?
6. О чём спра́шивает Пано́в своего́ дру́га, когда́ самолёт приближа́ется к Москве́?
7. Почему́ его́ интересу́ют Воробьёвы го́ры?
8. Что говори́т Пано́в, гля́дя с самолёта на Москву́?
9. Ско́лько в Москве́ церкве́й?
10. Куда́ е́дут Пано́в и Короле́нко с аэродро́ма?
11. Где они́ остана́вливаются?
12. Что у них спра́шивает слу́жащий гости́ницы?
13. Что удиви́ло Пано́ва?
14. Из чего́ состои́т челове́к по слова́м Короле́нко?

УРОК 30

Кремль
Krehml
The Kremlin

Короленко: С чего же мы начнём осмотр Москвы?
Koh-rol-YEN-*koh*: *S cheh*-VOH *zheh mee nahchn*-YOHM *os*-MOHTR *Mosk*-VEE?
Korolenko: With what shall we begin our inspection of Moscow?

Панов: Конечно с Кремля.
Pah-NOHV: *Kon*-YECH-*noh s Kreml*-YAH.
Panov: Naturally with the Kremlin.

Короленко: Хорошо. В таком случае мы пойдём на Москворецкий мост.
Khoh-roh-SHOH. *V tah*-KOHM SLOO-*chah-yeh mee poyd*-YOHM *nah Mosk-vor*-YETS-*kee mohst.*
Very well. In that case we shall go on the Moskva River bridge.

Оттуда хороший вид на Кремль.
Ot-TOO-*dah khoh*-ROH-*shee veed nah Krehml.*
From there, there is a good view of the Kremlin.

Панов: Не лучше ли нам пойти прямо в Кремль?
N'yeh LOOCH-*sheh lee nahm poy*-TEE *pr'*YAH-*moh v Krehml?*
Wouldn't it be better for us to go directly to the Kremlin?

Со стороны Красной площади, как мне помнится
Soh stoh-roh-NEE KRAHS-*noy* PLOHSH-*chah-dee, kahk mn'yeh* POHM-*neet-sah*
On the Red Square side, as I remember

из книг, есть ворота, Спасские . . .
eez kneeg, yest voh-ROH-*tah,* SPAHS-*skee-yeh . . .*
from books, there is a gate, (the Gate) of the Saviour . . .

Короленко: Ворота-то есть, но нас с тобой внутрь Кремля не впустят.
Voh-ROH-*tah-toh yest, noh nahs s toh*-BOY *vnootr Kreml*-YAH *n'yeh* POOST-*yaht.*
Yes, there is a gate there, but they won't let the two of us inside the Kremlin.

NOTE to STUDENT:

Нас с тобóй "us with you" meaning "the two of us." **Нас с тобóй** is the accusative. "The two of us," nominative, would be **мы с тобóй.**

Панов: Неужели не пустят? А я думал . . .
N'yeh-oo-ZHEH-*lee n'yeh* POOST-*yaht? Ah yah* DOO-*mahl . . .*
Is it possible that they won't let us in? And I thought . . .

Короленко: Мало что ты думал. Не пустят и только.
MAH-*loh shtoh tee* DOO-*mahl. N'yeh* POOST-*yaht ee* TOHL-*koh.*
It matters little what you thought. They won't let us in and that's all.

Но это ничего. Я покажу тебе все главные здания Кремля с моста.
Noh EH-*toh nee-cheh*-VOH. *Yah poh-kah*-ZHOO *t'yeb*-YEH *vs'yeh* GLAHV-*nee-yeh* ZDAH-*nee-yah Kreml*-YAH *s mos*-TAH.
But that doesn't matter. I'll show you all the principal buildings of the Kremlin from the bridge.

Панов: Коли так, идём на мост.
*Koh-*LEE *tahk, eed-*YOHM *nah mohst.*
If that is so, let's go onto the bridge.

Короленко: Вот мы на Москворецком мосту.
VOHT *mee nah Mosk-vor-*YETS*-kom mos-*TOO.
Here we are on the Moskva river bridge.

Отсюда лучший вид на Кремль.
*Ots-*YOO*-dah* LOOCH*-shee veed nah Krehml.*
From here is the best view of the Kremlin.

Панов: Какая красота! Как гордо и величественно стоит Кремль над рекой!
*Kah-*KAH*-yah krah-soh-*TAH! *Kahk* GOHR*-doh ee veh-*LEE*-chest-ven-noh stoh-*EET *Krehml nad r'yeh-*KOY!
What beauty! How proudly and majestically the Kremlin stands above the river!

Короленко: Вот в центре, над рекой, стоит Кремлёвский дворец,
Voht v TSENTR*-yeh, nahd r'yeh-*KOY, *stoh-*EET *Kreml-*YOHV*-skee dvor-*YETS,
There in the center above the river stands the Kremlin palace,

в котором живёт и работает Сталин.
*v koh-*TOH*-rom zheev-*YOHT *ee rah-*BOH*-tah-yet* STAH*-leen.*
in which Stalin lives and works.

К западу, налево, стоит Оружейная палата,
K ZAH*-pah-doo, nahl-*YEH*-voh, stoh-*EET *Oh-roo-*ZHAY*-nah-yah pah-*LAH*-tah,*
To the west, on the left, stands the Palace of Arms,

бывшая сокровищница царей, а теперь музей.
BEEV*-shah-yah soh-*KROH*-veeshch-nee-tsah tsah-*RAY, *ah t'yep-*YEHR *moo-*ZAY.
formerly the treasury of the tsars and now a museum.

К востоку, справа, блещут своими золотыми главами три собора.
*K vos-*TOH*-koo,* SPRAH*-vah bl'*YESH*-choot svoh-*EE*-mee zoh-loh-*TEE*-mee glah-*VAH*-mee tree soh-*BOH*-rah.*
To the east, on the right, shine the golden domes of three cathedrals.

Панов: А та высокая башня с золотой шапкой —
*Ah tah vee-*SOH*-kah-yah* BAHSHN*-yah s zoh-loh-*TOY SHAHP*-koy*—
And that tall tower with the golden top—

это, должно быть, колокольня Ивана Великого?
*EH-toh, dolzh-*NOH *beet, koh-loh-*KOHLN-*yah Ee-*VAH-*nah Veh-*LEE-*koh-voh?*
that is probably the Belfry of Ivan the Great?

Короленко: Совершенно верно.
*Soh-v'yehr-*SHEN-*noh v'*YEHR-*noh.*
Exactly so.

У её подножья стоит Царь-колокол,
*Oo yeh-*YOH *pod-*NOZH-*yah stoh-*EET TSAHR-KOH-*loh-kol,*
At its base stands the Tsar of the Bells,

весом в 12.000 пудов.
*v'*YEH-*som v dv'yeh-*NAHD-*tsaht* TEES-*yahch poo-*DOHV.
which weighs 12,000 puds.

NOTE on RUSSIAN MEASURES: A **пуд** is 40 pounds. Therefore the Tsar of the Bells, should weigh about 240 tons. A **верстá**, which has been mentioned previously, is about 2/3 of a mile.

Панов: Царь-колокол! И я его не увижу?
TSAHR-KOH-*loh-kol! Ee yah yeh-*VOH *n'yeh oo-*VEE-*zhoo?*
The Tsar of the Bells! And I shan't see it?

Коля, мой маленький племянник, попросил меня непременно посмотреть
KOHL-*yah, moy* MAHL-*yen-kee pl'yem-*YAHN-*neek, poh-proh-*SEEL
*men-*YAH *n'yeh-prem-*YEN-*noh pos-motr-*YET
Kolya, my little nephew, asked me by all means

на него и на Царь-пушку и рассказать ему о них, когда вернусь.
*nah n'yeh-*VOH *ee nah* TSAHR-POOSH-*koo ee rahs-skah-*ZAHT *yeh-*MOO
*oh neekh, kog-*DAH *v'yehr-*NOOS.
to look at it and at the Tsar of the Cannons and to tell him about them when I return.

Короленко: Ничего. Мы достанем снимки, ты их ему покажешь и скажешь ему,
*Nee-cheh-*VOH. *Mee doh-*STAHN-*yem* SNEEM-*kee, tee eekh yeh-*MOO
*poh-*KAH-*zhesh ee* SKAH-*zhesh yeh-*MOO,
It doesn't matter, we will get the pictures, you will show them to him and tell him

что ты всё видел. И он будет доволен.
shtoh tee vs'yoh VEED-*yel. Ee ohn* BOOD-*yet doh*-VOHL-*yen.*
that you saw everything, and he will be satisfied.

Панов: А где же находится Царь-пушка?
Ah gd'yeh zheh nah-KHOH-*deet-sah* TSAHR-POOSH-*kah?*
And where is the Tsar of the Cannons?

Короленко: Вон, за тем собором, позади колокольни
Vohn zah t'yem soh-BOH-*rom poh-zah*-DEE *koh-loh*-KOHL-*nee*
There behind that cathedral in back of the Belfry

Ивана Великого.
Ee-VAH-*nah Veh*-LEE-*koh-voh.*
of Ivan the Great.

Там же стоят сотни орудий, которые
Tahm zheh stoh-YAHT SOHT-*nee oh*-ROO-*dee, koh*-TOH-*ree-yeh*
There also are hundreds of cannons, which

были взяты у Наполеона в 1812-м году.
BEE-*lee vz'*YAH-*tee oo Nah-pol-yeh*-OH-*nah v* TEES-*yah-chah vos-yem*-SOHT *dv'yeh*-NAHD-*tsah-tom goh*-DOO.
were taken from Napoleon in 1812.

Панов: Скажи-ка, в тех соборах и других храмах
Skah-ZHEE-*kah, v t'yekh soh*-BOH-*rakh ee droo*-GGEEKH KHRAH-*makh*
Tell me, do they still have services in those

в Кремле ещё служат?
v Krehml-YEH *yesh*-CHOH SLOO-*zhaht?*
cathedrals and other churches in the Kremlin?

Короленко: Нет, не служат. С тех пор как в Кремле
N'yet, n'yeh SLOO-*zhaht. S t'yekh pohr kahk v Krehml*-YEH
No, they don't. Since the Soviet Government

поселилось советское правительство
pos-yeh-LEE-*los sov*-YETS-*koh-yeh prah*-VEET-*yelst-voh*
moved into the Kremlin,

в 1918-м году, там служить перестали,
v TEES-*yah-chah d'yev-yaht*-SOHT *vos-yem*-NAHD-*tsah-tom goh*-DOO, *tahm sloo*-ZHEET *p'yeh-reh*-STAH-*lee,*
in 1918, services have been stopped,

и народ в Кремль больше не пускают.
*ee nah-*ROHD *v Krehml* BOHL-*sheh n'yeh poos-*KAH-*yoot.*
and they don't let people into the Kremlin any more.

Храмы эти сохраняются только как памятники старины.
KHRAH-*mee* EH-*tee soh-khrahn-*YAH-*yoot-sah* TOHL-*koh kahk* PAHM-*yaht-nee-kee stah-ree-*NEE.
Those churches are only preserved as memorials of the past.

Ну, а теперь идём на Красную площадь.
*Noo, ah t'yep-*YEHR *eed-*YOHM *nah* KRAHS-*noo-yoo* PLOHSH-*chahd.*
So, now let's go to the Red Square.

THINKING IN RUSSIAN

(Answers on page 231)

1. С чего́ начина́ют Короле́нко и Пано́в осмо́тр Москвы́?
2. Куда́ они́ иду́т?
3. Отчего́ они́ пошли́ на мо́ст?
4. Почему́ они́ не пошли́ пря́мо в Кремль?
5. Что они́ ви́дят с моста́?
6. Что говори́т Пано́в, гля́дя на Кремль?
7. Како́е са́мое большо́е зда́ние в Кремле́?
8. Кто в нём живёт тепе́рь?
9. Кто в нём жил ра́ньше?
10. Как называ́ется са́мая высо́кая ба́шня в Кремле́?
11. Что стои́т у подно́жия Ива́на Вели́кого?
12. Ско́лько фу́нтов в одно́м пу́де?
13. Счита́ют ли в Сове́тском Сою́зе на фунты́ и пуды́?
14. Есть ли це́ркви в Кремле́?
15. Слу́жат ли в них?
16. Пуска́ют ли в Кремль наро́д?

УРОК 31

Красная площадь

KRAHS-*nah-yah* PLOHSH-*chahd*

The Red Square

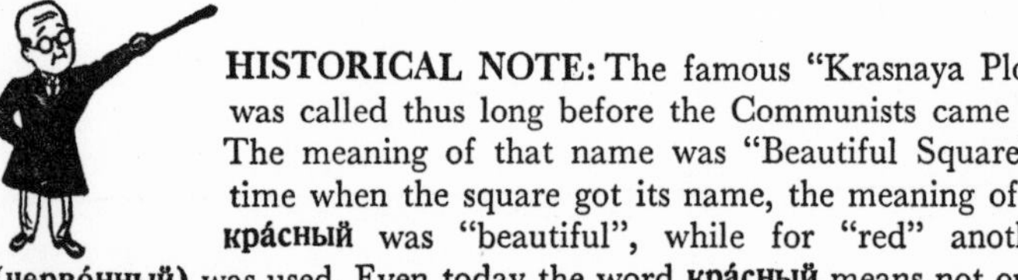

HISTORICAL NOTE: The famous "Krasnaya Plohshchad" was called thus long before the Communists came to power. The meaning of that name was "Beautiful Square". At the time when the square got its name, the meaning of the word **кра́сный** was "beautiful", while for "red" another word **(червóнный)** was used. Even today the word **кра́сный** means not only "red", but also "pretty".

Короленко: Отсюда, с Москворецкого моста,
*Ot-s'*YOO-*dah, s Mosk-vor*-YETS-*koh-voh mos*-TAH,
From here, from the Moskva river bridge,

рукой подать до Красной площади.
*roo-*KOY *poh-*DAHT *doh* KRAHS*-noy* PLOHSH*-chah-dee.*
it is very near to the Red Square.

Вот мы уже и пришли.
*Voht, mee oo-*ZHEH *ee preesh-*LEE.
Here, we have already arrived.

Панов: Я видел столько изображений Красной площади,
Yah VEED*-yel* STOHL*-koh eez-ob-rah-*ZHEH*-nee* KRAHS*-noy* PLOHSH*-chah-dee,*
I have seen so many pictures of the Red Square,

что, глядя на неё, мне кажется, что я здесь уже был.
*shtoh, gl'*YAHD*-yah nah n'yeh-*YOH, *mn'yeh* KAH*-zhet-sah, shtoh yah zd'yes oo-*ZHEH *beel.*
that, looking at it, it seems to me that I have already been here.

DON'T FORGET: **гля́дя** is the gerund of **глядéть** ("to look at"). **Ви́дя,** from **ви́деть** ("to see"), means "while seeing", **зна́я,** from **знать** ("to know"), means "knowing", **ду́мая,** from **ду́мать** ("to think"), means "thinking" etc.

Короленко: Это немудрено. Красную площадь знает весь русский народ,
EH*-toh n'yeh-moodr-yeh-*NOH, KRAHS*-noo-yoo* PLOHSH*-chahd* ZNAH*-yet v'yes* ROOS*-skee nah-*ROHD,
No wonder. The entire Russian people knows the Red Square,

ибо здесь веками создавалась русская история.
EE*-boh zd'yes v'yeh-*KAH*-mee soz-dah-*VAH*-lahs* ROOS*-skah-yah ees-*TOH*-ree-yah.*
because here through the centuries, Russian history was made.

THE PASSIVE: In Russian, there is no special form of the verb for the passive. It is expressed by using the reflexive form of the verb in the 3rd person, singular or plural.

Дом стрóится из кирпичá.	The house is being built of brick.
Как э́то дéлается?	How is it done?

For the past passive either the past reflexive form of the verb or the past participle combined with the past of the verb **быть** — "to be" is used. Notice the difference in the meaning:

дом продава́лся	"the house was on sale"
дом был про́дан	"the house was sold"

Панов: Я могу быть твоим проводником.
*Yah moh-*GOO *beet tvoh-*EEM *proh-vod-nee-*KOHM.
I can be your guide.

Вот видишь там, в конце площади,
Voht, VEE-*deesh tahm, v kon-*TSEH PLOHSH-*chah-dee,*
You see, there, at the end of the Square,

храм Василия Блаженного.
*khrahm Vah-*SEE-*lee-yah Blah-*ZHEN-*noh-voh.*
is the church of Basil the Blissful.

Короленко: Совершенно верно.
*Sov-yer-*SHEN-*noh v'*YEHR-*noh.*
Quite right.

Этот храм был построен
EH-*tot khrahm beel poh-*STROH-*yen*
This church was built

в шестнадцатом веке
*v shest-*NAHD-*tsah-tom v'*YEH-*keh*
in the 16th century

при царе Иоанне Грозном,
*pree tsahr-*YEH *Ee-oh-*AHN-*yeh* GROHZ-*nom,*
at the time of Ivan the Terrible,

покорившем Казань, татарскую столицу.
*poh-koh-*REEV-*shem Kah-*ZAHN, *tah-*TAHR-*skoo-yoo stoh-*LEE-*tsoo.*
who conquered Kazan, the Tatar capital.

AN APOLOGY: By calling the great Ivan "Ivan the Terrible", we are really doing him an injustice. The true meaning of **гро́зный** is "awe-inspiring". Therefore, by faulty translation generations of history students have considered Ivan as a cruel monster, although he was no more cruel than other absolute monarchs of his day.

Панов: Кстати, мне необходимо купить себе пару ботинок,
KSTAH-*tee, mn'yeh n'yeh-ob-khoh-*DEE-*moh koo-*PEET *s'yeb-*YEH PAH-*roo boh-*TEE-*nok,*
By the way, it is necessary for me to buy myself a pair of shoes,

а то у меня в дороге пропал чемодан,
ah TOH oo m'yen-YAH v doh-ROHG-yeh proh-PAHL cheh-moh-DAHN,
because during the trip I lost my bag,

в котором была вся моя обувь.
v koh-TOH-rom bee-LAH vs'yah moh-YAH OH-boov.
in which all my footwear was.

Короленко: Это мы можем сделать тут же рядом на улице Горького.
EH-toh mee MOH-zhem sd'YEH-laht TOOT zheh r'YAH-dom nah OO-lee-tseh GOHR-koh-voh.
This we can do here quite nearby in Gorky street.

Идём в универмаг.
Eed-YOHM v oo-neev-yehr-MAHG.
Let's go to the Univermag.

Панов: Куда?
Koo-DAH?
Where?

Короленко: В у-ни-вер-маг.
V oo-neev-yehr-MAHG.
to the U-ni-ver-mag.

Панов: Что это за чудовище?
Shtoh EH-toh zah choo-DOH-veesh-cheh?
What kind of monster is it?

Короленко: Это — универсальный магазин.
EH-toh — oo-neev-yehr-SAHL-nee mah-gah-ZEEN.
That is a general store.

Панов: О, понимаю, это что-то вроде наших "department store."
Oh, poh-nee-MAH-yoo, EH-toh SHTOH-toh v ROHD-yeh NAH-sheekh "department store."
Oh, I understand, it is something like our department stores.

(В магазине)
(V mah-gah-ZEEN-yeh)
(At the store)

Короленко: Где тут у вас продаётся обувь?
Gd'YEH toot oo VAHS proh-dah-YOHT-sah OH-boov?
Where do you sell footwear here?

Служащий магазина: Идите прямо до конца, а потом налево.
SLOO-zhash-chee mah-gah-ZEE-nah: Ee-DEET-yeh pr'YAH-moh doh kohn-TSAH, ah poh-TOHM nahl-YEH-voh.
Store employee: Go straight to the end, and then to the left.

Панов: Мне нужна пара башмаков, чёрных.
Mn'yeh noozh-NAH PAH-rah bash-mah-KOHV, CHOR-neekh.
I need a pair of shoes, black ones.

Продавец: Какой ваш номер?
Proh-dahv-YETS: *Kah*-KOY *vahsh* NOHM-*yer?*
Salesman: What is your size?

Панов: Право не знаю, как по-вашему. Я иностранец.
PRAH-*voh n'yeh* ZNAH-*yoo kahk poh*-VAH-*sheh-moo. Yah ee-nos*-TRAHN-*yets.*
I really don't know what it is according to you. I am a foreigner.

Продавец: Сейчас сниму мерку. Вот пара чёрных башмаков.
Say-CHAHS *snee*-MOO *m'*YEHR-*koo. Voht* PAH-*rah* CHOR-*neekh bash-mah*-KOHV.
I'll take the measure right away. Here is a pair of black shoes.

Панов: Кожа на них жёсткая. Нет ли у вас по-лучше?
KOH-*zhah nah* NEEKH ZHOHST-*kah-yah. N'yet lee oo* VAHS *poh*-LOOCH-*sheh?*
The leather (of them) is stiff. Don't you have better ones?

NOTE on COMPARATIVE: Лу́чше—"better" is the comparative of **хоро́ший** "good". The prefix **по-** here means "a little better". Otherwise **по** with the comparative intensifies it: **Беги́ по-скоре́е** — "run faster" — implying "as fast as possible".

Продавец: Нет. Эти башмаки высшего качества.
N'yet. EH-*tee bash-mah*-KEE VEES-*sheh-voh* KAH-*chest-vah.*
No. These shoes are of highest quality.

THE SUPERLATIVE:
The superlative is formed by adding to the stem the endings **-а́йший** or **-е́йший,** e.g. **но́вый** "new", **нове́йший** — "the newest". Another way is to add the prefix **наи-** to the comparative: **бо́льший** bigger, **наибо́льший** the biggest, **лу́чший** "better", **наилу́чший** "the best". Still another way is to have the adjective preceded by the word **са́мый,** for instance: **са́мый лу́чший** "the best", **са́мый большо́й** "the biggest".

In the above sentence the comparative **вы́сший** is used in the superlative sense. Other comparatives which are used in the superlative sense are: **лу́чший** — "the best", **ху́дший** — "the worst", **ста́рший** — "the oldest", **мла́дший**—"the youngest".

Панов: Неужели? Давайте попробуем.
*N'yeh-oo-*ZHEH-*lee? Dah-*VIGHT-*yeh poh-*PROH-*boo-yem.*
Is it possible? Let's try them on.

Они меня жмут.
*Oh-*NEE *m'yen-*YAH *zhmoot.*
They pinch me.

Продавец: Вот пара по-шире.
*Proh-dahv-*YETS: *Vot* PAH-*rah poh-*SHEE-*reh.*
Here is a pair which is wider.

Панов: Эти мне удобнее. Хорошо, я их возьму.
EH-*tee mn-yeh oo-*DOHBN-*yeh-yeh. Khoh-roh-*SHOH, *yah eekh voz-*MOO.
These are more comfortable. All right, I'll take them.

А сколько они стоят?
Ah SKOHL-*koh oh-*NEE STOH-*yaht?*
And how much do they cost?

Продавец: 120 рублей.
Stoh DVAHD-*tsaht roob-*LAY.
120 roubles.

Панов (прикинув в уме): Это что-то очень дорого.
(*pree-*KEE-*noov v oom-*YEH): EH-*toh* SHTOH-*toh* OH-*chen* DOH-*roh-goh.*
(after having figured it out in his mind): That is somehow very expensive.

У нас за эти деньги можно купить пять пар таких ботинок.
Oo NAHS *zah* EH-*tee d'*YEN-*ggee* MOHZH-*noh koo-*PEET *p'yaht pahr tah-*KEEKH *boh-*TEE-*nok.*
In our country one can buy five pairs of such shoes for that money.

Короленко: Ты американец. Ты ничего не понимаешь.
*Tee ah-meh-ree-*KAHN-*yets. Tee nee-cheh-*VOH *n'yeh poh-nee-*MAH-*yesh.*
You are an American. You don't understand anything.

У вас так, а у нас иначе.
Oo VAHS *tahk, ah oo* NAHS *ee-*NAH-*cheh.*
In your country it is so, and in our country it is otherwise.

Помни: "В чужой монастырь со своим уставом не ходи".
POHM-*nee*: *"V choo-*ZHOY *moh-nah-*STEER *so svoh-*EEM *oo-*STAH-*vom n'yeh khoh-*DEE"
Remember: "Don't go into somebody else's monastery with your rules."

Панов: Ничего не поделаешь. Придётся их взять.
*Nee-cheh-*VOH *n'yeh pod-*YEH-*lah-yesh. Preed-*YOHT-*sah eekh vz'yaht.*
There is nothing you can do. I'll have to take them.

Продавец: Вот ваш квиток. Уплатите в кассе.
*Voht vahsh kvee-*TOHK. *Oo-plah-*TEET-*yeh v* KAHS-*yeh.*
Here is your check. Pay the cashier.

THINKING IN RUSSIAN

(Answers on page 232)

1. Где нахо́дится Кра́сная пло́щадь?
2. Почему́ она́ так называ́ется?
3. Что ви́дно с Кра́сной пло́щади?
4. Как называ́ется храм, кото́рый стои́т на Кра́сной пло́щади?
5. Почему́ весь ру́сский наро́д зна́ет Кра́сную площадь?
6. Кем был постро́ен храм Васи́лия Блаже́нного?
7. Что постро́ил Ива́н Гро́зный?
8. Что хо́чет купи́ть Пано́в?
9. Что случи́лось с его́ чемода́ном?
10. Куда́ иду́т Пано́в и Короле́нко?
11. Каки́е боти́нки хо́чет купи́ть Пано́в?
12. Како́й но́мер его́ боти́нок?
13. Понра́вились ли Пано́ву башмаки́, кото́рые ему́ показа́л продаве́ц?
14. Почему́ они́ ему́ не понра́вились?
15. Кака́я ко́жа нра́вится вам, мя́гкая и́ли жёсткая?
16. Дёшево ли обошли́сь боти́нки Пано́ву и́ли до́рого?
17. Что говори́т Пано́в о цене́ башмако́в?

УРОК 32

В гостях у приятеля
V gost-YAHKH *oo pree*-YAHT-*yel-yah*
Visiting with a friend

Короленко: Вот мы уже и пришли.
Voht mee oo-ZHEH *ee preesh*-LEE.
Here, we have already arrived.

Мой приятель живёт на пятом этаже.
Moy pree-YAHT-*yel zheev*-YOHT *nah p'*YAH-*tom eh-tah*-ZHEH.
My friend lives on the fifth floor.

Соберитесь силами. Лифт не действует.
Sob-yeh-REET-*yes* SEE-*lah-mee. Leeft n'yeh d'*YAYST-*voo-yet.*
Pull yourself together. The elevator is out of order.

Панов: Ничего, одолеем как-нибудь.
*Nee-cheh-*VOH, *oh-dol-*YEH*-yem kahk nee-*BOOD.
Never mind. We will manage somehow.

Если б я знал, я привёз бы с собой из Америки геликоптер.
YES*-lee b yah znahl, yah preev-*YOHZ *bee s soh-*BOY *eez Ah-*MEH*-ree-kee ggeh-lee-*KOHP*-ter.*
If I had known I would have brought a helicopter with me from America.

NOTE on THE CONDITIONAL: Я бы знал is the conditional of **знать** "to know." The conditional is formed by the past tense with the particle **бы** or **б** which is put before or after the verb.

Я сказáл бы or **я бы сказáл**	(m.)	"I would say," or "I would have said."
Я сказáла бы or **я бы сказáла**	(f.)	
Я был бы or **я бы был**	(m.)	"I would be," or "I would have been."
Я былá бы or **я бы былá**	(f.)	

Короленко: Вот квартира номер пятнадцать. Это его квартира.
*Voht kvahr-*TEE*-rah* NOHM*-yehr p'yaht-*NAHD*-tsaht.* EH*-toh yeh-*VOH *kvahr-*TEE*-rah.*
This is apartment number 15. This is his apartment.

Панов: А это что за список на дверях?
Ah EH*-toh shtoh zah* SPEE*-sok nah dv'yehr-*YAKH?
And what kind of list is this on the door?

Короленко: Это список жильцов. Давай посмотрим:
EH*-toh* SPEE*-sok zheel-*TSOHV. *Dah-*VIGH *pos-*MOHT*-reem:*
That's the list of the tenants. Let's see:

Сосо Каландаришвили — звонить 1 раз.
*Soh-*SOH *Kah-lahn-dah-reesh-*VEE*-lee—zvoh-*NEET *oh-*DEEN *rahz.*
Soso Kalandarishvili—ring once.

Богос Тер-Тотомянц — звонить 2 раза.
*Boh-*GOHS *Tehr-toh-tom-*YANTS*—zvoh-*NEET *dvah* RAH*-zah.*
Bogos Ter-Totomyants—ring twice.

Йонас Балтрушайтис — звонить 3 раза.
*Yoh-*NAHS *Bahl-troo-*SHIGH*-tees—zvoh-*NEET *tree* RAH*-zah.*
Yonas Baltrushaitis—ring 3 times.

Султан Атабекоглу — звонить 4 раза.
Sool-TAHN *Ah-tah-bek-oh*-GLOO—*zvoh*-NEET *cheh*-TEE-*reh* RAH-*zah*.
Sultan Atabekoglu—ring 4 times.

А вот наш Григорий Петров — звонить 5 раз.
Ah voht nahsh Gree-GOH-*ree Pet*-ROHV—*zvoh*-NEET *p'yaht rahz*.
And here is our Grigory Petrov—ring 5 times.

Это мне напоминает Ноев ковчег.
EH-*toh mn'yeh nah-poh-mee*-NAH-*yet* NOH-*yev kov*-CHEG.
This reminds me of Noah's Ark.

Грузин, армянин, литовец, татарин и русский — все в одной квартире.
Groo-ZEEN, *ahrm-yah*-NEEN, *lee*-TOHV-*yets*, *tah*-TAH-*reen ee* ROOS-*skee*—*vs'yeh v od*-NOY *kvahr*-TEER-*yeh*.
A Georgian, an Armenian, a Lithuanian, a Tatar, and a Russian—all in one apartment!

Панов: За этой дверью, значит, несколько квартир?
Zah EH-*toy dv'*YEHR-*you*, ZNAH-*cheet*, *n'*YES-*kol-koh kvahr*-TEER?
That means that behind that door there are several apartments?

Короленко: Нет, всего только одна квартира
N'yeht, vs'yeh-VOH TOHL-*koh od*-NAH *kvahr*-TEE-*rah*
No, only one apartment

из пяти комнат, одной кухни и одной уборной.
eez p'yah-TEE KOHM-*naht*, *od*-NOY KOOKH-*nee ee od*-NOY *oo*-BOHR-*noy*.
consisting of five rooms, a kitchen and a bathroom.

Панов: Неужели в одной квартире
N'yeh-oo-ZHEH-*lee v od*-NOY *kvahr*-TEER-*yeh*
Is it possible that

ютятся пять семейств? Разве это возможно?
yoot-YAHT-*sah p'yaht s'yem*-AYSTV? RAHZV-*yeh* EH-*toh voz*-MOHZH-*noh*?
five families should crowd into one apartment? Is it really possible?

Короленко: В Москве большинство смертных живёт именно так.
*V Mosk-v'*YEH *bol-sheen*-STVOH SMEHRT-*neekh zheev*-YOHT EE-*men-noh tahk*.
In Moscow most mortals live exactly like that.

(Слышны шаги. Из-за двери кто-то спрашивает): Кто там?
(SLEESH-*nee shah* GGEE. *Eez-zah dv'*YEH-*ree* KTOH-*toh* SPRAH-*shee-vah-yet*): *Ktoh tahm?*
(Footsteps are heard. Somebody asks from behind the door): Who is it?

Короленко: Гриша, это я.
GREE-*shah,* EH-*toh yah.*
Grisha, it's I.

Голос из-за двери: Вам кого?
GOH-*los eez-zah dv'*YEH-*ree*: *Vahm koh*-VOH*?*
The voice from behind the door: Whom do you want?

Короленко: Петрова . . .
Pet-ROH-*vah* . . .
Petrov . . .

Сердитый голос из-за двери: Я не Петров. Вы позвонили четыре раза.
Sehr-DEE-*tee* GOH-*los eez-zah dv'*YEH-*ree*: *Yah n'yeh Pet*-ROHV. *Vwee poz-voh*-NEE-*lee cheh*-TEE-*reh* RAH-*zah.*
(An angry voice from behind the door:) I am not Petrov. You rang four times.

Позвоните пять раз. (Шаги удаляются).
Poz-voh-NEET-*yeh p'yaht rahz.* (*Shah*-GGEE *oo-dahl*-YAH-*yoot-sah*).
Ring five times. (The footsteps go away).

(Короленко звонит пять раз. Дверь открывается).
(*Koh-rol*-YEN-*koh zvoh*-NEET *p'yaht rahz. Dv'yehr ot-kree*-VAH-*yet-sah*).
(Korolenko rings five times. The door opens).

Петров: Как я рад! Добро пожаловать!
Pet-ROHV: *Kahk yah rahd! Dob*-ROH *poh*-ZHAH-*loh-vaht!*
I am so glad. Welcome!

Короленко: Здравствуй, Гриша! А вот мой приятель — Панов из Америки.
ZDRAHV-*stvooy,* GREE-*shah! Ah voht moy pree*-YAHT-*yel Pah*-NOHV *eez Ah*-MEH-*ree-kee.*
Hello, Grisha! And this is my friend Panov from America.

Петров: Очень рад познакомиться.
OH-*chen rahd poz-nah*-KOH-*meet-sah.*
Very glad to meet you.

Я пойду вперёд. Вот наша комната.
Yah poy-DOO *vpehr*-YOHD. *Voht* NAH-*shah* KOHM-*nah-tah.*
I'll go first. Here is our room.

Идите, пожалуйста, за мной.
Ee-DEET-*yeh, poh*-ZHAH-*looy-stah, zah mnoy.*
Please follow me.

Лиза! Наши гости пришли.
LEE-*zah!* NAH-*shee* GOHS-*tee pree*-SHLEE.
Lisa! Our guests have come.

Мишу ты, надеюсь, узнаёшь,
MEE-shoo tee, nahd-YEH-yoos, ooz-nah-YOHSH,
I hope you recognize Misha,

а это его приятель, Панов.
ah EH-toh yeh-VOH pree-YAHT-yel Pah-NOHV, ah-meh-ree-KAHN-yets.
and this is his friend Panov, an American.

Лиза: Очень приятно. А как ваше имя и отчество?
LEE-zah: OH-chen pree-YAHT-noh. Ah kahk VAH-sheh EEM-yah ee OHT-chest-voh?
Liza: I am very pleased. What are your first and (your) middle names?

Панов: Владимир Васильевич . . .
Vlah-DEE-meer Vah-SEEL-yeh-veech . . .
Vladimir Vasilyevitch.

Лиза: Это мои дочери Маня и Шура,
EH-toh moh-EE DOH-cheh-ree MAHN-yah ee SHOO-rah,
These are my daughters Manya and Shura,

а это их подруга Варя,
ah EH-toh eekh pod-ROO-gah VAHR-yah,
and this is their friend Varya,

Варвара Антоновна Панина . . .
Vahr-VAH-rah Ahn-TOH-nov-nah PAH-nee-nah.
Varvara Antonovna Panin.

Петров: Звезда московского балета . . .
Zv'yez-DAH mos-KOHV-skoh-voh bahl-YEH-tah . . .
A star of the Moscow ballet . . .

Варя: Что вы! . . . Вы меня смущаете . . . Вы шутите . . .
VAHR-yah: Shtoh vwee! Vwee m'yen-YAH smoosh-CHAH-yet-yeh . . . Vwee SHOO-teet-yeh.
Don't say that . . . You are confusing me . . . You are joking . . .

Петров: Скажем — будущая звезда.
SKAH-zhem—BOO-doosh-chah-yah zv'yez-DAH.
Let's say, a future star . . .

Лиза: Садитесь, пожалуйста, поужинаем
Sah-DEET-yes, poh-ZHAH-looy-stah, poh-oo-zhee-nah-yem
Sit down, please. We will have supper

сразу, чтобы вы не опоздали в театр.
SRAH-zoo, SHTOH-bee vwee n'yeh oh-poz-DAH-lee v t'yeh-AHTR.
at once, so you will not be late for the theatre.

Короленко: А вы разве в театр не пойдёте?
Ah vwee RAHZ-*v'yeh v t'yeh*-AHTR *n'yeh poyd*-YOHT-*yeh?*
And you won't really come to the theatre?

Лиза: Нет, не пойду. Грише не удалось
N'yet, n'yeh poy-DOO. GREE-*sheh n'yeh oo-dah*-LOHS
No, I won't go because Grisha didn't succeed

получить больше трёх билетов.
poh-loo-CHEET BOHL-*sheh tr'*YOHKH *beel*-YEH-*tov.*
in getting more than three tickets.

Панов: Это очень досадно . . .
EH-*toh* OH-*chen doh*-SAHD-*noh* . . .
I am very sorry (This is very annoying).

Лиза: Ничего.
Nee-cheh-VOH.
Never mind.

С вами пойдёт Варя.
S VAH-*mee poyd*-YOHT VAHR-*yah.*
Varya will go with you.

Петров: Выпьем по рюмочке?
VWEEP-*yem poh r'*YOO-*moch-keh?*
Shall we each drink a glass?

Короленко: Я не откажусь, а ты?
Yah n'yeh ot-kah-ZHOOS, *ah tee?*
I won't refuse, and you?

NOTE to STUDENT: по with the dative means "each":

Гру́ши сто́ят по пяти́ копе́ек	The pears cost 5 kopecks each
Мы получи́ли по пяти́ рубле́й	We got five roubles each

Панов: С удовольствием.
S oo-doh-VOHLS-*tvee-yem.*
With pleasure.

Петров: За ваше здоровье!
Zah VAH-*sheh zdoh*-ROHV-*yeh.*
To your health!

Короленко: За здоровье милой хозяйки!
Zah zdoh-ROHV-*yeh* MEE-*loy kho*-ZIGH-*kee!*
To the health of our charming hostess!

За здоровье милых барышень!
Zah zdoh-ROHV-*yeh* MEE-*leekh* BAH-*ree-shen!*
To the health of the charming young ladies!

Петров: Мне очень жаль, что нет дома моего сына.
Mn'yeh OH-*chen zhahl, shtoh n'yet* DOH-*mah moh-yeh*-VOH SEE-*nah.*
I am very sorry that my son is not home.

Если бы он был здесь, он бы засыпал
YES-*lee bee ohn beel zd'*YES, *ohn bee zah*-SEE-*pahl*
If he were here, he would flood

нашего американского гостя вопросами
NAH-*sheh-voh ah-meh-ree*-KAHN-*skoh-voh* GOHST-*yah vop*-ROH-*sah-mee*
our American guest with questions

об Америке. У нас все очень интересуются Америкой.
ob Ah-MEH-*ree-keh. Oo* NAHS *vs'yeh* OH-*chen eent-yeh-reh-*
SOO-*yoot-sah Ah*-MEH-*ree-koy.*
about America. Here everybody is greatly interested in America.

Панов: Мне было бы очень интересно познакомиться с ним.
Mn'yeh BEE-*loh bee* OH-*chen eent-yeh*-REHS-*noh*
poz-nah-KOH-*meet-sah s neem.*
It would be very interesting for me to meet him.

Маня: А не привезли ли вы с собой из Америки модные журналы?
MAHN-*yah*: *Ah n'yeh preev-yez*-LEE *lee vwee s soh*-BOY *eez Ah*-MEH-*ree-kee*
MOHD-*nee-yeh zhoor*-NAH-*lee?*
Manya: And didn't you bring fashion magazines with you from Ameria?

Панов: К сожалению, не привёз. Если б я знал, я привёз бы.
K soh-zhahl-YEH-*nee-yoo n'yeh preev*-YOHZ. YES-*lee b yah znahl yah preev*-
YOHZ *bee.*
I am sorry I didn't bring any. If I had known, I would have brought some.

Я холостяк и мне до сих пор ещё
Yah khoh-lost-YAHK *ee mn'yeh doh seekh pohr yesh*-CHOH
I am a bachelor and up to now

не приходилось интересоваться **дамскими модами.**
n'yeh pree-khoh-DEE-*los eent-yeh-reh-soh*-VAHT-*sah* DAHM-*skee-mee* MOH-*dah-mee.*
I haven't yet had to be interested in women's fashions . . .

NOTE to STUDENT: **Мне прихóдится** "I have to" is one of the numerous impersonal expressions which are so frequent in Russian. Other very useful impersonal expressions are: **мне хóчется**—"I want to . . . " **мне хотéлось бы** "I would like to." The past of **прихóдится** is **пришлóсь**: **мне пришлóсь** "I had to," and the future is **придётся**—"I shall have to."

Короленко: Мы тебя женим . . .
Mee t'yeb-YAH ZHEH-*neem . . .*
We will get you married . . .

USEFUL HINT: женить "to marry" is one of the few Russian verbs which can be used without any change in the perfective and imperfective sense.

Панов: Ты ещё сам не женат. Подумай сперва о себе.
*Tee yesh-*CHOH *sahm n'yeh zheh-*NAHT.
*Poh-*DOO-*migh sp'yehr-*VAH *oh s'yeb-*YEH.
You yourself are not married yet. Think of yourself first.

А вы, Варвара Антоновна, тоже интересуетесь модами?
*Ah vwee, Var-*VAH-*rah An-*TOH-*nov-nah,* TOH-*zheh eent-yeh-reh-*SOO-*yet-yes* MOH-*dah-mee?*
And you, Varvara Antonovna, are you also interested in fashions?

Варя: Конечно интересуюсь, в особенности бальными платьями.
VAHR-*yah*: *Kon-*YECH-*noh eent-yeh-reh-*SOO-*yoos, v oh-*SOB-*yen-nos-tee* BAHL-*nee-mee* PLAHT-*yah-mee.*
Naturally I am interested, particularly in evening gowns.

Лиза: Вот борщ.
Voht borshch.
Here is the borshch.

Панов: Борщ замечательный. Я его очень люблю.
*Borshch zahm-yeh-*CHAHT-*yel-nee. Yah yeh-*VOH OH-*chen l'yoobl-*YOO.
The borshch is remarkable. I like it very much.

В Америке я часто хожу в русские рестораны.
*V Ah-*MEH-*ree-keh yah* CHAHS-*toh khoh-*ZHOO *v* ROOS-*skee-yeh res-toh-*RAH-*nee.*
In America I often go to Russian restaurants.

Варя: Разве у вас в Америке есть русские рестораны?
RAHZ-*v'yeh oo* VAHS *v Ah-*MEH-*ree-keh yest* ROOS-*skee-yeh res-toh-*RAH-*nee?*
Do you really have Russian restaurants in America?

Панов: Есть сколько угодно, в особенности в Нью-Йорке.
Yest SKOHL-*koh oo-*GOHD-*noh, v oh-*SOH-*ben-nos-tee v N'yoo-*YOR-*keh.*
There are as many as you want, especially in New York.

Варя: А есть ли у вас балет?
Ah yest lee oo VAHS *bahl-*YET?
And do you have a ballet?

Панов: Да, у нас есть несколько русских балетов.
Dah, oo NAHS *yest n'*YES-*kol-koh* ROOS-*skeekh bahl-*YEH-*tov.*
Yes, we have several Russian ballets.

Варя: Мне так хотелось бы посмотреть Америку.
*Mn'yeh tahk khot-*YEH-*los bee pos-motr-*YET *Ah-*MEH-*ree-koo.*
I would like so much to see America.

Панов: Приезжайте к нам на гастроли в Нью-Йорк. **Вы наверное имели бы успех.**
*Pree-yez-*ZHIGHT-*yeh k nahm nah gast-*ROH-*lee v N'yoo-*YORK. *Vwee nahv-*YEHR-*noh-yeh eem-*YEH-*lee bee oosp-*YEKH.
Come to us in New York for a star performance. You would surely be a success.

Варя: По чём вы знаете? Вы ведь не видели как я танцую.
Poh CHOHM *vwee* ZNAH-*yet-yeh? Vwee v'yed n'yeh* VEED-*yeh-lee kahk yah tahn-*TSOO-*you.*
How do you know? You haven't seen me dance.

Панов: Вы член балета Большого театра; **значит вы танцуете хорошо.**
*Vwee chlen bahl-*YEH-*tah Bol-*SHOH-*voh t'yeh-*AHT-*rah*: ZNAH-*cheet vwee tan-*TSOO-*yet-yeh khoh-roh-*SHOH.
You are a member of the ballet of the Bolshoy theatre: that means that you dance well.

Варя: Странно. Отчего это вы так уверены?
STRAHN-*noh. Ot-cheh-*VOH EH-*toh vwee tahk oov-*YEH-*reh-nee?*
Strange. Why are you so sure of it?

Панов: Я вижу вас и я могу вас уверить в том, **что американцы ценят красоту.**
Yah VEE-*zhoo vahs ee yah moh-*GOO *vahs oov-*YEH-*reet v tohm,* *shtoh ah-meh-ree-*KAHN-*tsee* TSEHN-*yaht krah-soh-*TOO.
I see you and I can assure you that Americans appreciate beauty.

Варя: Эх вы, мужчины! Все вы одинаковы. **Все вы льстецы.**
*Ekh vwee moozh-*CHEE-*nee. Vs'yeh vwee oh-dee-*NAH-*koh-vee!* *Vs'yeh vwee lst'yeh-*TSEE*!*
Oh you men! You are all alike. You are all flatterers!

Панов: Если бы я был директором нью-йоркской оперы,
YES-*lee bee yah beel dee-*REK-*toh-rom n'yoo-*YORK-*skoy* OH-*peh-ree,*
If I were the director of the New York Opera,

я бы вас непременно пригласил на гастроли.
*yah bee vahs n'yeh-prehm-*YEN*-noh pree-glah-*SEEL *nah gast-*ROH*-lee.*
I would not fail to invite you for a star performance.

Лиза: Извините, что я прерываю ваш интересный разговор, но борщ стынет.
*Eez-vee-*NEET*-yeh shtoh yah preh-ree-*VAH*-yoo vahsh eent-yeh-*RES*-nee rahz-goh-*VOR*, noh borshch* STEEN*-yet.*
I am sorry to interrupt your interesting conversation but the borshtch is getting cold.

Панов: Борщ превкусный. Можно мне попросить ещё?
*Borshch preh-*VKOOS*-nee.* MOHZH*-noh mn'yeh poh-proh-*SEET *yesh-*CHOH*?*
The borshtch is very tasty. May I ask for more?

Лиза: Я очень рада, что угодила гостям.
Yah OH*-chen* RAH*-dah shtoh oo-goh-*DEE*-lah gost-*YAHM.
I am very happy to please my guests.

Петров: Мы засиделись за столом.
*Mee zah-seed-*YEH*-lees zah stoh-*LOHM.
We have been sitting too long at the table.

Надо нам поторопиться,
NAH*-doh nahm poh-toh-roh-*PEET*-sah,*
We must hurry,

иначе мы опоздаем на балет.
*ee-*NAH*-cheh mee oh-poz-*DAH*-yem nah bahl-*YET.
otherwise we shall be late for the ballet.

Панов: А далеко нам ехать?
*Ah dahl-yeh-*KOH *nahm* YEH*-khaht?*
And have we far to go?

Петров: Да, довольно далеко.
*Dah, doh-*VOHL*-noh dahl-yeh-*KOH.
Yes, quite far.

Лиза: А вот кисель. Только извините,
*Ah voht kees-*YEL. TOHL*-koh eez-vee-*NEET*-yeh*
Here is the jello. But excuse me

сливок я достать не могла.
SLEE*-vok yah dos-*TAHT *n'yeh mog-*LAH.
I could not get any cream.

Петров: Пора нам двигаться. Времени осталось не много.
*Poh-*RAH *nahm* DVEE*-gaht-sah.* VREH*-meh-nee os-*TAH*-los n'yeh* MNOH*-goh.*
It is time to go. There is not much time left.

Лиза: Я вас не задерживаю.
Yah vahs n'yeh zahd-YEHR-*zhee-vah-yoo.*
I am not holding you back.

Короленко, Панов, Петров (хором): Спасибо за всё, дорогая хозяюшка!
(KHOH-*rom*:) *Spah*-SEE-*boh zah vs'*YOH, *doh-roh*-GAH-*yah khoz*-YAH-*yoosh- kah.*
(in a chorus:) Thanks for everything, dear little hostess.

Короленко: Ты, Вася, пойдёшь с Варварой Антоновной,
Tee, VAHS-*yah, poyd*-YOHSH *s Var*-VAH-*roy An*-TOH-*nov-noy,*
You, Vasya, will go with Varvara Antonovna,

как её будущий антрепренёр,
kahk yeh-YOH BOO-*doosh-chee ahn-treh-pren*-YOR,
as her future impresario,

а мы с Гришей будем идти позади, как ваши шапроны . . .
a mee s GREE-*shey* BOOD-*yem eed*-TEE *poh-zah*-DEE, *kahk* VAH-*shee shap*-ROH-*nee . . .*
Grisha and I will follow you as your escorts . . .

THINKING IN RUSSIAN

(Answers on Page 232)

1. Как зову́т прия́теля Короле́нко?
2. На како́м этаже́ он живёт?
3. Кака́я у него́ кварти́ра?
4. Ско́лько у него́ ко́мнат?
5. Кто живёт в други́х ко́мнатах?
6. Что сказа́л Короле́нко об э́той кварти́ре?
7. Ско́лько раз звони́л Короле́нко?
8. Кто ему́ откры́л дверь?

9. Что сказа́л Петро́в?
10. Что сказа́ла Ли́за Пано́ву?
11. Как зову́т дочере́й Ли́зы?
12. Что сказа́л Петро́в о Ва́ре?
13. Где танцу́ет Ва́ря?
14. Како́е у Петро́вых меню́?
15. Что го́сти пьют пе́ред обе́дом?
16. Пьёте ли вы во́дку?
17. Чем интересу́ются до́чери Петро́ва?
18. Что интересу́ет Ва́рю?
19. Есть ли в Нью-Йо́рке ру́сские рестора́ны?
20. Почему́ Пано́в приглаша́ет Ва́рю в Нью-Йо́рк?
21. Почему́ Пано́в ду́мает, что Ва́ря име́ла бы успе́х в Нью-Йо́рке?
22. Се́рдится ли Ва́ря на Пано́ва?
23. Что она́ говори́т Пано́ву?
24. Почему́ Ва́ря прерыва́ет их разгово́р?
25. Пано́ву борщ понра́вился?
26. Что он говори́т Ли́зе?
27. Зна́ете ли вы, что тако́е кисе́ль?
28. Далеко́ ли от Петро́вых до теа́тра?
29. Почему́ го́сти торо́пятся?
30. Почему́ г-жа́ Петро́ва их не заде́рживает?
31. Что говоря́т Ли́зе го́сти, уходя́?
32. Что говори́т Короле́нко Пано́ву на у́лице?

УРОК 33

Балет в Большом Театре
Bahl-YET *v Bol*-SHOHM *T'yeh*-AHTR-*yeh*
A ballet in the Bolshoi Theatre

Панов: Какое красивое здание! Когда его построили?
Kah-KOH-*yeh krah*-SEE-*voh-yeh* ZDAH-*nee-yeh! Kog*-DAH *yeh*-VOH *pos*-TROH-*ee-lee?*
Panov: What a beautiful building! When was it built?

Петров: Больше ста лет тому назад.
Pet-ROHV: BOHL-*sheh stah l'yet toh*-MOO *nah*-ZAHD.
Petrov: More than a hundred years ago.

Панов: А что сегодня ставят?
Ah shtoh seh-VOHD-*n'yah* STAHV-*yaht?*
And what are they playing today?

Варя: Лебединое озеро Чайковского.
VAHR-*yah*: *L'yeb-yeh*-DEE-*noh-yeh* OHZ-*yeh-roh Chigh*-KOHV-*skoh-voh.*
Varya: Tchaikovsky's "Swan Lake."

Панов: Неужели Лебединое озеро всё ещё имеет успех?
N'yeh-oo-ZHEH-*lee L'yeb-yeh*-DEE-*noh-yeh* OHZ-*yeh-roh vs'yoh yesh*-CHOH *eem*-YEH-*yet oosp*-YEKH?
Is it possible that the "Swan Lake" is still popular?

Я думал, что революция всё переменила.
Yah DOO-*mahl, shtoh reh-vol*-YOO-*tsee-yah vs'yoh p'yeh-rem-yeh*-NEE-*lah.*
I thought that the revolution had changed everything.

Варя: Революция переменила многое,
Reh-vol-YOO-*tsee-yah p'yeh-rem-yeh*-NEE-*lah* MNOH-*goh-yeh,*
The revolution has changed a lot,

но искусство осталось и остаётся искусством.
noh ees-KOOST-*voh os*-TAH-*los ee os-tah*-YOHT-*sah ees*-KOOST-*vom.*
but art has remained and remains art.

Панов: Но ведь есть же и новые балеты.
Noh v'yed yest zheh ee NOH-*vee-yeh bahl*-YEH-*tee.*
But no doubt there are new ballets too.

Варя: Конечно есть. Мне хотелось бы, чтобы вы посмотрели Золушку Прокофьева.
Kon-YECH-*noh yest. Mn'yeh khot*-YEH-*los bee* SHTOH-*bee vwee pos-motr*-YEH-*lee* ZOH-*loosh-koo Proh*-KOHF-*yeh-vah.*
There certainly are. I would like you to see Prokofiev's "Cinderella."

IMPORTANT NOTE:

Here is the subjunctive which is expressed in Russian in several ways.

1) The particle **бы** is added to **что** (**чтобы**) and the verb is put into the past tense. For example:

Я хочу, чтобы ты пошёл домой—I want you to go home.

2) **бы** can also be used without **что**, in which case the verb usually precedes it:

Пошёл бы ты лучше домой—You had better go home.

3) **бы** can also follow a pronoun or an adverb: **кто, котóрый, какóй, как, кудá, где** etc. Thus

кудá бы вы ни пошлú—wherever you go
кто бы он ни был—whoever he might be

Панов: Кто сегодня выступает в главной роли?
Ktoh s'yeh-VOHDN-*yah vee-stoo*-PAH-*yet v* GLAHV-*noy* ROH-*lee?*
Who plays the leading role today?

Варя: Вам очень повезло. Главную роль исполняет Галина Уланова.
Vahm OH-*chen poh-vez*-LOH. GLAHV-*noo-yoo rohl ees-poln*-YAH-*yet Gah*-LEE-*nah Oo*-LAH-*noh-vah.*
You are very lucky. Galina Ulanova is playing the leading role.

Панов: Я этого имени ещё не слыхал.
Yah EH-*toh-voh* EE-*meh-nee yesh*-CHOH *n'yeh slee*-KHAHL.
I haven't heard that name yet.

Варя: Не может быть. Уланову знают все.
N'yeh MOH-*zhet beet. Oo*-LAH-*noh-voo* ZNAH-*yoot vs'yeh.*
That's impossible. Everybody knows Ulanova.

Панов: Каюсь, но не слыхал. Я ведь американец.
KAH-*yoos, noh n'yeh slee*-KHAHL. *Yah v'yed ah-meh-ree*-KAHN-*yets.*
I confess my guilt, but I haven't heard it. I'm an American, you know.

Короленко: Пора нам идти в театр,
Poh-RAH *nahm eed*-TEE *v t'yeh*-AHTR,
It's time (for us) to go into the theatre

чтобы мы не опоздали, а то нас не впустят.
SHTOH-*bee mee n'yeh oh-poz*-DAH-*lee, ah toh nahs n'yeh* VPOOST-*yaht.*
lest we be late, otherwise they won't let us in.

Панов: Какой великолепный зал!
Kah-KOY *v'yeh-lee-kol*-YEP-*nee zahl!*
What a magnificent hall!

Петров: Уже тушат свет. Вот поднимается занавес.
Oo-ZHEH TOO-*shaht sv'yet. Voht pod-nee*-MAH-*yet-sah* ZAH-*nahv-yes.*
The lights are already being put out. Here, the curtain is raised.

(Во время антракта).
(*Voh vrehm-yah ahn*-TRAHK-*tah.*)
(During the intermission.)

Короленко: Как тебе понравилась Уланова?
Kahk t'yeb-YEH *pon*-RAH-*vee-lahs Oo*-LAH-*noh-vah?*
How did you like Ulanova?

Панов: Удивительно, поразительно, восхитительно!
*Oo-dee-*VEET*-yel-noh, poh-rah-*ZEET*-yel-noh, vos-khee-*TEET*-yel-noh.*
Marvelous, striking, ravishing!

Петров: Неудивительно, что даже ваш генерал Маршалл загорелся.
*N'yeh-oo-dee-*VEET*-yel-noh, shtoh* DAH*-zheh vahsh ggen-yeh-*RAHL *Mar-shal zah-gor-*YEL*-sah.*
No wonder that even your General Marshall caught fire.

Панов: Как загорелся?
*Kahk zah-gor-*YEL*-sah?*
How did he catch fire?

Варя: Да так. Он был с вашим послом Смитом
Dah tahk. On beel s VAH*-sheem pos-*LOHM SMEE*-tom*
Yes, so it is! He was with your ambassador Smith

в Большом театре и смотрел балет Щелкунчики . . .
*v Bol-*SHOHM *t'yeh-*AHTR*-yeh ee smotr-*YEL *bahl-*YET *Shchel-*KOON*-chee-kee.*
in the Bolshoi theatre and he saw the "Nutcracker" ballet.

Панов: И загорелся? Надеюсь, что театр не сгорел.
*Ee zah-gor-*YEL*-sah? Nahd-*YEH*-yoos shtoh t'yeh-*AHTR *n'yeh sgor-*YEL.
And he caught fire? I hope the theatre didn't burn down.

Варя: Театр не пострадал.
*T'yeh-*AHTR *n'yeh post-rah-*DAHL.
The theatre was not harmed.

Но балерина Плисецкая ему так понравилась,
*Noh bahl-yeh-*REE*-nah Plees-*YETS*-kah-yah yeh-*MOO *tahk pon-*RAH*-vee-las,*
But he was so pleased by the ballerina Plisetskaya

что он послал ей корзину цветов.
*shtoh ohn pos-*LAHL *yay kor-*ZEE*-noo tsv'yeh-*TOHV.
that he sent her a basket of flowers.

Панов: Молодец!
*Moh-lod-*YETS*!*
A splendid fellow!

Варя: Да, молодец. Этот жест всем очень понравился.
*Dah, moh-lod-*YETS. EH*-tot zhest vs'yem* OH*-chen pon-*RAH*-veel-sah.*
Yes, a splendid fellow. Everybody liked that gesture very much.

А то у нас привыкли думать, что американцы
*Ah toh oo nahs pree-*VEEK-*lee* DOO-*maht, shtoh ah-meh-ree-*KAHN-*tsee*
because we were used to thinking that the Americans

интересуются только долларами.
*eent-yeh-reh-*SOO-*yoot-sah* TOHL-*koh* DOHL-*lah-rah-mee.*
were interested only in dollars.

Панов: Скажите, пожалуйста, Плисецкая очень красива?
*Skah-*ZHEET-*yeh, poh-*ZHAHL'*stah, Plee-s'*YETS-*kah-yah* OH-*chen krah-*SEE-*vah?*
Please, tell (me) is Plisetskaya very pretty?

Варя: Да, очень, и она хорошо танцует.
Dah, OH-*chen, ee oh-*NAH *khoh-roh-*SHOH *tahn-*TSOO-*yet.*
Yes, very, and she dances well.

Панов: Но она, наверное, не лучше вас . . .
*Noh oh-*NAH, *nahv-*YEHR-*noh-yeh, n'yeh* LOOCH-*sheh vahs . . .*
But I am sure she is not more beautiful than you . . .

Варя: Вы уже опять начинаете.
*Vee oo-*ZHEH *op-*YAHT *nah-chee-*NAH-*yet-yeh.*
Now you are starting in again.

Пора нам идти обратно в зал.
*Poh-*RAH *nahm eed-*TEE *ob-*RAHT-*noh v zahl.*
It's time to go back to the hall.

Панов: Я хотел спросить ещё об одном:
*Yah khot-*YEL *sproh-*SEET *yesh-*CHOH *ob od-*NOHM:
I wanted to ask you one more thing:

Сегодня какой-то военный праздник?
*Seh-*VOHDN-*yah kah-*KOY-*toh voh-*YEN-*nee* PRAHZD-*neek?*
Is today some military holiday?

Петров: Отчего вы так думаете?
*Ot-cheh-*VOH *vee tahk* DOO-*mah-yet-yeh?*
Why do you think so?

Панов: В театре столько офицеров в парадных формах.
*V t'yeh-*AHTR-*yeh* STOHL-*koh oh-fee-*TSEH-*rov v pah-*RAHD-*neekh* FOR-*makh.*
There are so many officers in full-dress uniforms.

Все первые ряды блестят погонами . . .
*Vs'yeh p'*YEHR-*vee-yeh r'yah-*DEE *blest-*YAHT *poh-*GOH-*nah-mee . . .*
All the first rows are glittering with epaulets . . .

Петров: Офицеров всегда много и лучшие места предоставляются им.
Oh-fee-TSEH-*rov vs'yeg*-DAH MNOH-*goh, ee* LOOCH-*shee-yeh m'yes*-TAH *pred-os-tahv-l'*YAH-*yoot-sah eem.*
There always are many officers and the best seats are given to them.

Короленко: Поднимается занавес. Тише!
Pod-nee-MAH-*yet-sah* ZAH-*nahv-yes.* TEE-*sheh!*
The curtain is rising. Quiet!

Панов: Ах!
Akh!
Ah!

Варя: Чего вы вздыхаете?
Cheh-VOH *vwee vzdee*-KHAH-*yet-yeh?*
Why are you sighing?

Панов: Я думаю о том, как хороши были бы вы в роли Улановой.
Yah DOO-*mah-yoo o tohm, kahk khoh-roh*-SHEE BEE-*lee bee vwee v* ROH-*lee Oo*-LAH-*noh-voy.*
I am thinking of how beautiful you would be in the role of Ulanova.

Варя: Вы неисправимы.
Vee n'yeh-ees-prah-VEE-*mee.*
You are incorrigible.

(После представления).
(POHSL-*yeh pr'yed-stahv-l'*YEH-*nee-yah.*)
(After the performance.)

Панов: Да, из-за одного только балета стоило приехать в Москву.
Dah, eez-zah od-noh-VOH TOHL-*koh bahl*-YEH-*tah* STOH-*ee-loh pree*-YEH-*khaht v Mosk*-VOO.
Yes, it was worthwhile to come to Moscow for the ballet alone.

Варя: А больше вам делать нечего в Москве?
Ah BOHL-*sheh vahm d'*YEH-*laht n'*YEH-*cheh-voh v Mosk-v'*YEH*?*
And you have nothing else to do in Moscow?

Панов: Я конечно приехал бы в Москву ради вас.
Yah kon-YECH-*noh pree*-YEH-*khahl bee v Mosk*-VOO RAH-*dee vahs.*
Naturally, I would come to Moscow because of you.

Варя: Вы, право, несносный. Я хотела сказать,
Vee PRAH-*voh n'yes*-NOHS-*nee. Yah khot*-YEH-*lah skah*-ZAHT*,*
You really are unbearable. I wanted to say

что вы ведь приехали в Москву по делам.
shtoh vwee v'yed pree-YEH-*khah-lee v Mosk*-VOO *poh d'yeh*-LAHM.
that you came to Moscow on business.

Петров: Не пойти ли нам куда-нибудь выпить чашку чаю?
N'yeh poy-TEE *lee nahm koo*-DAH-*nee*-BOOD VEE-*peet* CHASH-*koo* CHAH-*yoo?*
Shouldn't we go somewhere for a cup of tea?

IMPORTANT NOTE:

Do you notice the infinitive in combination with the dative of a pronoun to express "should?" In the same way you say: **не взять ли мне зóнтик?**—"shouldn't" I take the umbrella? **Не взять ли вам пальтó?**—"shouldn't" you take an overcoat?

Варя: Здесь поблизости есть ресторанчик, недорогой, куда ходят артисты.
Zd'yes poh BLEE-*zos-tee yest res-toh*-RAHN-*cheek, n'yeh-doh-roh*-GOY, *koo*-DAH KHOHD-*yaht ar*-TEE-*stee.*
Here near-by is a little restaurant, inexpensive, where artists go.

Идёмте туда. Я вас познакомлю с балеринами.
Eed-YOHMT-*yeh too*-DAH. *Yah vahs poz-nah*-KOHML-*yoo s bahl-yeh*-REE-*nah-mee.*
Let's go there. I will introduce you to some ballerinas.

Петров: Идёмте. Это интересно.
Eed-YOHMT-*yeh.* EH-*toh eent-yeh*-RES-*noh.*
Let's go. This is interesting.

NOTE on POLITENESS:

If you use the familiar **ты** "thou" in speaking to a friend, you say **идём** meaning "let's go!"

As Petrov is still relatively formal with his guests, he uses the polite form **идёмте,** for "let's go!"

THINKING IN RUSSIAN

(Answers on page 233)

1. Что ви́дели Короле́нко и Пано́в в Большо́м теа́тре?
2. Понра́вился ли Пано́ву теа́тр?
3. Давно́ ли постро́или Большо́й теа́тр?
4. Что сказа́ла Ва́ря о револю́ции и об иску́сстве?
5. Кто игра́ет гла́вную роль в Лебеди́ном о́зере?
6. Зна́ете ли вы Ула́нову?
7. Слы́шали ли вы об Ула́новой?
8. Почему́ Пано́в ничего́ не зна́ет об Ула́новой?
9. Како́й бале́т смотре́л генера́л Ма́ршалл?
10. Кто ему́ понра́вился?
11. Что он посла́л балери́не?
12. Хо́дите ли вы ча́сто в теа́тр?
13. Есть ли в ва́шем го́роде бале́т?
14. Мно́го ли офице́ров быва́ет в Большо́м теа́тре?
15. Где сидя́т офице́ры?
16. Почему́ прие́хал Пано́в в Москву́?
17. Понра́вился ли ему́ бале́т?
18. Что он сказа́л по по́воду бале́та?
19. Что сказа́ла Ва́ря?
20. Что на э́то отве́тил Пано́в?

ANSWERS

NOTE: For better practice in the following exercises we have followed a system of an imaginary conversation between Professor Berlitz and the student. For instance, page 21, question 5:

Professor: **Кто я?**

Student: **Вы господи́н Бе́рлиц.**

Professor Berlitz, although invisible in this conversation, will always be present to help you towards acquiring knowledge of Russian.

ANSWERS TO THE QUESTIONS OF LESSON 1 ON PAGE 3

1. Это кни́га.
2. Да, э́то кни́га.
3. Нет, э́то не коро́бка.
4. Нет, э́то не стол.
5. Это не зе́ркало.
6. Это коро́бка.
7. Это не ла́мпа.
8. Это не стул.
9. Это ключ.
10. Это каранда́ш.
11. Это не карти́на.
12. Это не кни́га.
13. Это не дверь.
14. Это не ключ.
15. Это стол.

ANSWERS TO THE QUESTIONS OF LESSON 2 ON PAGE 6

1. Это не чуло́к.
2. Это не плато́к.
3. Это не га́лстук и не су́мка.
4. Это боти́нок.
5. Это не пла́тье
6. Это не часы́ и не де́ньги.
7. Это не каранда́ш.
8. Это перча́тка.
9. Это не костю́м.
10. Это не пальто́.
11. Это не боти́нок.
12. Это не пиджа́к и не брю́ки.
13. Это не га́лстук.
14. Это ни носо́к, ни перча́тка.
15. Да, э́то шля́па.
16. Это шля́па.

ANSWERS TO THE QUESTIONS OF LESSON 3 ON PAGE 11

1. Нет, э́то перо́ не си́нее.
2. Перо́ не кра́сное.
3. Это перо́ не се́рое.
4. Перо́ э́то не бе́лое и не чёрное.
5. Это перо́ зелёное.
6. Это каранда́ш.
7. Да, э́то каранда́ш.
8. Этот каранда́ш не кра́сный и не зелёный.
9. Этот каранда́ш жёлтый.
10. Это не стол и не стул.
11. Нет, э́то не карти́на.
12. Да, э́то ла́мпа.
13. Нет, э́та ла́мпа не кра́сная и не жёлтая.
14. Нет, э́та ла́мпа не зелёная.
15. Ла́мпа си́няя.
16. Это кни́га.
17. Да, э́то кни́га.
18. Нет, э́та кни́га не чёрная.
19. Эта кни́га не кори́чневая и не се́рая.
20. Эта кни́га кра́сная.

ANSWERS TO THE QUESTIONS OF LESSON 4 ON PAGE 15

1. Да, кра́сная кни́га дли́нная.
2. Да, она́ широ́кая.
3. Она́ больша́я.
4. Да, зелёная кни́га коро́ткая.
5. Она́ у́зкая.
6. Да, она́ ма́ленькая.
7. Больша́я кни́га кра́сная.
8. Ма́ленькая кни́га зелёная.
9. Дли́нное пла́тье чёрное.
10. Нет, оно́ не кра́сное.
11. Да, чёрное пла́тье дли́нное.
12. Нет, оно́ не коро́ткое.
13. Коро́ткое пла́тье жёлтое.
14. Оно́ не чёрное и не зелёное.
15. Широ́кое окно́ си́нее.
16. Узкое окно́ кра́сное.
17. Нет, оно́ не се́рое.
18. Кра́сное окно́ не широ́кое.
19. Си́нее окно́ широ́кое.
20. Да, си́нее окно́ большо́е.
21. Да, кра́сное окно́ ма́ленькое.
22. Ма́ленькое окно́ кра́сное.
23. Большо́е окно́ си́нее.

ANSWERS TO THE QUESTIONS OF LESSON 5 ON PAGE 21

1. Я...
2. Да, я америка́нец. (Я америка́нка).
3. Я учени́к. (Я учени́ца).
4. Я не ру́сский, я америка́нец. (Я не ру́сская, я америка́нка).
5. Вы господи́н Бе́рлиц.
6. Гали́на Ула́нова — ру́сская.
7. Она́ балери́на.
8. Она́ не италья́нка, она́ кита́янка.
9. Толсто́й — ру́сский.
10. Ваш га́лстук зелёный.
11. Моя́ шля́па се́рая.
12. Это мой пиджа́к.
13. Это ва́ша кни́га.
14. Это моё пальто́.
15. Он не япо́нец, он америка́нец.
16. Генера́л Ма́ршалл — америка́нец.

ANSWERS TO THE QUESTIONS OF LESSON 6 ON PAGE 27

1. Кни́га на столе́.
2. Нет, она́ не под сту́лом.
3. Шля́па на сту́ле.
4. Она́ в шля́пе.
5. Нет, он не под сту́лом.
6. Он о́коло стола́.
7. Он пе́редо мной.
8. Пе́ред столо́м стул.
9. На сту́ле шля́па.
10. Надо мно́й потоло́к.
11. Ме́жду учи́телем и коро́бкой стол.
12. Оно́ в коро́бке.
13. Над столо́м виси́т ла́мпа.
14. Перо́ под столо́м в коро́бке.
15. Там перо́.
16. Я тут.
17. Япо́ния в Азии.
18. Ки́ев в Малоро́ссии.
19. Малоро́ссия в Росси́и.
20. Го́род Баку́ на Кавка́зе.

ANSWERS TO THE QUESTIONS OF LESSON 7 ON PAGE 35

1. Он берёт кни́гу.
2. Да, учи́тель берёт кни́гу.
3. Он не кладёт кни́гу на стол.
4. Нет, он не берёт коро́бку.
5. Нет, он не сиди́т, он стои́т.
6. Да, он открыва́ет окно́.
7. Учи́тель открыва́ет окно́.
8. Он открыва́ет окно́.
9. Да, я открыва́ю дверь.
10. Он не открыва́ет дверь.
11. Нет, учи́тель не е́дет в Нью-Йо́рк.
12. Он не е́дет в Ло́ндон.
13. Он лети́т в Москву́.
14. Москва́ больша́я.
15. Нет, я не е́ду в Москву́.
16. Учи́тель е́дет в Москву́.

ANSWERS TO THE QUESTIONS OF LESSON 8 ON PAGE 43

1. Я счита́ю: оди́н, два, три и так да́лее.
2. Вы счита́ете.
3. Учи́тель счита́ет.
4. Он счита́ет де́ньги.
5. В э́той ко́мнате два сту́ла.
6. Да, есть.
7. На столе́ коро́бка и де́ньги.
8. Я зна́ю слов три́ста.
9. Она́ сто́ит пять це́нтов.
10. В до́лларе сто це́нтов.
11. Она́ не сто́ит ста до́лларов.
12. До́ллар не сто́ит ста рубле́й.
13. Нет, не мно́го, то́лько два окна́.
14. Это ци́фра четы́рнадцать.
15. В э́той ко́мнате то́лько одна́ дверь.
16. Лет де́сять. (Го́да три).

ANSWERS TO THE QUESTIONS OF LESSON 9 ON PAGE 51

1. Пе́рвая бу́ква — А.
2. Тре́тья — В.
3. Вы спра́шиваете меня́, кака́я пе́рвая бу́ква а́збуки.
4. Я отвеча́ю на ваш вопро́с.
5. Да, я отвеча́ю на его́ вопро́сы.
6. Это господи́н Бе́рлиц.
7. Это четвёртая бу́ква.

8. Вы спрáшиваете, какáя бýква Г.
9. В шкóле я учýсь.
10. Учи́тель меня́ ýчит.
11. Да, я её читáю.
12. Да, я читáю по-рýсски.
13. Я читáю рýсскую кни́гу.
14. В шкóле я говорю́ по-рýсски.
15. В шкóле я по-англи́йски не говорю́.
16. Да, пишý.
17. Да, я пишý урóки.
18. Я читáю тóлько э́ту кни́гу.
19. Не читáю.

ANSWERS TO THE QUESTIONS OF LESSON 10 ON PAGE 57

1. Ученики́ идýт в шкóлу Бéрлица.
2. Они́ там ýчатся говори́ть по-рýсски.
3. Хожý. (Не хожý).
4. Идý. (Не идý).
5. Да, хожý.
6. Мы вéшаем пальтó на вéшалку.
7. Шля́па виси́т на вéшалке.
8. Мы её берём с вéшалки.
9. Кольцó в корóбке.
10. Мы егó берём из корóбки.
11. Идý. (Не идý).
12. Еду. (Не éду).
13. Да, я éду в ресторáн. (Нет, не éду).
14. Нет, не éдут.
15. Они́ éдут в Одéссу.

ANSWERS TO THE QUESTIONS OF LESSON 11 ON PAGE 62

1. У негó под мы́шкой газéта.
2. Есть.
3. Да, у негó в кармáне трýбка.
4. На крéсле.
5. Нет, линéйка не под егó прáвой ногóй.
6. В егó прáвой рукé два перá.
7. Да, пéрья у негó в прáвой рукé.
8. Есть.
9. Да, на столé.
10. На столé.
11. Да, есть.
12. На столé четы́ре кни́ги.
13. Да, есть. (Нет, у негó в кармáне дéнег нет).
14. Да, на стýле лежи́т шля́па.

ANSWERS TO THE QUESTIONS OF LESSON 12 ON PAGE 67

1. У Лёли четвертáк.
2. Нет, у неё мéньше дéнег.
3. У учи́теля бóльше.
4. Да, у негó зá ухом два карандашá.
5. Да, у негó бóльше.
6. У Лёли бóльше книг.
7. У тёти Мáши.
8. У учи́теля мéньше всех.
9. Нет, у неё не мнóго.
10. У негó тóлько однá кни́га.
11. Да, я читáю мнóго рýсских книг.
12. Я пишý бóльше.

13. Да, мно́го. (Нет, не мно́го).
14. В Нью Йо́рк Таймс ме́ньше страни́ц.
15. У вас мно́го де́нег.
16. У меня́ ма́ло де́нег. (Мно́го).
17. Да, мно́го. (Нет, ма́ло).

ANSWERS TO THE QUESTIONS OF LESSON 13 ON PAGE 73

1. Да, он ей даёт кни́гу.
2. Он ей даёт де́ньги.
3. Она́ сиди́т на сту́ле.
4. Нет, не даёт.
5. С ней никто́ не говори́т.
6. Он ей не говори́т ничего́.
7. Нет, она́ ей ничего́ не говори́т.
8. Она́ ей что́-то даёт.
9. Она́ ничего́ не говори́т.
10. Говоря́т. (Не говоря́т).
11. Да, они́ ему́ говоря́т "здра́вствуйте".
12. Он говори́т им "до свида́ния".
13. В ле́вой руке́ у неё мяч.
14. Я говорю́ вам, что у неё в руке́ мяч.
15. Она́ говори́т ему́ спаси́бо.
16. Меня́ зову́т Робе́рт Яковлевич.
17. Её зову́т Магдали́на Васи́льевна.
18. Его́ зову́т Карл Ка́рлович.

ANSWERS TO THE QUESTIONS OF LESSON 14 ON PAGE 78

1. Да, у него́ в пра́вой руке́ папиро́са.
2. У неё в ле́вой руке́ плато́к.
3. В ле́вой руке́ у неё нет ничего́.
4. В пра́вой руке́ у неё то́же ничего́ нет.
5. Во́зле него́ стол.
6. Около него́ никто́ не стои́т.
7. Да, ме́жду ни́ми стол.
8. Да, в пра́вой руке́ она́ де́ржит кни́гу.
9. На сту́ле никто́ не сиди́т.
10. На столе́ нет ничего́.
11. У учи́теля под мы́шкой нет ничего́.
12. Напра́во стои́т тётя Ма́ша.
13. Нале́во нет никого́.
14. На сту́ле ничего́ не лежи́т.
15. Нет, она́ стои́т пе́ред ним.
16. Под столо́м никого́ нет.
17. У него́ на голове́ нет шля́пы.
18. На голове́ у него́ нет ничего́.

ANSWERS TO THE QUESTIONS OF LESSON 15 ON PAGE 85

1. Он ню́хает лук но́сом.
2. Нет, лук па́хнет скве́рно.
3. Да, ро́за па́хнет хорошо́.
4. Она́ ню́хает ро́зу.
5. Нет, я не ви́жу предме́тов, кото́рые за мной.
6. Да, мы ви́дим предме́ты пе́ред на́ми.
7. Да, я слы́шу.
8. Да, я вас слы́шу.
9. Да, мы еди́м хлеб. (Нет, мы хле́ба не еди́м).
10. Да, в кинемато́графе мы ви́дим карти́ну.
11. Да, мы кладём в чай са́хар.

(Нет, мы са́хар в чай не кладём).
12. Да, америка́нцы едя́т бе́лый хлеб.
13. Да, ру́сские пьют мно́го ча́ю.
14. Нет, мы не еди́м карто́фель с са́харом.
15. Да, я пью чай с молоко́м. (Нет, я не пью чай с молоко́м).
16. Мы ре́жем мя́со ножо́м.
17. Нет, мы горо́х ножо́м не еди́м.
18. Мы ре́жем бума́гу но́жницами.

ANSWERS TO THE QUESTIONS OF LESSON 16 ON PAGE 92

1. Да, у ро́зы прия́тный за́пах.
2. У сы́ра неприя́тный за́пах.
3. Нет, суп с са́харом неприя́тен на вкус.
4. За́пах капу́сты мне не нра́вится.
5. Вкус мали́ны мне нра́вится.
6. Я зелёных я́блок не люблю́.
7. Я люблю́ сыр. (Я не люблю́ сыр).
8. Да, де́ти лю́бят конфе́ты.
9. Да, я люблю́ говори́ть по-ру́сски.
10. Ста́туя Вене́ры о́чень краси́ва.
11. Она́ мне нра́вится.
12. Му́зыка Чайко́вского мне нра́вится.
13. Мне его́ му́зыка нра́вится.
14. Из стака́на.
15. Из стака́на и́ли ча́шки.
16. Из рю́мки.
17. Сова́ некраси́ва.
18. Да, ру́сский язы́к краси́в.
19. Да, мне прия́тно его́ слу́шать.
20. Да, я ем мя́со.
21. Я ры́бы не ем.

ANSWERS TO THE QUESTIONS OF LESSON 17 ON PAGE 98

1. Да, она́ её тро́гает.
2. Нет, она́ её тро́нуть не мо́жет.
3. Да, он мо́жет тро́нуть её шля́пу.
4. Нет, он её не тро́гает.
5. Да, она́ ни́зкая.
6. Да, он мо́жет её тро́нуть.
7. Он ничего́ не тро́гает.
8. Да, у него́ есть очки́.
9. Да, он мо́жет ви́деть без очко́в. (Нет, не мо́жет).
10. Да, я могу́ вы́йти из ко́мнаты, е́сли дверь откры́та.
11. Нет, без пера́ и́ли карандаша́ вы не мо́жете писа́ть.
12. Нет, не мо́жем.
13. Нет, они́ потоло́к тро́нуть не мо́гут. (Нет, они́ потолка́ тро́нуть не мо́гут).
14. Да, могу́.
15. Нет, я не могу́ сосчита́ть звёзды на не́бе. (Нет, не могу́).
16. Нет, не могу́. (Нет, я не могу́ есть суп ви́лкой).

ANSWERS TO THE QUESTIONS OF LESSON 18 ON PAGE 104

1. Да, хо́чет.
2. Нет, она́ его́ доста́ть не мо́жет.
3. Он его́ ей не даёт.
4. Потому́, что он хо́чет её подразни́ть.
5. Да, хо́чет.

6. Да, мы должны́ откры́ть дверь, что́бы вы́йти.
7. Да, мы должны́ откры́ть глаза́, что́бы ви́деть.
8. Да, мы должны́ име́ть де́ньги.
9. Мы должны́ име́ть перо́ и́ли каранда́ш.
10. Мы должны́ её откры́ть.
11. Нет, он без очко́в чита́ть не мо́жет.
12. Он до́лжен име́ть очки́.
13. Для того́, что́бы пойти́ в о́перу, у нас должны́ быть биле́ты.
14. Нет, ножо́м я суп есть не могу́.
15. У меня́ должна́ быть ло́жка.
16. Нет, я до́лжен име́ть ло́жку.
17. Нет, не до́лжен.
18. Нет, вы не должны́.

ANSWERS TO THE QUESTIONS OF LESSON 19 ON PAGE 112

1. Да, есть.
2. Одни́ на столе́, а други́е на стене́.
3. Да, есть. (Нет, у меня́ нет часо́в).
4. Да, они́ у меня́ в карма́не. (Нет, они́ не в карма́не).
5. На́ стену.
6. Да, пока́зывают. (Нет, не пока́зывают).
7. Не зна́ю (I don't know). Без пяти́ час. Пять часо́в.
8. В три часа́.
9. В четы́ре.
10. Шестьдеся́т мину́т.
11. Из двадцати́ четырёх часо́в.
12. Шестьдеся́т секу́нд.
13. Иду́т. (Нет, они́ стоя́т).
14. На́до их завести́.
15. Нет, они́ отстаю́т. (Да, они́ спеша́т).
16. Нет, не отстаю́т. (Да, отстаю́т).
17. Да, они́ бо́льше карма́нных.
18. Он бо́льше сту́ла.
19. Да, она́ длинне́е карти́ны.
20. Да, коро́че.
21. Нет, окно́ ши́ре. (Оно́ тако́е же широ́кое, как и две́рь).
22. Нет, руба́шка длинне́е жиле́та.
23. Да, да́мские шля́пы краси́вее.
24. Да, лу́чше. (Нет, не лу́чше).
25. Да, фиа́лка па́хнет лу́чше.
26. Нет, не ху́же. (Да, ху́же).
27. Да, моё англи́йское произноше́ние лу́чше.
28. Нет, моё ру́сское произноше́ние непра́вильное.
29. У моего́ учи́теля произноше́ние лу́чше.
30. Нет, я пишу́ ху́же. (Я пишу́ та́к же хорошо́, как и вы).
31. Да, у меня́ хоро́шие глаза́. (Нет, у меня́ глаза́ плохи́е).
32. Да, я ви́жу хорошо́. (Нет, я ви́жу пло́хо).
33. Нет, он без очко́в ви́дит пло́хо.
34. Да, в очка́х он ви́дит лу́чше.

ANSWERS TO THE QUESTIONS OF LESSON 20 ON PAGE 120

1. В году́ три́ста шестьдеся́т пять дней.
2. Из семи́ дней.
3. Пе́рвого января́.
4. Три́дцать пе́рвого декабря́.
5. Пе́рвый ме́сяц — янва́рь, тре́тий — март, пя́тый — май, восьмо́й — а́вгуст.

6. Понедéльник, втóрник, средá, четвéрг, пя́тница, суббóта, воскресéнье.
7. Он называ́ется воскресéньем.
8. Сегóдня — понедéльник, втóрник и т. д.
9. Да, воскресéнье. Нет, суббóта.
10. По воскресéньям и по прáздникам.
11. Да, пятнáдцатое. (Нет, шестнáдцатое).
12. Сегóдня двенáдцатое.
13. В бýдущий понедéльник бýдет седьмóе числó.
14. В прóшлый четвéрг бы́ло трéтье.
15. Да, зáвтра конéц мéсяца. (Нет, зáвтра не конéц месяца).
16. Тепéрь чéтверть пя́того, полови́на шестóго, без чéтверти семь.
17. Мы рабóтаем в бýдни.
18. Нет, в воскресéнье я не рабóтаю.
19. Нет, по воскресéньям они́ урóков не даю́т.
20. На ю́ге жить прия́тнее.
21. Нет, не хóлодно.
22. Да, под Москвóй лéтом прия́тно.

ANSWERS TO THE QUESTIONS OF LESSON 21 ON PAGE 126

1. Днём.
2. Темнó. (Не темнó).
3. От сóлнца.
4. На нéбе.
5. Нет, не ви́дно.
6. Электри́чеством.
7. Мы зажигáем свет.
8. Лунý и звёзды.
9. Сéвер, востóк, юг и зáпад.
10. Сóлнце всхóдит ýтром.
11. В шесть часóв утрá.
12. Нет, онó захóдит пóздно.
13. Лéтом.
14. Нет, не могý.
15. Я ложýсь спать вéчером.
16. В семь часóв.
17. Да, люблю́. (Нет, не люблю́).
18. Свет луны́ слабéе свéта сóлнца.
19. Нóчью.
20. Нет, нельзя́.
21. На востóке.
22. На зáпаде.
23. Я ложýсь в дéсять часóв.
24. Да, лéтом я ложýсь пóзже.

ANSWERS TO THE QUESTIONS OF LESSON 22 ON PAGE 133

1. Нéбо сéрое.
2. Онó покры́то облакáми.
3. Нет, не идёт. (Да, идёт).
4. Снег.
5. Нет, неприя́тно.
6. У меня́ в рукé зóнтик.
7. Сегóдня хорóшая погóда. (Сегóдня пáсмурно).
8. Да, выхожý. (Нет, не выхожý).
9. Да, сли́шком. (Нет, не сли́шком).
10. Да, хóлодно.
11. Снег идёт с октября́ по апрéль.
12. Да, чáсто.
13. Нет, не чáсто.
14. Нет, в áвгусте никогдá не идёт снег.
15. В мáрте вéтер дýет чáсто.
16. Я люблю́ грозý.
(Я не люблю́ грозы́).

ANSWERS TO THE QUESTIONS OF LESSON 23 ON PAGE 141

1. Нет, нé был. (Нет, не былá). Был. (Былá).
2. Я тудá éздил (éздила) мóрем.
3. Да, бывáл (бывáла). — Не бывáл (не бывáла).
4. Да, рóзы цвелй.
5. Онá жилá в большóй гостйнице.
6. Кавкáзская Ривьéра.
7. Москóвский купéц.
8. Онá национализйрована.
9. Да, был.
10. Нá море.
11. Да, купáлась.
12. Да, плáвала.
13. На Крáсную Полянý.
14. В автомобйле и на лошадях.
15. Нет, онá не éздила пóездом.
16. Нет, онá не ходйла пешкóм.
17. Нет, я тудá не éздил (не éздила). — Да, éздил (éздила).
18. Онá гуляла в лесý и собирáла грибы́ и ягоды.
19. Да, онá ходйла в лес.
20. Онá собирáла грибы́ и ягоды.

ANSWERS TO THE QUESTIONS OF LESSON 24 ON PAGE 148

1. Мóжет быть поéдут.
2. Если бýдет хорóшая погóда.
3. Нет, не знáю.
4. Не знáю.
5. Онй поéдут пóездом.
6. Зáвтра воскресéнье.
7. Онй бýдут сидéть под берёзой.
8. Под берёзой.
9. У Попóвых.
10. Потомý что татáры бы́ли незвáными гостями.
11. Да, бýдут, éсли бýдет хорóшая погóда.
12. Онй остáнутся в гóроде.
13. Да, остáнутся.
14. Да, пойдýт.
15. В магазйне.
16. Онй пойдýт гулять.
17. Да, пойдýт.
18. Онй бýдут смотрéть витрйны.
19. В ресторáне.
20. Нет, не пойдýт.
21. Потомý что у них не хвáтит дéнег.
22. Нет, не идý. (Да, идý).
23. Да, я хожý чáсто в теáтр. (Нет, рéдко).
24. Онó бýдет стóить стóлько, скóлько Кóля зарабáтывает в два мéсяца.

ANSWERS TO THE QUESTIONS OF LESSON 25 ON PAGE 154

1. На рисýнке мы вйдим льва, тйгра, слонá и жирáфа.
2. Это дйкие живóтные.
3. Да, онй полéзны.
4. Онá даёт нам молокó.
5. Пчелá нам даёт мёд.
6. Лóшадь нас вóзит.
7. Собáка стережёт дом.
8. Кóшка лóвит мышéй.
9. У лóшади четы́ре ногй.
10. У негó четы́ре лáпы.
11. У негó два крылá.
12. Онй летáют в вóздухе.
13. Шéрстью.
14. Онá ползёт по землé.
15. Нет, онá не хóдит.

16. Нет, у неё нет ног.
17. Нет, у ры́бы нет ног.
18. Они́ пла́вают.
19. Они́ живу́т в воде́.
20. Да, лягу́шки пла́вают.
21. Нет, они́ бесполе́зны.
22. В на́шем до́ме ма́ло мух (мно́го мух, нет мух).
23. Я зна́ю орла́, ку́рицу, петуха́, воробья́, ла́сточку.
24. Ло́шадь, коро́ву, соба́ку, ко́шку, овцу́, свинью́.

ANSWERS TO THE QUESTIONS OF LESSON 26 ON PAGE 162

1. Оттого́ что у него́ мно́го де́нег.
2. Потому́ что она́ разби́ла свою́ ку́клу.
3. Да, она́ грусти́т.
4. Свои́м умо́м.
5. В мозгу́.
6. Мо́згом.
7. Ло́шадь бежи́т быстре́е.
8. Ры́ба пла́вает лу́чше.
9. Орёл ви́дит лу́чше.
10. Челове́к.
11. Сейча́с я ду́маю об уро́ке.
12. О посте́ли.
13. Да, па́мять у меня́ хоро́шая.
14. Да, я их запомина́ю легко́.
15. Нет, я не по́мню всех слов.
16. Я ча́сто сержу́сь.
17. Да, я дово́лен.
18. Мы называ́ем хра́брым челове́ка, кото́рый не бои́тся.
19. Лу́чше смея́ться.
20. Нет, я пауко́в не бою́сь.
21. Нет, меня́ не легко́ испуга́ть.

ANSWERS TO THE QUESTIONS OF LESSON 27 ON PAGE 169

1. Пано́в прие́хал из Аме́рики.
2. Его́ зову́т Са́шей.
3. Он вспомина́ет войну́.
4. То́лько на оди́н день.
5. Что́бы повида́ться со свои́м прия́телем.
6. Потому́ что он до́лжен быть послеза́втра в Москве́.
7. Нет, он Москвы́ не зна́ет.
8. Нет, я Оде́ссы не зна́ю.
9. Да, я в Вашингто́не быва́л.
10. Потому́ что он зна́ет Москву́.
11. Нет, у меня́ о́тпуска не́т. (Да, у меня́ о́тпуск).
12. У меня́ бу́дет о́тпуск ле́том (че́рез ме́сяц).
13. Я отдыха́ю. (Я уезжа́ю в дере́вню).
14. Они́ летя́т в Москву́.
15. В конто́ре.
16. Они́ за́втракают в рестора́не.
17. Поза́втракав, они́ осма́тривают Ки́ев.
18. Короле́нко берёт биле́т в оди́н коне́ц.
19. Да, он берёт обра́тный биле́т.
20. Потому́ что Ки́ев пе́рвая столи́ца ру́сского госуда́рства, "мать ру́сских городо́в".

ANSWERS TO THE QUESTIONS OF LESSON 28 ON PAGE 176

1. Нет, он не вста́л во́ время.
2. Потому́ что он проспа́л.
3. Его́ буди́ли два ра́за.
4. Ма́льчик взял его́ бага́ж.

5. У него́ был оди́н чемода́н и ма́ленький саквоя́ж.
6. Его́ зва́ли Фе́дей.
7. Он его́ оста́вил в ко́мнате.
8. Касси́р пожела́л ему́ счастли́вого пути́.
9. Что́бы он не бра́л ма́ленького саквоя́жа.
10. Потому́ что в нём бы́ли все его́ доку́менты.
11. Нет, недалеко́.
12. За ним зае́хал Короле́нко.
13. Он спроси́л Пано́ва, отчего́ он опозда́л.
14. До отлёта оста́лось ещё со́рок мину́т.
15. Всего́ лишь три ме́ста.
16. Два чемода́на и оди́н саквоя́ж.
17. Нет, не успе́ли.
18. Потому́ что он ещё ничего́ не ел.
19. Да, люблю́. (Не люблю́).
20. Я уже́ лета́л. (Я ещё не лета́л ни ра́зу).

ANSWERS TO THE QUESTIONS OF LESSON 29 ON PAGE 184

1. Нет, Пано́в на аэродро́ме не за́втракал.
2. Потому́ что не́ было вре́мени.
3. Нет, и на самолёте ему́ не удало́сь поза́втракать.
4. Он удивля́ется, что на самолёте не ко́рмят "голода́ющих".
5. Терпи́, каза́к, атама́ном бу́дешь.
6. Он спра́шивает, где Воробьёвы го́ры.
7. Потому́ что с Воробьёвых гор Наполео́н впервы́е уви́дел Москву́.
8. Эх, краси́ва Москва́.
9. Наро́д говори́т, что в Москве́ "со́рок сороко́в" церкве́й.
10. Они́ е́дут в го́род.
11. Они́ остана́вливаются в гости́нице.
12. Он у них спра́шивает па́спорты.
13. Что и Короле́нко до́лжен был дать свой па́спорт.
14. По его́ слова́м челове́к состои́т из души́, те́ла и па́спорта.

ANSWERS TO THE QUESTIONS OF LESSON 30 ON PAGE 191

1. Они́ начина́ют с Кремля́.
2. На Москворе́цкий мост.
3. Для того́, что́бы посмотре́ть на Кре́мль.
4. Потому́ что в Кремль их бы не пусти́ли.
5. Они́ ви́дят все гла́вные зда́ния Кремля́.
6. Кака́я красота́!
7. Большо́й кремлёвский дворе́ц.
8. Тепе́рь в нём живёт Ио́сиф Виссарио́нович Ста́лин.
9. Ра́ньше в нём жи́ли цари́.
10. Ива́н Вели́кий.
11. У его́ подно́жия стои́т Царь-ко́локол.
12. В одно́м пу́де со́рок фу́нтов.
13. Нет, в Сове́тском Сою́зе счита́ют на килогра́ммы и це́нтнеры.
14. Да, в Кремле́ есть це́ркви.
15. Нет, в них тепе́рь не слу́жат.
16. Нет, в Кремль наро́д не пуска́ют.

ANSWERS TO THE QUESTIONS OF LESSON 31 ON PAGE 198

1. Кра́сная пло́щадь в це́нтре Москвы́.
2. Потому́ что она́ краси́ва.
3. С Кра́сной пло́щади ви́ден Кремль.
4. Васи́лий Блаже́нный.
5. Потому́ что там века́ми создава́лась его́ исто́рия.
6. Иоа́нном Гро́зным.
7. Он постро́ил храм Васи́лия Блаже́нного.
8. Он хо́чет купи́ть па́ру боти́нок.
9. Его́ чемода́н пропа́л.
10. Они́ иду́т в универма́г.
11. Он хо́чет купи́ть чёрные боти́нки.
12. Пано́в не зна́ет, како́й но́мер его́ боти́нок.
13. Нет, башмаки́ ему́ не понра́вились.
14. Потому́ что они́ жёсткие.
15. Мне нра́вится мя́гкая ко́жа.
16. Боти́нки обошли́сь ему́ до́рого.
17. Он говори́т, что за э́ти де́ньги в Аме́рике он мог бы купи́ть не́сколько пар таки́х боти́нок.

ANSWERS TO THE QUESTIONS OF LESSON 32 ON PAGE 210

1. Его́ фами́лия — Петро́в.
2. Он живёт на пя́том этаже́.
3. У него́ нет кварти́ры.
4. У него́ то́лько одна́ ко́мната.
5. Четы́ре други́х семе́йств.
6. Он сказа́л, что э́та кварти́ра напомина́ет ему́ Но́ев ковче́г.
7. Он позвони́л снача́ла четы́ре ра́за, а пото́м пять раз.
8. По́сле четырёх звонко́в никто́ ему́ две́ри не откры́л. По́сле пяти́ звонко́в ему́ откры́л Петро́в.
9. Петро́в сказа́л: добро́ пожа́ловать.
10. Здра́вствуйте! Как вас зову́т?
11. Их зову́т Ма́ня и Шу́ра.
12. Он сказа́л, что она́ звезда́ бале́та.
13. Она́ танцу́ет в Большо́м теа́тре.
14. Борщ, отварна́я говя́дина и кисе́ль.
15. Они́ пьют во́дку.
16. Да, я пью во́дку. (Нет, я во́дки не пью).
17. Они́ интересу́ются мо́дами.
18. Ва́рю интересу́ют ба́льные пла́тья.
19. Да, в Нью-Йо́рке есть не́сколько ру́сских рестора́нов.
20. Потому́ что он ду́мает, что она́ име́ла бы в Нью-Йо́рке успе́х, а та́кже потому́ что она́ ему́ нра́вится.
21. Потому́ что она́ балери́на Большо́го теа́тра.
22. Нет, она́ не се́рдится. Она́ то́лько де́лает вид, что се́рдится.
23. Она́ говори́т ему́, что он несно́сный.
24. Потому́ что борщ сты́нет.
25. Борщ ему́ о́чень понра́вился.
26. Он про́сит ещё.
27. Зна́ю. Это что́-то вро́де америка́нского jello.
28. Да, дово́льно далеко́.

29. Потому́ что они́ боя́тся опозда́ть.
30. Она́ бои́тся, что́бы они́ не опозда́ли.
31. Спаси́бо за всё.
32. Ты, Ва́ся, пойдёшь с Варва́рой Анто́новной, а мы с Гри́шей бу́дем идти́ позади́.

ANSWERS TO THE QUESTIONS OF LESSON 33 ON PAGE 219

1. Они́ ви́дели бале́т "Лебеди́ное о́зеро".
2. Да, теа́тр ему́ о́чень понра́вился.
3. Бо́льше чем сто лет тому́ наза́д.
4. Она́ сказа́ла, что револю́ция переменила мно́гое, но иску́сства она́ не перемени́ла.
5. Балери́на Ула́нова.
6. Нет, я её не зна́ю. (Да, я её зна́ю).
7. Нет, не слыха́л. (Да, слыха́л).
8. Потому́ что он прие́хал из Аме́рики.
9. Генера́л Ма́ршалл смотре́л бале́т "Щелку́нчики".
10. Ему́ понра́вилась балери́на Плисе́цкая.
11. Он посла́л ей корзи́ну с цвета́ми.
12. Да, я хожу́ ча́сто в теа́тр. (Нет, я хожу́ ре́дко).
13. Да, есть. (Нет, в на́шем го́роде бале́та нет).
14. Да, в Большо́м теа́тре всегда́ мно́го офице́ров.
15. Они́ сидя́т в пе́рвых ряда́х.
16. Он прие́хал в Москву́ по дела́м.
17. Да, ему́ бале́т о́чень понра́вился.
18. Он сказа́л, что ра́ди одного́ э́того бале́та сто́ило прие́хать в Москву́.
19. А бо́льше вам не́чего де́лать в Москве́?
20. Пано́в отве́тил, что он прие́хал бы в Москву́ ра́ди неё.

GLOSSARY

NOTE ON ABBREVIATIONS: acc.—accusative, adj.—adjective, adv.—adverb, dat.—dative, f.—feminine, gen.—genitive, i.—imperfective, instr.—instrumental, intr.—intransitive, m.—masculine, n.—neuter, p.—perfective, plur.—plural, prep.—prepositional, tr.—transitive.

The gender of nouns is given only in cases where it differs from the following rule: nouns ending in a hard consonant, i.e. a consonant not followed by **-ь**, are masculine; nouns ending in **-а, -я** or **-ь** are feminine; those ending in **-о** or **-е** are neuter.

А

А and, but
абрико́с apricot
а́вгуст August
автомоби́ль *m.* automobile
а́збука alphabet
Азия Asia
алфави́т alphabet
Аме́рика America
америка́нец *m.* American
америка́нка *f.* American
америка́нский *adj.* American
англи́йский English
англича́нин Englishman
англича́нка Englishwoman
Англия England
антра́кт intermission
антрепренёр theatrical producer
апельси́н orange
апре́ль *m.* April
апте́ка pharmacy
армяни́н Armenian
Африка Africa
аэродро́м airdrome
аэропла́н airplane

Б

Ба́ба (peasant) woman
ба́бочка butterfly
ба́бушка grandmother
база́р market
бал ball, dance
бале́т ballet

Балти́йское мо́ре Baltic Sea
ба́льный ball- *adj.*
банк bank
бара́ний mutton- *adj.*
ба́рышня young lady
башма́к shoe
ба́шня tower
бе́гать *i.* to run
бе́дный poor
бежа́ть *i.* to flee
без *gen.* without
бесполе́зный useless
безразли́чный indifferent
бе́лый white
бе́рег shore, bank
береги́сь! watch out!
берёза birchtree
бере́чься *i.* to be careful
библиоте́ка library
биле́т ticket
бито́к cutlet
бифште́кс beefsteak
блаже́нный blissful
бланк form, blank
блесте́ть *i.* } to shine
блесну́ть *p.* }
блестя́щий shiny
бли́зкий near
бли́зость nearness
блю́дечко saucer
блю́до platter
бога́тый rich
бога́ч wealthy man
бо́лее more
боле́ть *i.* to ail; ache
больни́ца hospital
больно́й sick, ailing
бо́льше more
большинство́ majority
большо́й large, big
борода́ beard
боти́нок shoe
борщ borshch
боя́ться *i.* to fear, be afraid
брат brother
брать *i.* to take
бри́ться *i.* to shave (oneself)
броса́ть *i.* } to throw
бро́сить *p.* }
брю́ки trousers
бу́блик bublik, doughnut
буди́льник alarm clock
буди́ть *i.* to wake up *tr.*
бу́дущий future
бу́ква letter (of the alphabet)
бума́га paper
бума́жный paper- *adj.*
бу́ря storm
буты́лка bottle
быва́ть *i.* to be, to visit, to exist
бы́вший former
бык bull
бы́стрый swift, quick
быть to be

В

в in
ваго́н railroad car
ва́нна tub
ва́нная bathroom
вас you *acc.*
ваш your
вдоль *gen.* along
взве́шивать *i.* } to weigh
взве́сить *p.* }
вздыха́ть *i.* } to sigh
вздохну́ть *p.* }
взять *p.* to take
ведь surely, you know
везде́ everywhere
везти́ *i.* to carry (in a vehicle)
век century, life time
вели́кий great
великоле́пный magnificent
вели́чественный majestic
Вене́ра Venus
ве́рить *i.* to believe

вернýть *p.* to return *tr.*, to call back
верóятно probably
вéрхний upper
вес weight
весёлый gay
весéнний spring- *adj.*
веснá spring
вести́ *i.* to lead, to conduct
весь all, entire
вéтер wind
ветчинá ham
вéчер evening
вéшалка rack
вéшать *i.* to hang *tr.*
вещь thing, object
вид *m.* view
ви́деть *i.* to see
ви́дный noticeable; prominent
ви́лка fork
винó wine
виногрáд grapes
висéть *i.* to hang *intr.*
витри́на show-window
ви́шня sour cherry
включáть *i.* to include
вкус *m.* taste
вкýсный tasty
владéлец owner
вмéсте together
вмéсто instead
вниз down, downwards
внизý beneath, down (stairs)
внутри́ *gen.* inside
внутрь *acc.* inside, inwards
водá water
води́ть *i.* to lead
вóдка vodka, whisky
воéнный military
вóздух air
вози́ть *i.* to carry (in a vehicle)
вóзле *gen.* near, at
возмóжно it is possible
возмóжность possibility
войнá war
вокзáл railroad station
вол ox
волк wolf
вóлос hair
вóля will; freedom
вон over-there
вообщé in general
воробéй sparrow
ворóта *pl.* gate
восемнáдцать eighteen
вóсемь eight
вóсемьдесят eighty
восемьсóт eight hundred
воскресéнье Sunday
востóк east
восхити́тельный entrancing, charming
восьмóй eighth
вот here
впервы́е for the first time
вперёд forwards
вполнé completely
впусти́ть *p.* to let in
врéдный harmful
врéмя *n.* time
врóде sort of
вряд ли hardly, it's doubtful
всегó in all
всё everything
всё же nevertheless
вспоминáть *i.* } to remember
вспóмнить *p.* }
вставáть *i.* } to get up
встать *p.* }
встарь in olden times
встречáть to meet
всходи́ть *i.* } to rise (sun)
взойти́ *p.* }
вся́кий every
втóрник Tuesday
вторóй second
вчерá yesterday
вход entrance
входи́ть *i.* } to enter
войти́ *p.* }

вы you
высо́кий high
выбира́ть *i.* to choose
выступа́ть *i.* to step forward
вы́сший highest
вы́учить *p.* to learn, to master
вы́ход exit
выходи́ть *i.* } to go out
вы́йти *p.* }

Г

Газ gas
газе́та newspaper
га́лстук tie
гастро́ль star performance
где where
генера́л general
Герма́ния Germany
глава́ chapter
гла́вный main, chief *adj.*
глаз eye
гла́сная vowel
глу́пый stupid
глухо́й deaf
гляде́ть *i.* to look
говори́ть *i.* to speak
говя́дина beef
год year
годи́ться *i.* to suit, to fit
голова́ head
голода́ть *i.* to be hungry, to starve
голо́дный hungry
го́лос voice
голубо́й (light) blue
го́лубь *m.* pigeon
гора́ mountain
гора́здо much, by far
горди́ться *i.* to be proud
го́рдый proud
горе́ть *i.* to burn
го́род town, city
горо́х pea(s)
го́рький bitter
горя́чий hot
господи́н gentleman, Mr.
госпожа́ lady, Mrs.
гости́ная living room
гости́ница hotel
гость *m.*, **го́стья** *f.* guest
госуда́рство state, country
гото́вый ready
граждани́н *m.*, **гражда́нка** *f.* citizen
грани́ца frontier
гриб mushroom
гроза́ (thunder) storm
гро́зный awe-inspiring, menacing
гром thunder
грудь chest; breast
грузи́н Georgian
гру́ша pear
гуля́ть *i.* to stroll, to go for a walk
гусь *m.* goose

Д

Да yes
дава́ть *i.* } to give
дать *p.* }
давно́ *p.* long ago
далёкий far
да́льше farther
да́ма lady
дари́ть *i.* to present
да́ром gratis
два two
два́дцать twenty
двена́дцать twelve
дверь door
две́сти 200
дви́гать *i.* to move
двор yard, court
дворе́ц palace
деви́ца girl, maiden
де́вочка little girl
де́вушка girl, maid
девятна́дцать nineteen
девя́тый ninth

де́вять nine
девятьсо́т 900
де́душка grandfather
де́йствовать *i.* to act
дека́брь *m.* December
де́лать *i.* to do
день *m.* day
де́ньги *plur.* money
дере́вня village
де́рево tree
держа́ть *i.* to hold
деся́ток ten (*collective*)
деся́тый tenth
де́сять ten
де́ти children
дешёвый cheap
дива́н sofa
дире́ктор director, manager
ди́кий wild
дитя́ *n.* child
дли́нный long
для *gen.* for
до *gen.* to, up to
до́брый good, kind
дово́льный satisfied
дово́льно enough
дождь *m.* rain
долг debt; duty
до́лгий long
до́лжен must
дом house
до́ма at home
домо́й home, homewards
доро́га road
дорого́й dear
доса́да disappointment
доса́дный disappointing
доска́ board, blackboard
достава́ть *i.* } to fetch, bring,
доста́ть *p.* } get, procure
дре́вний ancient
друг friend
друг дру́га one another
друго́й another
дуб oak
ду́мать *i.* to think
дух spirit
ду́шный stuffy, hot
душа́ soul
дыша́ть *i.* to breath
дю́жина dozen
дя́дя *m.* uncle

Е

Евро́па Europe
европе́йский European
его́ him *acc.*
еда́ food
едва́ scarcely
её her *acc.*
ежедне́вный daily
е́здить *i.* to go repeatedly (not on foot)
е́ле hardly
ёлка Christmas tree
ель fir tree
е́сли if
есть is
есть *i.* to eat
е́хать *i.* to drive, to go in a vehicle
ещё still; yet; more

Ж

Жаль it is a pity
жале́ть *i.* to pity
жара́ heat
жа́рить *i.* to fry
жа́ркий hot
ждать *i.* to wait
же but, and, then
жела́ть *i.* to wish, desire
желе́зный iron *adj.*
желе́зная доро́га railroad
желе́зо iron
жёлтый yellow
жена́ wife

женить *i.* and *p.* to marry (a man to a woman)
же́нщина woman
жест gesture
жёсткий stiff, tough
живо́й alive
живо́тное animal
жизнь life
жиле́т vest
жиле́ц tenant
жи́тель *m.* inhabitant
жить *i.* to live
журна́л magazine

З

За behind, beyond
забыва́ть *i.* / **забы́ть** *p.* } to forget
заво́д factory
заводи́ть *i.* / **завести́** *p.* } to wind
за́втра tomorrow
за́втрак breakfast
за́втракать *i.* to have breakfast
загоре́ться *p.* to start burning to catch fire
за-грани́цей (to live) abroad
за-грани́цу abroad (to go)
задава́ть вопро́с *i.* / **зада́ть вопро́с** *p.* } to ask a question
заде́рживать *i.* / **задержа́ть** *p.* } to hold back
заезжа́ть *i.* / **зае́хать** *p.* } to call on the way, to drop in
зажига́ть *i.* / **зажéчь** *p.* } *i.* to light
зака́зывать *i.* / **заказа́ть** *p.* } to order
заключа́ть *i.* / **заключи́ть** *p.* } to conclude
закрыва́ть *i.* / **закры́ть** *p.* } to close, to shut
заку́ривать *i.* / **закури́ть** *p.* } to light a cigarette, cigar, pipe
зал, за́ла hall, salon
замеча́тельный remarkable
за́муж (выходи́ть) *i.* / **за́муж (вы́йти)** *p.* } to marry (appl. only to women)
за́мужем married (woman)
за́навес curtain
занести́ *p.* / **заноси́ть** *i.* } to write down
записа́ть *p.* / **запи́сывать** *i.* } to make a note
запи́ска note
занято́й busy
за́пад west
за́падный western
за́пах smell, odor
запира́ть *i.* / **запере́ть** *p.* } to lock
запомина́ть *i.* / **запо́мнить** *p.* } to remember
за́работок earnings
заси́живаться *i.* / **засиде́ться** *p.* } to stay too long
заставля́ть *i.* / **заста́вить** *p.* } to induce, compel
засыпа́ть *i.* / **засну́ть** *p.* } to fall asleep
зате́м then; for the purpose of
заходи́ть *i.* / **зайти́** *p.* } to set (sun); to call on the way, drop in
звать *i.* to call *tr.*
звезда́ star
зверь *m.* wild animal
звони́ть *i.* to ring
звоно́к bell
звук sound
зда́ние building
здесь here
здоро́ваться *i.* to greet
здоро́вый healthy
здра́вствуйте! Good health! (How do you do?)
зелёный green
земля́ earth, soil
земляни́ка (wild) strawberry

зима́ winter
зи́мний winter *adj.*
зли́ться *i.* to be angry
злой angry, vicious
змея́ snake
знак sign
знако́мый acquaintance
знако́мить *i.* to introduce
знако́миться *i.* to become acquainted
зна́мя *n.* banner
знать *i.* to know
зна́чить *i.* to mean
зо́лото gold
золото́й golden
зо́лушка Cinderella
зо́нтик umbrella
зре́ние eyesight
зуб tooth

И

И and
и́бо because
игра́ть *i.* to play
иде́я idea
идти́ *i.* to go
из *gen.* from
изба́ peasant hut
извести́ть *p.* } to let know
извеща́ть *i.* }
изве́стный well known, famous
извини́ть *p.* } to excuse
извиня́ть *i.* }
извини́ться *p.* } to apologize
извиня́ться *i.* }
из-за *gen.* from behind; because of
изображе́ние picture, image
из-под *gen.* from under
и́ли or
и́менно namely
име́ть to have
и́мя *n.* name, first name
ина́че otherwise, else
иногда́ sometimes
ино́й other
иностра́нец *m.* } foreigner
иностра́нка *f.* }
интересова́ть *i.* to interest
интересова́ться *i.* to be interested
иска́ть *i.* to seek, look for
иску́сство art
испо́лнить *p.* } to fulfil, execute
исполня́ть *i.* }
испуга́ть *p.* to frighten
исто́рия history
Ита́лия Italy
италья́нец *m.* Italian
италья́нка *f.* Italian woman
италья́нский Italian *adj.*
их them (*acc.*)
ию́ль *m.* July
ию́нь *m.* June

К

К, ко *dat.* to, towards
Кавка́з Caucasus
кавка́зский Caucasian
ка́ждый every
каза́к Cossack
каза́рма barracks
каза́ться *i.* to seem
ка́жется it seems
как how
как-нибу́дь somehow
како́й what kind of, what
како́й-то some, a certain
как раз just, exactly
календа́рь *m.* calendar
кана́л canal
капу́ста cabbage
карма́н pocket
ка́рта card; map
карти́на picture
ка́сса cashier's office
касси́р cashier
ката́ться *i.* to drive, to go on horseback, to skate etc. (for pleasure)
ка́ша porridge

ка́яться *i.* to repent
кварти́ра apartment
квас drink made of bread or fruits
квита́нция receipt
кинемато́граф, кино́ cinema
кирпи́ч brick
кисе́ль *m.* jello
ки́слый sour
кита́ец *m.* Chinese (man)
Кита́й China
кита́йский *adj.* Chinese
китая́нка Chinese woman
класс class, -room
кла́ссный class- *adj.*
класть *i.* to put
кли́мат climate
ключ key
кни́га book
ковче́г ark
когда́ when
ко́е-как somehow
коли́ when
кольцо́ *n.* ring
кома́р mosquito
ко́мик comedian
ко́мната room
компа́ния company
коне́ц end
коне́чно of course
конто́ра office
конфе́ты sweets, candy
конча́ть *i.* } to finish
ко́нчить *p.* } to finish
конь *m.* horse
коньки́ *pl.* skates
копе́йка kopeck
корзи́на basket
коридо́р corridor
кори́чневый brown
корми́ть *i.* to feed
коро́ва cow
коро́ткий short
костю́м suit
кото́рый who
ко́фе *m.* coffee
кошелёк purse
ко́шка cat
краса́вица beauty, belle
краси́вый beautiful
красота́ beauty
кремлёвский Kremlin- *adj.*
Кремль *m.* the Kremlin
кре́сло armchair
крича́ть *i.* } to shout
кри́кнуть *p.* } to shout
кровь blood
кро́ме *gen.* except
кру́глый round
кру́пный large; coarse
крыло́ wing
Крым Crimea
кры́ша roof
кста́ти by the way
кто who?
кто́-либо somebody, anybody
кто-нибу́дь anybody, somebody
кто́-то somebody
куда́-нибу́дь anywhere, somewhere
куда́-то (to) somewhere
кузи́на cousin *f.*
купа́ться *i.* to bathe
купе́ц merchant
купи́ть *p.* to buy
ку́пол cupola
кури́ть *i.* to smoke
ку́рица hen
куса́ть *i.* to bite
кусо́к piece
ку́хня kitchen
ку́шать *i.* to eat

Л

Ла́вка shop, store
ла́мпа lamp
ла́ндыш lily-of-the-valley
ла́па paw
ле́бедь *m.* swan
лебеди́ный swan- *adj.*
лев lion

ле́вый left
лёгкий light (weight); easy
лежа́ть *i.* to lie
лени́вый lazy
лес forest, woods
ле́стница stairway
лета́ть, лете́ть *i.* to fly
ле́то summer
ле́тний summer- *adj.*
ли *interr. particle*
лимо́н lemon
лимона́д lemonade
лине́йка ruler
лист, *pl.* **ли́стья** leaf;
лист, *pl.* **листы́** sheets (paper)
лицо́ face; person
ли́чный personal
ли́шний superfluous, spare-
лифт elevator
лови́ть *i.* to catch
ло́дка boat
ложи́ться *i.* / **лечь** *p.* } to lie down
ло́жка spoon
ложь *f.* lie, untruth
лома́ть *i.* to break
ло́шадь *f.* horse
луг meadow
лук onion
луна́ moon
лу́чше better
лы́жа ski
льстец flatterer, adulator
льстить *i.* to flatter
любе́зный kind, friendly
люби́ть *i.* to love
любо́й any
любо́вь love
лю́ди people
лягу́шка frog

М

Магази́н shop, store
май May
ма́ленький little, small
мали́на raspberry (-ies)
ма́ло *adv.* little
ма́льчик little boy
ма́ма mother
маргари́тка dairy
март March
ма́сло butter
мать mother
Ма́ша Mary
маши́на machine, car
ме́бель furniture
мёд honey
медве́дь *m.* bear
меда́ль medal
ме́жду *instr., gen.* between
мел chalk
мелька́ть *i.* flash by
ме́нее less
ме́ньше less
ме́рка measure
мёртвый dead
ме́сто place, spot
ме́сяц month
метро́ subway
мех fur
мехово́й fur- *adj.*
мечта́ть *i.* to day-dream
ми́лый kind, dear
ми́мо *gen.* past, by
мину́та minute
мир peace; world
мла́дший younger, youngest
мне́ние opinion
мо́да fashion, mode
мо́дный fashionable
мо́жет быть maybe, perhaps
мо́жно it is possible, allowed
мозг brain
мой, моя́, моё my
мо́крый wet
молоде́ц lad, splendid fellow
молодо́й young
молоко́ milk
молча́ть *i.* to be silent

монасты́рь *m.* monastery, convent
мо́ре sea
морко́вка carrot(s)
моро́з frost
морско́й sea *adj.*
Москва́ Moscow
моско́вский Moscow *adj.*
мост bridge
мочь *i.* to be able
муж husband
мужи́к peasant; boor
мужчи́на *m.* man, male
музе́й museum
му́зыка music
му́ха fly
мы we
мы́ло soap
мы́слить *i.* to think
мысль thought
мы́ть to wash
мы́шка armpit
мышь mouse
мя́гкий soft
мясно́й meat *adj.*
мя́со meat

Н

На on, upon
наве́рно surely, certainly
наве́рх upstairs (to go)
наверху́ upstairs (to be)
наводи́ть *i.* / **навести́** *p.* **спра́вку** } to inquire
над *instr.* above
надева́ть *i.* / **наде́ть** *p.* } to put on
наде́жда *f.* hope
наде́яться *i.* to hope
на днях lately; one of these days
на́до it is necessary
наза́д back (wards)
назва́ть *p.* / **называ́ть** *i.* } to call
называ́ться *i.* to be called
наизу́сть by heart
найти́ *p.* / **находи́ть** *i.* } to find
наконе́ц at last
накрыва́ть *i.* / **накры́ть** *p.* } to cover
нале́во to the left
налива́ть *i.* / **нали́ть** *p.* } to pour
нам us *dat.*
напи́ток beverage
напомина́ть *i.* / **напо́мнить** *p.* } to remind
напра́во to the right
напра́сно in vain
наприме́р for instance
напро́тив *gen.* opposite; on the contrary
наро́д people; nation
наро́чно on purpose
нас us *acc.*
насеко́мое insect
находи́ться *i.* to be found, to be
нача́ло beginning
нача́ть *p.* / **начина́ть** *i.* } to begin
наш, -а, -е our
национализи́ровать *i.* & *p.* to nationalize
не not
не́бо sky, heaven
невозмо́жно impossible *adv.*
недалеко́ not far
неде́ля week
недово́льный dissatisfied
недорого́й unexpensive
не́жели than
незва́ный uninvited
некраси́вый ugly
не́который some
нельзя́ impossible; not allowed
не́мец German (man)
неме́цкий German *adj.*
не́мка German (woman)
немно́го a little

немудрено́ no wonder
ненави́деть *i.* to hate
необходи́мый necessary
непоправи́мый irreparable
непреме́нно without fail
неприя́тность annoyance, trouble
неприя́тный unpleasant
не́сколько several, a few
несмотря́ на in spite of
несно́сный unbearable
нести́ *i.* to carry
несча́стный unhappy, unlucky
нет no
неуже́ли is it possible? really?
не́чего nothing; no use . . .
не́что something
ни not even
ни . . . ни neither . . . nor
нигде́ nowhere
ни́зкий low
ника́к by no means
никогда́ never
никто́ nobody
ничего́ nothing
ниче́й, -ья́, -ьё nobody's
ничто́ nothing
но but
но́вый new
нога́ leg, foot
нож knife
но́жницы scissors
но́мер number; size
но́рка mink
но́рковый mink *adj.*
нос nose
носи́льщик porter
носи́ть *i.* to carry, to wear
ночь night
ночно́й night-
ноя́брь *m.* November
нра́виться *i.* to please,
мне нра́вится I like
ну well, now, indeed?
ну́жный necessary
ну́жно it is necessary
ню́хать *i.* to smell *tr.*
ня́ня nurse

О

О, об, о́бо *prep.*: about, concerning; *acc.*: against
о́ба *m.*, **о́бе** *f.* both
обе́д noon-time meal, dinner
обе́дать *i.* to have dinner
обезья́на monkey, ape
обеща́ть *i.* to promise
о́блако cloud
образова́ть *i.* to form
обра́тно back(wards)
о́бувь footwear; shoes
о́бщий common
объясни́ть *p.* } to explain
объясня́ть *i.* } to explain
обыкнове́нный usual
о́вощи vegetables
овца́ sheep
ого́нь *m.* fire
одева́ть *i.* } to clothe
оде́ть *p.* } to clothe
одева́ться, оде́ться to dress (oneself)
оде́жда clothes
оди́и, одна́, одно́ *pl.* **одни́** alone
оди́н, *pl.* **одни́** alone
оди́ннадцать eleven
одолева́ть *i.* } to overcome, to conquer
одоле́ть *p.* } to overcome, to conquer
ожида́ть *i.* to wait, to expect
о́зеро lake
о́ко, *pl.* **о́чи** eye
окно́ window
о́коло *gen.* near, at
октя́брь *m.* October
он, она́, оно́ he, she, it
опа́здывать *i.* } to be late
опозда́ть *p.* } to be late
опа́сный dangerous
о́пера opera
опя́ть again

орёл eagle
ору́дие tool; artillery piece
ору́жие weapon; arms
освеща́ть *i.* to light
осёл ass, donkey
осе́нний autumn *adj.*
о́сень autumn
осмо́тр inspection, survey
осмотре́ть *p.* / **осма́тривать** *i.* } to inspect
осо́бенный particular
осо́бенность particularity
остава́ться *i.* / **оста́ться** *p.* } to remain, stay
оставля́ть *i.* / **оста́вить** *p.* } to leave *tr.*
остана́вливаться *i.* / **останови́ться** *p.* } to stop (*intr.*)
о́стров island
о́стрый sharp; spicy
от (*gen.*) from
отбира́ть *i.* / **отобра́ть** *p.* } to take away
отварно́й cooked, boiled
отве́т answer
отвеча́ть *i.* / **отве́тить** *p.* } to answer
о́тдых rest
отдыха́ть *i.* / **отдохну́ть** *p.* } to rest
оте́ц father
оте́чество fatherland
отка́зываться *i.* / **отказа́ться** *p.* } to renounce, to refuse
открыва́ть *i.* / **откры́ть** *p.* } to open
откры́тка post-card
отку́да where from
отлета́ть *i.* / **отлете́ть** *p.* } to fly away
отпира́ть *i.* / **отпере́ть** *p.* } to unlock,
отстава́ть *i.* / **отста́ть** *p.* } to fall, lag behind
отсю́да from here
оттого́ что because
отту́да from there
отправля́ться *i.* / **отпра́виться** *p.* } to depart
о́тпуск leave, vacation
отсу́тствовать *i.* to be absent
отчего́ why
о́тчество patronymic (middle name)
офице́р officer
официа́нт waiter
охо́та hunting
о́чень very
о́чередь turn; line, queue
о́чи see **о́ко**
очки́ eyeglasses
ощуще́ние feeling; sensation

П

Па́дать *i.* / **пасть** *p.* } to fall
пала́та palace
па́лец finger
па́лка stick
пальто́ overcoat
па́мятник monument
па́мять memory
папиро́са cigarette
па́ра pair
Пари́ж Paris
па́смурный murky, gloomy (weather)
па́спорт passport
пассажи́р passenger
пау́к spider
па́хнуть *i.* to smell *intr.*
пе́рвый first
пе́ред *instr., acc.* before, in front of
переменя́ть *i.* / **перемени́ть** *p.* } to change
перестава́ть *i.* / **переста́ть** *p.* } to cease, to stop *intr.*
перо́ feather

пéрсик peach
перчáтка glove
петýх rooster
пи́во beer
пиджáк jacket, coat
писáть *i.* to write
пить *i.* to drink
плáвать *i.* to swim
плáкать *i.* to cry, weep
план plan
плати́ть *i.* to pay
платóк handkerchief; shawl
племя́нник nephew
плохóй bad
плóщадь square, plaza
пляж beach
по *dat.* according to, along *acc.* up to; *prep.* on, after
побережье sea shore
повернýть *p.* / **повóрачивать** *i.* } to turn
пóвод reason, ground
повидáть *p.* to visit, to see
повóзка carriage
погóда weather
погóн epaulet
погуля́ть *p.* to go for a walk
под *instr., acc.* under
подавáть *i.* / **подáть** *p.* } to give; to serve
поднимáть *i.* / **подня́ть** *p.* } to raise, lift
поднóжие, у поднóжия at the foot of
поднóс tray
подéлать *p.,* **ничегó не подéлаешь** there is nothing to be done
подойти́ *p.* / **подходи́ть** *i.* } to approach; to suit
поéздить *p.* to drive around
поéхать *p.* to go (not on foot)
пожáловать *p.,* **добрó пожáловать!** Welcome!
пожáлуйста please
пожáр fire
поживáть *i.* to live, get on

позади́ *gen.* behind
позвáть *p.* to call
позвони́ть *p.* to ring
пóздно late
пóзже later
познакóмиться *p.* to meet, get acquainted
покá meanwhile
показáть *p.* / **покáзывать** *i.* } to show
покоря́ть *i.* / **покори́ть** *p.* } to conquer
покрывáть *i.* / **покры́ть** *p.* } to cover
пол floor
пол half
полагáть *i.* to think, suppose
пóлдень *m.* noon
ползти́ *i.* to creep
полéзный useful
поливáть *i.* to water
пóлный full
пóлно (-те) enough, that's enough; don't talk any more
пóлночь midnight
полови́на half
получáть *i.* / **получи́ть** *p.* } to receive
пóлюс pole
помидóр tomato
помогáть *i.* / **помóчь** *p.* } to help
пóмнить *i.* to remember
понимáть *i.* / **поня́ть** *p.* } to understand, to grasp
понрáвиться *p.* to please
пообéдать *p.* to have dinner
попадáть *i.* / **попáсть** *p.* } to hit (target)
потрéбовать *p.* to ask, demand
порá it is time
порази́тельно striking
поря́док order
посели́ться *p.* to settle
посидéть *p.* to sit for a while

посла́ть *p.*, **посыла́ть** *i.* to send
по́сле *gen.* after
послеза́втра after tomorrow
после́дний last
посло́вица proverb
послу́шать *p.* to listen
посмотре́ть *p.* to look
посо́л ambassador
постро́ить *p.* to build
потеря́ть *p.* to lose
потоло́к ceiling
пото́м then
почему́ why
пра́вда truth
пра́вильный correct, accurate
прави́тельство government
пра́во *adv.* really, truly
пра́вый right *adj.*
пра́здник holiday
превку́сный very tasty
превосходи́ть *i.* to surpass
предложе́ние sentence
предпочита́ть *i.*, **предпоче́сть** *p.* to prefer
представле́ние performance
пре́жний former
прекра́сный beautiful, excellent
прекра́сно *adv.* very well
прерыва́ть *i.*, **прерва́ть** *p.* to interrupt
при *prep.* by, at, near
приближа́ться *i.*, **прибли́зиться** *p.* to approach
привезти́ *p.*, **привози́ть** *i.* to bring (not on foot)
привыка́ть *i.*, **привы́кнуть** *p.* to get used
пригласи́ть *p.*, **приглаша́ть** *i.* to invite
пригото́вить *p.*, **приготовля́ть** *i.* to prepare
приземи́ться *p.*, **приземля́ться** *i.* to land (airplane)
прие́зд arrival
приезжа́ть *i.*, **прие́хать** *p.* to arrive
прийти́ *p.*, **приходи́ть** *i.* to come
приказа́ть *p.*, **прика́зывать** *i.* to order, command
прики́нуть *p.*, **прики́дывать** *i.* to reckon
принадлежа́ть *i.* to belong
присла́ть *p.*, **присыла́ть** *i.* to send (here)
прису́тствовать *i.* to be present
прихо́дится (мне, нам, вам etc.**)** (I, we, you etc.) have to . . .
приходи́ть *i.* to come
причеса́ться *p.*, **причёсываться** *i.* to comb (oneself)
прия́тель *m.* friend
про *acc.* about, concerning
проводни́к guide
продолжа́ть *i.*, **продо́лжить** *p.* to continue
прожива́ть *i.*, **прожи́ть** *p.* to live, reside
проезжа́ть *i.*, **прое́хать** *p.* to pass (not on foot)
произноси́ть *i.*, **произнести́** *p.* to pronounce
произноше́ние pronunciation
промока́ть *i.*, **промо́кнуть** *p.* to get wet
пропада́ть *i.*, **пропа́сть** *p.* to get lost
проси́ть *i.* to ask
просто́й simple
простужа́ться *i.*, **простуди́ться** *p.* to catch cold
про́шлый former
пры́гать *i.*, **пры́гнуть** *p.* to jump
прямо́й straight
публи́чный public *adj.*
пуд pud (40 pounds)
пуска́ть *i.*, **пусти́ть** *p.* to let

путешéствие trip, voyage
путь *m.* way, road, journey
пчелá bee
пшени́ца wheat
пятнáдцать fifteen
пя́тница Friday
пятóк five (coll.)
пя́тый fifth
пять five
пятьдеся́т fifty
пятьсóт five hundred

Р

Рабóта work
рабóтать *i.* to work
рад glad
рáди *gen.* for the sake of
радиáтор radiator
рáдоваться *i.* to be glad
раз once, one time; . . . . times
разбуди́ть *p.* waken
размéр measure, size
разрывáть *i.* to tear (asunder)
рако early *adj.*
расскáзывать *i.* } to relate;
рассказáть *p.* } narrate
рвать *i.* to tear
ребёнок child
револю́ция revolution
реди́ска radish(es)
рéдко seldom
рéзать *i.* to cut
ресторáн restaurant
рисýнок drawing
рóвно exactly
род sort, kind
рóдина homeland, fatherland
роди́тели parents
рóдственник relative
Росси́я Russia
рот mouth
рубáшка shirt
руби́ть *i.* to chop, cut, hack
рýбленый chopped
рубль *m.* ruble
рукá hand; arm
рýсский Russian (*adj.* and noun)
Русь Russia
ры́ба fish
рю́мка wine glass
ряд row, string, line
ря́дом side by side

С

С, со *gen.* from, off,
acc. about, approximately,
instr. with
сад garden, orchard
сади́ться *i.* to sit down
саквоя́ж handbag
салáт lettuce; salad
салфéтка napkin
сам, самá, самó self
самолёт airplane
сáмый same
сáни *plur.* sleigh
сáхар sugar
сáхарница sugar bowl
свáдьба wedding
свёкла beet(s)
свет light; world
свети́ть *i.* to shine
свéтлый light, bright
свидáние meeting, rendezvous
свини́на pork
свинóй pork- *adj.*
свинья́ pig, swine
свобóда freedom
свобóдный free
свой my, his, her, its, our, your, their (reflexive pronoun)
сгорéть *p.* to burn out
сдáча change (money)
сдéлать *p.* to do, make
себé myself, yourself etc. *dative*
себя́ myself, yourself etc. *acc.*

се́вер north
се́верный northern
сего́дня today
седьмо́й seventh
сей this
сейча́с now, immediately
секу́нда second (in time)
семе́йство family
семна́дцать seventeen
семь seven
се́мьдесят seventy
семьсо́т seven hundred
семья́ family
сентя́брь *m.* September
серди́тый angry
серди́ться to be angry
серебро́ silver
сере́бряный silver- *adj.*
се́рый gray
сестра́ sister
сиби́рский Siberian
Сиби́рь Siberia
сиде́ть *i.* to sit
си́льный strong
си́ний blue
сказа́ть *p.* to say
ска́терть table-cloth
ско́лько how much
ско́рый quick, fast
сла́дкий sweet
сле́ва on the left
сле́довать *i.* to follow
сле́дующий following
сли́ва plum
сли́вки *f. pl.* cream
сли́шком too
сло́во word
слон elephant
слу́жащий employee
служи́ть *i.* to serve
слу́чай case, occurrence
случа́ться *i.* } to occur
случи́ться *p.* }
слу́шать *i.* to listen
слу́шаться *i.* to obey

слы́шать *i.* to hear; to perceive odor
слы́шный audible
сме́ртный mortal
смерть death
смешно́й funny, comical
смея́ться *i.* to laugh
смотре́ть *i.* to look
смуща́ть *i.* } to embarrass
смути́ть *p.* }
(смя́тка) яйцо́ в смя́тку soft boiled egg
снег snow
снижа́ться *i.* } to descend (airplane)
сни́зиться *p.* }
снима́ть *i.* } to take off; to take a picture
снять *p.* }
сни́мок photo, snapshot
соба́ка dog
собира́ть *i.* } to gather
собра́ть *p.* }
собира́ться *i.* } to get ready
собра́ться *p.* }
собо́р cathedral
собы́тие occurrence
сова́ owl
соверше́нно completely
совсе́м quite, altogether
согла́сный consenting; **я согла́сен** I agree
согла́сная consonant (letter)
согласи́ться *p.* } to agree
соглаша́ться *i.* }
сожале́ние regret; pity, compassion
Соединённые Шта́ты United States
соедини́ть *p.* } to unite, join
соединя́ть *i.* }
сойти́ *p.* **(сойдёт)** it will do
со́лнце sun
соль salt
сообща́ть *i.* } to communicate
сообщи́ть *p.* }
со́рок forty
сосчита́ть *p.* to count
со́тня a hundred

со́тый hundredst
сохраня́ть *i.* } to keep,
сохрани́ть *p.* }
спаси́бо thanks, thank you
спать *i.* to sleep
сперва́ at first
спеши́ть *i.* to hurry
спи́сок list
спи́чка match
спра́ва to (from) the right
спра́вка information
справля́ться *i.* } to inquire
спра́виться *p.* }
спра́шивать *i.* } to ask
спроси́ть *p.* }
сра́зу at once
среда́ Wednesday
среди́ *gen.* among, amidst
ста́вить *i.* to put (upright)
стака́н glass, tumbler
сталь *f.* steel
стара́ться *i.* to endeavour
станови́ться *i.* } to become
стать *p.* }
стать, с како́й ста́ти? for what purpose? why?
старина́ old times
ста́туя statue
статья́ article
стена́ wall
стенно́й wall- *adj.*
стере́чь *i.* to guard
сто hundred
стой! halt! stop!
сто́ить *i.* to cost
стол table
столи́ца capital (city)
сто́лько as much, as many
сторожи́ть *i.* to guard
сторона́ side
стоя́ть *i.* to stand
страна́ country
страни́ца page
страх fear
стра́шный terrible
стро́ить *i.* to build
стул chair
стуча́ть *i.* to knock
суббо́та Saturday
су́мка handbag
суп soup
су́тки *pl.* day and night, 24 hours
сухо́й dry
сходи́ть *i.* to go down
счастли́вый happy, lucky
сча́стье good luck
счита́ть *i.* to count
съе́здить *p.* to make a trip
сын son
сыно́к little son
сы́тый sated, not hungry
сыр cheese
сюда́ here, hither

Т

Та see **тот**
так so
тако́й such
такси́, таксомото́р taxi
там there
танцова́ть *i.* to dance
таре́лка plate
тата́рин *m.* Tartar
тата́рка *f.* Tartar woman
тата́рский Tartar *adj.*
твой thine, your
теа́тр theater
телефо́н telephone
телефони́ст *m.*, **-ка** *f.* telephone operator
те́ло body
теля́тина veal
темнота́ darkness
тёмный dark
тепе́рь now
тёплый warm
терпе́ть *i.* to tolerate, to endure suffer

терпели́вый patient
тётя aunt
тигр tiger
ти́хий quiet
ти́ше comp. of **ти́хий**
то see **тот**
то́лько only
и то́лько that's all, that's enough
то́лько-что just (now)
тот, та, то that
тот же the same
тре́тий third
три three
три́дцать thirty
трина́дцать thirteen
три́ста three hundred
тро́гать *i.* / **тро́нуть** *p.* } to touch
туда́ there (to), thither
тут here
туши́ть *i.* to put out
ты thou, you
ты́сяча thousand
тяну́ть *i.* to pull, to drag

У

у *gen.* at, by
убива́ть *i.* / **уби́ть** *p.* } to kill
убо́рная bathroom, toilet
уве́ренный sure, confident
уверя́ть *i.* / **уве́рить** *p.* } to assure
уви́деть *p.* to perceive
угоди́ть *i.* / **угожда́ть** *p.* } to satisfy
уго́дно, ско́лько уго́дно as much as you want
у́гол corner
у́голь *m.* coal
удава́ться *i.* / **уда́ться** *p.* } to succed, to turn out well
удиви́тельный marvelous, astonishing
удиви́ть *p.* / **удивля́ть** *i.* } to astonish
удо́бный comfortable
удово́льствие pleasure
уезжа́ть *i.* / **уе́хать** *p.* } to go away, leave (not on foot)
уже́ already
у́жин supper
у́жинать *i.* to have supper
у́зкий narrow
узнава́ть *i.* / **узна́ть** *p.* } to learn; to recognize
уйти́ *p.* to go away, to leave
у́лица street
ум mind *noun,* intellect
уме́ть *i.* / **суме́ть** *p.* } to know how
умира́ть *i.* / **умере́ть** *p.* } to die
у́мный clever, intelligent
умыва́ться *i.* / **умы́ться** *p.* } to wash (oneself)
универма́г department store
университе́т university
уплати́ть *p.* to pay
упражне́ние exercise
уро́к lesson
успева́ть *i.* / **успе́ть** *p.* } to have time, to succeed
успе́х success
уста́в by-laws, rules
у́тка duck
у́тренний morning- *adj.*
у́тро morning
у́хо, *pl.* **у́ши** ear
уходи́ть *i.* / **уйти́** *p.* } to go away, leave
учени́к student, pupil *m.*
учени́ца student, pupil *f.*
учи́тель *m.* teacher
учи́тельница *f.* teacher
учи́ть *i.* (*with dat.*) to teach; (*with acc.*) to learn
учи́ться *i.* (*with dat.*) to learn

Ф

Факт fact
фами́лия surname, family name
фасо́ль bean(s)
февра́ль *m.* February
фиа́лка violet
фо́рма form; uniform
Фра́нция France
францу́женка French woman
францу́з Frenchman
францу́зский French
фрукт, *pl.* **фру́кты** fruit

Х

ха́та peasant hut
хвали́ть *i.* to praise
хлеб bread
ходи́ть *i.* to go, to walk
хозя́ин host; proprietor
хозя́йка hostess, proprietress
холо́дный cold
холостя́к bachelor
хор choir
хоро́ший good
хоро́шенький pretty
хоте́ть *i.* to want
хотя́, хоть although
хра́брый brave
храм church, temple
храни́ть *i.* to keep, preserve
ху́же worse

Ц

Царь *m.* tsar
цари́ца tsarina
цвести́ *i.* to bloom
цвет, *pl.* **цвета́** color
цвето́к, *pl.* **цветы́** flower
це́лый whole, entire
цена́ price
цени́ть *i.* to esteem; to price
центр center
це́рковь church
ци́фра, цы́фра figure, cipher

Ч

Чай tea;
  дать на чай to give a tip
ча́йник tea-pot
час hour
ча́сто often
часы́ *pl.* watch; clock
часы́-брасле́т wrist-watch
часть *f.* part
ча́шка cup
чей, чья, чьё whose
челове́к man, person, human
чем *instr.* with what
чем than
чемода́н bag, trunk
чере́шня cherry, -tree
черни́ла *neut. plur.* ink
Чёрное мо́ре Black Sea
черномо́рский Black Sea *adj.*
чёрный black
че́стный honest
четве́рг Thursday
четвёртый fourth
че́тверть a quarter
четы́ре four
четы́реста four hundred
четы́рнадцать fourteen
число́ number; date
чи́стый clean
чита́тель *m.,* **-ница** *f.* reader
чита́ть to read
член member
что what; that (conj.)
что́бы in order that
что-ли́бо any-thing, something
что-нибу́дь something, anything
что́-то something
чу́вство feeling
чу́вствовать *i.* to feel

чу́дный wonderful
чудо́вище monster
чужо́й strange, foreign
чуло́к, *pl.* **чулки́** stocking

Ш

Шаг pace, step
шанс chance
ша́йка gang
ша́пка cap
шапро́н chaperon
ше́я neck
шерсть wool
шерстяно́й woolen
шестна́дцать sixteen
шесто́й sixth
шесть six
шестьдеся́т sixty
шестьсо́т six hundred
широ́кий wide
шкаф cupboard, closet
шко́ла school
шля́па hat
шокола́д chocolate
шофёр driver, chauffeur
шу́ба fur coat
шум noise
шути́ть *i.* to joke
шу́тка joke

Щ

Щека́, *pl.* **щёки** cheek
щелку́нчик nut-cracker
щи cabbage soup

Э

Эй! look here! I say!
электри́ческий electric
электри́чество electricity
эта́ж floor
э́тот, э́та, э́то this

Ю

Юбка skirt
юг south
ю́жный southern
ю́ный youthful
ю́ноша youth, young man
юти́ться *i.* to crowd (*intr.*), to be cooped up

Я

Я I
я́блоко apple
я́года berry
язы́к tongue; language
янва́рь *m.* January
япо́нец Japanese (man)
Япо́ния Japan
япо́нка Japanese (woman)
япо́нский Japanese *adj.*
я́ркий bright (color, light)
я́сный clear
яйцо́ egg
я́щик box; drawer
почто́вый я́щик letter box

APPENDIX

Below is a breakdown of some of the more elaborate phases of Russian grammar. Don't shy away from it because it looks difficult; it is really easier than it appears! Remember that we use cases in English too. That is why we say, "I see him", instead of "I see he". So, to speak Russian well, watch your grammar!

There are six cases in Russian, which we shall take up one by one and tell why they are used. The first is:

THE NOMINATIVE

The nominative case answers the question **кто?** ("who?") or **что?** ("what?"). It is used when the noun is the subject or the predicate of a sentence. **Со́лнце све́тит** ("The sun shines"). **Со́лнце** is the subject. **Москва́—столи́ца** ("Moscow is the capital"). **Столи́ца** is the predicate.

THE GENITIVE

I. After a Substantive the genitive is used:

1. To designate a person to whom, or an object to which somebody or something belongs or refers (possessive genitive): **глаза́ де́вушки**—"the eyes of the girl"; **за́пах ча́я**—"the odor of the tea".
2. It is used to modify another noun: **министе́рство иностра́нных дел**—"the ministry of foreign affairs"; **дека́н факульте́та**—"the dean of the faculty".
3. It is used after a substantive derived from a transitive verb: **перево́зка ме́бели**—"the moving of the furniture", (**перевози́ть**—"to move"); **ата́ка неприя́теля**—"the attack of the enemy", (**атакова́ть**—"to attack").

4. It also is used after nouns denoting a quantity or measure: **стака́н воды́**—"a glass of water"; **фунт са́хару**—"a pound of sugar"; **метр полотна́**—"a meter of linen".

Notice that in all these instances (1-4) *the word "of" is used in English.*

II. After Numerals:

1. After all numerals over 4 the genitive plural is used (with the exception of compound numerals whose last figure is 1, 2, 3 or 4): **пять па́льцев**—"five fingers", **два́дцать домо́в**—"twenty houses", but **два́дцать оди́н дом**—"twenty one houses".
2. Also indefinite numerals like **не́сколько**—"several", **мно́го**—"much, many", **ма́ло**—"little, few", **немно́го**—"a little, a few", **дово́льно**—"enough", require the genitive (singular or plural): **мно́го наро́ду**—"many people", **ма́ло люде́й**—"few people", **немно́го мёду**—"a little honey", **дово́льно со́ли**—"enough salt".

III. After Certain Verbs:

1. After **нет** (which is a contraction of **не есть**—"there is not"), **не́ было**—"there wasn't", and **не бу́дет**—"there won't be" the noun (or pronoun) is put in the genitive: **не́т воды, не́ было воды́, не бу́дет воды́**—"there is no water, there was no water, there won't be water".
2. After other verbs in the negative the noun (or pronoun) referred to is usually put in the genitive: **я не беру́ шля́пы**—"I don't take the hat"; **я не ви́жу сту́ла**—"I don't see the chair".
3. If a verb refers not to the whole but only to a part of something the ('partitive') genitive is used: **вы́пить воды́**—"to drink (some) water", but **вы́пить во́ду** (acc.)—"to drink (all) the water" (which was in the bottle or in the glass etc.).
4. The genitive is also used after some verbs, e.g.: **боя́ться, опаса́ться**—"to fear", **избега́ть**—"to avoid", **добива́ться**—"to make efforts to obtain, to achieve": **боя́ться огня́**—"to fear fire", **доби́ться успе́ха**—"to achieve success".

IV. In Expressing Comparison:

The noun denoting a person with whom, or a thing with which another person or thing is compared is put in the genitive after the comparative of an adjective: **соба́ка бо́льше ко́шки**—"the dog is bigger than the cat"; **де́рево вы́ше до́ма**—"the tree is taller than the house".

V. After Prepositions:

Many Russian prepositions require the genitive. See the Table of prepositions on pages 275 and 276.

VI. After Certain Adjectives:

по́лон эне́ргии—"full of energy";
досто́ин награ́ды—"worthy of an award".

THE DATIVE

The dative—**да́тельный паде́ж** (the "giving-case", **дать**—"to give") designates the person to whom something is given or done, or the object to which something is given or done:

Я даю́ де́ньги бра́ту	I am giving money to my brother
Я иду́ к бра́ту	I am going to my brother

Notice the difference: in the first sentence the dative is used without a preposition while in the second sentence the preposition **к** with the dative is used. The reason is that in the latter motion ("towards" the brother) is indicated.

Three prepositions require the dative: **к, (ко)**—"to, towards", **по**—"along" (**идти́ по у́лице**—"to walk in the street") and **вопреки́**—"in spite of", "contrary to".

Certain verbs are also followed by the dative, e.g.:

Я ра́дуюсь его́ прие́зду	I am glad he is arriving
ве́рить кому́-то	to believe somebody
учи́ться ру́сскому языку́	to learn the Russian language

THE ACCUSATIVE

The noun in the accusative case usually denotes the direct object of an action: **Я беру́ кни́гу**—"I take the book".

Also certain prepositions (**в, на, под, пе́ред, че́рез, по** etc.) govern the accusative:

Он кладёт кни́гу на стол. He puts the book on the table.

The accusative is also used to express time and distance: **в суббо́ту**—"on Saturday"; **он прое́хал со́тню вёрст**—"he rode 100 verst".

THE INSTRUMENTAL

This case is used without a preposition

1. When a noun (or pronoun) denotes the instrument or means by which something is done, or the person by whom something is done:

писа́ть перо́м	to write with a pen
ходи́ть нога́ми	to walk with the legs
Дом стро́ится архите́ктором	The house is being built by an architect

2. In order to express the way in which something is done:

Ло́шадь бежи́т гало́пом	The horse goes at a gallop
Он говори́т шо́потом	He speaks in whispers
Он у́мер геро́ем	He died a hero

3. After certain verbs instead of the accusative:

управля́ть име́нием	to manage an estate
дыша́ть во́здухом	to breathe air
кома́ндовать полко́м	to command a regiment

4. After some verbs as a predicate instead of the nominative:

быть офице́ром	to be an officer
служи́ть по́варом	to serve as a cook
счита́ться геро́ем	to be reputed a hero

5. In adverbial expressions like **днём**—"by day" **но́чью**—"by night", **ле́том**—"in summer", **зимо́й**—"in winter", etc.

6. In expressing dimensions:

гора́ высото́ю в 1000 фут	a mountain 1000 feet high
о́зеро глубино́ю в 40 ме́тров	a lake 40 meters deep

7. Several prepositions govern the instrumental case: **пе́ред**—"before, in front of", **за**—"behind", **под**—"under", **ме́жду**—"between", **с (со)**—"with".

THE PREPOSITIONAL

It is used only after prepositions which require that case. It cannot be used without a preposition, hence its name. After **в** and **на** it denotes the place where something is located or where something occurs. Therefore it is also called, in English, the Locative case.

The following prepositions require the prepositional: **в**—"in", **на**—"on", **по**—"after", **при**—"at, in the presence of, at the time of".

Now that you know *why* the cases are used, here are a series of tables that will save you many a linguistic faux pas.

DECLENSION OF MASCULINE NOUNS

Remember: The accusative of masculine nouns is like the nominative if the noun denotes an inanimate object, but if it denotes an animate being the accusative is like the genitive. To remind you of this the accusative cases of all the nouns below are marked with asterisks.*

Some nouns ending in a syllable containing **о** or **е** between two consonants and also some monosyllabic nouns containing **о** or **е** drop these vowels in all the oblique cases and in the nom. plural: **оте́ц** ("father"), gen.: **отца́**, plur.: **отцы́**; **лоб** ("forehead"), gen.: **лба**, plur.: **лбы**.

Nouns ending in a hard consonant

N.	**стол**	**стол-ы́**[2]
G.	**стол-а́**	**стол-о́в**[3]
D.	**стол-у́**	**стол-а́м**
A.	**стол***	**стол-ы́***
I.	**стол-о́м**[1]	**стол-а́ми**
P.	**стол-е́**	**стол-а́х**

[1] The instrumental sing. ends in **-ем,** if the ending is not accented and if the stem ends in **-ц: пе́рец** ("pepper")—**пе́рцем; па́лец** ("finger")—**па́льцем.**

[2] The nominative plural ends in **-и** after gutturals **(г, к, х): пиро́г** ("cake")—**пироги́; ма́льчик** ("boy") — **ма́льчики; вздох** ("sigh")—**вздо́хи.**

Some nouns have the nominative pl. in an accented **-а** (instead of **-ы** or **-и**): **дом** ("house")—**дома́; глаз** ("eye")—**глаза́; рог** ("horn")— **рога́.**

Some have two different endings for the nom. pl., **-ы** and **-а,** which impart to them different meanings: **цветы́** ("flowers"), **цвета́** ("colors").

[3] The genitive plural ends in **-ев** (instead of **-ов**) if the ending is not accented and if the stem ends in **-ц: па́льцы** ("fingers")—**па́льцев.**

A few nouns have the gen. pl. like the nominative singular: **челове́к** ("man", used only after numerals), **глаз** ("eye"), **солда́т** ("soldier"), **сапо́г** ("boot"), **чуло́к** ("stocking"), **во́лос** ("hair"), gen. pl.—**воло́с.**

Some nouns ending in a hard consonant form the plural in -ья

N.	**стул**	**сту́л-ья**
G.	**сту́л-а**	**сту́л-ьев**[1]
D.	**сту́л-у**	**сту́л-ьям**
A.	**стул***	**сту́л-ья***
I.	**сту́л-ом**	**сту́л-ьями**
P.	**сту́л-е**	**сту́л-ьях**

[1] Some nouns have the genitive plur. in **-ей: муж** ("husband"), plur.: **мужья́,** gen.: **муже́й; друг** ("friend"), plur.: **друзья́,** gen.: **друзе́й.** Also **сын** ("son"), plur.: **сыновья́,** gen.: **сынове́й.** The plural of **брат** ("brother") is **бра́тья,** gen.: **бра́тьев.**

Nouns ending in a soft consonant

N.	**гвоздь**	**гво́зд-и**[2]
G.	**гвозд-я́**	**гвозд-е́й**
D.	**гвозд-ю́**	**гвозд-я́м**
A.	**гвоздь***	**гво́зд-и***
I.	**гвозд-ём**[1]	**гвозд-я́ми**[3]
P.	**гвозд-е́**	**гвозд-я́х**

[1] The instrumental ends in **-ем** if the ending is not accented: **гость** ("guest"), instrum.: **го́стем.**

[2] Some nouns have the nom. pl. in an accented **-я: учи́тель** ("teacher")—**учителя́,** genitive: **учителе́й.**

Some end in **-ья: зять** ("brother-in-law")—**зятья́,** gen.: **зяте́й,** dat.: **зятья́м;** alike: **князь** ("prince")—**князья́, князе́й.**

[3] Some have the instr. pl. also in **-ьми: гостьми́, гвоздьми́.**

Nouns ending in -ж, -ч, -ш or -щ

N.	**ключ**	**ключ-и́**
G.	**ключ-а́**	**ключ-е́й**
D.	**ключ-у́**	**ключ-а́м**
A.	**ключ***	**ключ-и́***
I.	**ключ-о́м**[1]	**ключ-а́ми**
P.	**ключ-е́**	**ключ-а́х**

On this pattern all masculine nouns ending in the sibilants **ж, ч, ш** or **щ** are declined, e.g.: **нож** ("knife"), **врач** ("physician"), **вы́игрыш** ("the gain", "winnings"), **това́рищ** ("comrade").

[1] If the ending is not accented, the instrumental ends in: **-ем: това́рищем.**

Nouns ending in -й

N.	**слу́чай**	**слу́ча-и**[3]
G.	**слу́ча-я**[1]	**слу́ча-ев**[2]
D.	**слу́ча-ю**	**слу́ча-ям**
A.	**слу́чай***	**слу́ча-и***
I.	**слу́ча-ем**[2]	**слу́ча-ями**
P.	**слу́ча-е**	**слу́ча-ях**

[1] If the **й** is preceded by an **е** as in **воробе́й** ("sparrow"), **руче́й** ("brook") the **е** changes, in the oblique cases and in the nominative plural, into **-ь:** gen. singular: **воробья́,** plur.: **воробьи́,** gen.: **воробьёв; ручья́, ручьи́, ручьёв.**

[2] If the ending is accented, the instrumental sing. ends in **-ём** and the genitive plural in **-ёв: ручьём, ручьёв.**

Some nouns of this category have the nominative plural in an accented **-я,** e.g.: **край** ("land", "region"), plur.: **края́,** gen. **краёв.**

Nouns ending in -ин

N.	**южа́нин**	**южа́н-е**
G.	**южа́нин-а**	**южа́н**
D.	**южа́нин-у**	**южа́н-ам**
A.	**южа́нин-а**	**южа́н**
I.	**южа́нин-ом**	**южа́н-ами**
P.	**южа́нин-е**	**южа́н-ах**

Nouns in **-анин, -янин,** usually denoting nationalities, classes, or domicile, have the nominative plural in **-е,** e.g.: **англича́нин** ("Englishman"), plur.: **англича́не; северя́нин** ("Northerner"), plur.: **северя́не; горожа́нин** ("city dweller"), plur.: **горожа́не.**

The plural of **господи́н** ("Mr.", "gentleman") is **господа́,** gen.: **госпо́д.** That of **хозя́ин** ("master", "proprietor") is **хозя́ева,** gen.: **хозя́ев.**

Nouns ending in -ёнок

N.	**ребёнок**	**ребя́т-а**
G.	**ребён-ка**	**ребя́т**
D.	**ребён-ку**	**ребя́т-ам**
A.	**ребён-ка**	**ребя́т**
I.	**ребён-ком**	**ребя́т-ами**
P.	**ребён-ке**	**ребя́т-ах**

Most nouns denoting the young animals belong to this category: **жеребёнок** ("foal"), gen. plur.: **жеребя́т; телёнок** ("calf")—**телят; котёнок** ("kitten")—**котя́т; цыплёнок** ("chicken")—**цыпля́т.** Also **щено́к** ("cub")—**щеня́т.**

DECLENSION OF FEMININE NOUNS

The instrumental case of the singular has two endings: **-ою** (or **-ею**) and **-ой** (or **-ей**). Both endings can be used indiscriminately though the shorter form (**-ой, -ей**) is more common.

The accusative plural has, as it is the case with masculine nouns, two different endings depending on whether the noun denotes an inanimate object or an animate being. But in the singular the accusative has only one ending.

If the stem ends in two consonants, an **е** or an **о** is inserted in the genitive plural to facilitate pronunciation: **спи́чка** ("match"), gen. plur.: **спи́чек; па́лка** ("stick"), gen. pl.: **па́лок.**

Nouns ending in -а (after a hard consonant)

N.	трав-á	трáв-ы
G.	трав-ы́	трав[2]
D.	трав-é	трáв-ам
A.	трав-ý	трáв-ы
I.	трав-óй (-óю)[1]	трáв-ами
P.	трав-é	трáв-ах

[1] The instrumental sing. ends in **-ей, -ею** after **ж, ч, ш, щ** and **ц** if the ending is not accented: **дáча** ("country house")—**дáчей; ýлица** ("street")—**ýлицей.**

[2] After gutturals **г, к, х** and sibillants **ж, ч, ш, щ** the genitive singular and the nominative and accusative plural end in **-и** instead of **-ы: кни́га** ("book")—**кни́ги; свечá** ("candle")—**свéчи.**

Nouns ending in -я (after a soft consonant)

N.	недéл-я	недéл-и
G.	недéл-и	недéль
D.	недéл-е	недéл-ям
A.	недéл-ю	недéл-и
I.	недéл-ей (ею)[1]	недéл-ями
P.	недéл-е	недéл-ях

[1] The instrumental ends in **-ёй, -ёю** if the ending is accented: **земля́** ("earth"), instr.: **землёй, землёю.**

Nouns ending in -ня after a consonant or a й

N.	ви́шн-я	ви́шн-и
G.	ви́шн-и	ви́шен[1]
D.	ви́шн-е	ви́шн-ям
A.	ви́шн-ю	ви́шн-и
I.	ви́шн-ей (-ею)	ви́шн-ями
P.	ви́шн-е	ви́шн-ях

[1] Notice that the genitive plural ends in **-ен** with the exception of these nouns which end in a soft sign: **дерéвня** ("village")—**деревéнь, бáрышня** ("young lady")—**бáрышень, кýхня** ("kitchen")—**кýхонь.** Notice that nouns ending in **-ня** after a vowel are declined like **недéля,** the preceding paradigm, e.g. **ня́ня** ("nurse"), gen. pl.: **нянь.**

Nouns ending in -я after a vowel with the exception of и:

N.	стá-я	стá-и
G.	стá-и	стá-й
D.	стá-е	стá-ям
A.	стá-ю	стá-и
I.	стá-ей (-ею)	стá-ями
P.	стá-е	стá-ях

Nouns ending in -я after и:

N.	áрми-я	áрми-и
G.	áрми-и	áрми-й
D.	áрми-и	áрми-ям
A.	áрми-ю	áрми-и
I.	áрми-ей (-ею)	áрми-ями
P.	áрми-и	áрми-ях

Like **áрмия** are declined the names of countries ending in **-ия: Росси́я, Англия,** etc.

Nouns ending in ь

N.	**степь**	**сте́п-и**
G.	**сте́п-и**	**степ-е́й**
D.	**сте́п-и**	**степ-я́м**
A.	**степь**	**сте́п-и**
I.	**сте́п-ью**	**степ-я́ми**[2]
P.	**сте́п-и**[1]	**степ-я́х**

[1] After the prepositions **в** and **на** the stress is on the last syllable: **в степи́.**

[2] Some nouns belonging to this group have the instrumental plur. in **-ьми** in addition to the regular form in **-ями: дверь** ("door") —**дверьми́** and **дверя́ми.**

Two nouns, **мать** ("mother") and **дочь** ("daughter") use the original stems **ма́тер** and **до́чер** in forming the oblique cases of the singular with the exception of the accusative which is **мать, дочь,** and also in forming all the cases of the plural. Accordingly, the gen. sing. is **ма́тери, до́чери,** the nominative plur.—**ма́тери, до́чери,** the gen. plur.—**матере́й** and **дочере́й.**

There is one masculine noun belonging to this group, **путь,** which is declined like **степь** with the exception of the instrumental sing. whose form is **путём.**

DECLENSION OF NEUTER NOUNS

Neuter nouns are in most respect declined like masculine nouns. The accusative is always like the nominative.

Nouns ending in -о

N.	**блю́д-о**	**блю́д-а**
G.	**блю́д-а**	**блюд**[2]
D.	**блю́д-у**	**блю́д-ам**
A.	**блю́д-о**	**блю́д-а**
I.	**блю́д-ом**	**блю́д-ами**
P.	**блю́д-е**	**блю́д-ах**

[1] Some nouns ending in **-ко** have the plural in **-и: я́блоко** ("apple"), plur.: **я́блоки; ли́чико** ("little face"), plur.: **ли́чики;** also **у́хо** ("ear")—**у́ши; плечо́** ("shoulder")—**пле́чи; о́ко** ("eye")—**о́чи; коле́но** ("knee") —**коле́ни.**

Не́бо ("sky") and **чу́до** ("miracle") add **-ес** to the stem in the plural: **небеса́** ("skies"), **чудеса́** ("miracles").

[2] If the stem ends in two consonants, an **е** or an **о** is inserted in the genitive plural: **пятно́** ("spot"), plur.: **пя́тна,** gen.: **пя́тен; окно́** ("window"), plur.: **о́кна,** gen.: **око́н.** If there is a **ь** between the two consonants, it changes into **е: письмо́** ("letter"), plur.: **пи́сьма,** gen. **пи́сем.**

Nouns ending in -е, -ие and -ье

N.	**по́л-е**	**пол-я́**	**зда́н-ие**	**зда́н-ия**	**поме́ст-ье**	**поме́ст-ья**
G.	**по́л-я**	**пол-е́й**	**зда́н-ия**	**зда́н-ий**	**поме́ст-ья**	**поме́ст-ий**
D.	**по́л-ю**	**пол-я́м**	**зда́н-ию**	**зда́н-иям**	**поме́ст-ью**	**поме́ст-ьям**
A.	**по́л-е**	**пол-я́**	**зда́н-ие**	**зда́н-ия**	**поме́ст-ье**	**поме́ст-ья**
I.	**по́л-ем**	**пол-я́ми**	**зда́н-ием**	**зда́н-иями**	**поме́ст-ьем**	**поме́ст-ьями**
P.	**по́л-е**	**пол-я́х**	**зда́н-ии**	**зда́н-иях**	**поме́ст-ье**	**поме́ст-ьях**

The genitive plural of nouns ending in **-ье** usually ends in **-ий.** However some nouns form the genitive plural in **-ьев,** e.g.: **пла́тье** ("dress"), gen.: plural: **пла́тьев.**

Nouns ending in **-мя**

N.	**и́м-я**	**им-ена́**
G.	**и́м-ени**	**им-ён**
D.	**и́м-ени**	**им-ена́м**
A.	**и́м-я**	**им-ена́**
I.	**и́м-енем**	**им-ена́ми**
P.	**и́м-ени**	**им-ена́х**

There are only ten words belonging to this category. Among them are: **вре́мя** ("time"), **зна́мя** ("banner"), **се́мя** ("seed"), **пла́мя** ("flame"), **бре́мя** ("burden"), **пле́мя** ("tribe").

DECLENSION OF PRONOUNS

N.	**я**	**ты**	**он** *m.*, **оно́** *n.*	**она́**	**мы**	**вы**	**они́**
G.	**меня́**	**тебя́**	**его́**	**её**	**нас**	**вас**	**их**
D.	**мне**	**тебе́**	**ему́**	**ей**	**нам**	**вам**	**им**
A.	**меня́**	**тебя́**	**его́**	**её**	**нас**	**вас**	**их**
I.	**мной (-бю)**	**тобо́й (-бю)**	**им**	**ей (е́ю)**	**на́ми**	**ва́ми**	**и́ми**
P.	**мне**	**тебе́**	**нём**	**ней**	**нас**	**вас**	**них**

If **он, она́, оно́** is preceded and governed by a preposition an **н** is prefixed: **к нему́**—"to him", **с ней**—"with her". This is not the case if **его́, её** correspond to the English "his", "her": **У его́ отца́ дом**—"His father has a house". The reflexive pronoun **себя́** which has no nominative and no special endings for the plural is declined like **я** or **ты:** gen. and acc.—**себя́,** dat.—**себе́,** instr.—**собо́й, собо́ю,** prep.—**себе́.**

N.	**мой**	**моя́**	**мои́**	**наш**	**на́ша**	**на́ши**
G.	**моего́**	**мое́й**	**мои́х**	**на́шего**	**на́шей**	**на́ших**
D.	**моему́**	**мое́й**	**мои́м**	**на́шему**	**на́шей**	**на́шими**
A.	**мой (моего́)***	**мою́**	**мои́ (мои́х)***	**наш (на́шего)***	**на́шу**	**на́ши (на́ших)***
I.	**мои́м**	**мое́й**	**мои́ми**	**на́шим**	**на́шей (-ею)**	**на́шими**
P.	**моём**	**мое́й**	**мои́х**	**на́шем**	**на́шей**	**на́ших**

Твой—"thy", **свой**—"one's own", are declined like **мой; ваш**—"your", is declined like **наш.**

The neuter **моё** is declined like the masculine **мой** with the exception of the accusative which is always **моё.**

The neuter **на́ше, ва́ше** is declined like the masculine **наш** with the exception of the accusative which always is **на́ше, ва́ше** (sing.) and **на́ши, ва́ши** (plur.).

N.	**э́тот**	**э́та**	**э́ти**	**тот**	**та**	**те**
G.	**э́того**	**э́той**	**э́тих**	**того́**	**той**	**тех**
D.	**э́тому**	**э́той**	**э́тим**	**тому́**	**той**	**тем**
A.	**э́тот**	**э́ту**	**э́ти**	**тот**	**ту**	**те**
	(э́того)*		**(э́тих)***	**(того́)***		**(тех)***
I.	**э́тим**	**э́той**	**э́тими**	**тем**	**той**	**тем**
P.	**э́том**	**э́той**	**э́тих**	**том**	**той**	**тех**

The neuter **э́то** is declined like the masculine **э́тот** with the exception of the accusative which is **э́то** (sing.) and **э́ти** (plur.).

The neuter **то** is declined like the masculine **тот** with the exception of the accusative which is **то** (sing.) and **те** (plur.).

* If animate.

N.	**кто**	**что**	**никто́**	**ничто́**	—	—
G.	**кого́**	**чего́**	**никого́**	**ничего́**	**не́кого**	**не́чего**
D.	**кому́**	**чему́**	**никому́**	**ничему́**	**не́кому**	**не́чему**
A.	**кого́**	**что**	**никого́**	**ничто́**	**не́кого**	**не́чего**
I.	**кем**	**чем**	**нике́м**	**ниче́м**	**не́кем**	**не́чем**
P.	**ком**	**чём**	**ни (о) ко́м**	**ни (о) чём**	**не́ (о) ком**	**не́ (о) чём**

Like **кто** are declined the compound pronouns **кто-нибу́дь,** gen.: **кого́-нибу́дь, ко́е-кто,** gen.: **ко́е-кого́** etc. If a pronoun, one part of which is **ни** or **не,** is used with a preposition, the preposition is inserted between the two parts and they are written as two separate words: **никто́** ("nobody"), **ни с кем** ("with nobody").

N.	**чей**	**чья**	**чьи**	**сам**	**сама́**	**са́ми**
G.	**чьего́**	**чьей**	**чьих**	**самого́**	**само́й**	**сами́х**
D.	**чьему́**	**чьей**	**чьим**	**самому́**	**само́й**	**сами́ми**
A.	**чей**	**чью**	**чьи**	**самого́**	**самоё**	**сами́х**
	(чьего́)*		**(чьих)***			
I.	**чьим**	**чьей (-е́ю)**	**чьи́ми**	**сами́м**	**само́й (-о́ю)**	**сами́ми**
P.	**чьём**	**чьей**	**чьих**	**само́м**	**само́й**	**сами́х**

* If animate.

The neuter **чьё** is declined like the masculine with the exception of the accusative singular which is **чьё.**

The neuter **camó** is declined like the masculine **cam** with the exception of the accusative which is **camó.**

Don't confuse **cam** ("self"), **oн cam** ("he himself") with **cáмый** (used in forming the superlative) which is declined like an adjective.

N.	**скóлько**	**стóлько**	**весь**	**вся**	**все**
G.	**сколькúх**	**столькúх**	**всегó**	**всей**	**всех**
D.	**сколькúм**	**столькúм**	**всемý**	**всей**	**всем**
A.	**скóлько (сколькúх)***	**стóлько (столькúх)***	**весь (всегó)***	**всю**	**все (всех)***
I.	**сколькúми**	**столькúми**	**всем**	**всей (-éю)**	**всéми**
P.	**сколькúх**	**столькúх**	**всём**	**всей**	**всех**

* If animate.

Нéсколько ("several") is declined like **скóлько,** but has the stress on the first syllables: **нéскольких, нéскольким** etc.

The neuter **всё** is declined like the masculine **весь** with the exception of the accusative which is **всё.**

The pronouns **вся́кий, инóй, какóй, такóй, никакóй, котóрый, нéкоторый** are declined like adjectives.

* If animate.

DECLENSION OF NUMERALS

Cardinal Numerals

Nom.	gen.	dat.	acc.	instr.	prep.
одúн	**одногó**	**одномý**	**одúн (одногó)***	**однúм**	**однóм**
однó	**одногó**	**одномý**	**однó**	**однúм**	**однóм**
однá	**однóй**	**однóй**	**однý**	**однóй**	**однóй**
		Plural (for all genders)			
однú	**однúх**	**однúм**	**однú (однúх)***	**однúми**	**однúх**

* If animate.

два *m. & n.* / **две** *fem.*	**двух**	**двум**	**два** / **две** **двух***	**двумя́**	**двух**
три	**трёх**	**трём**	**три (трёх)**	**тремя́**	**трёх**
четы́ре	**четырёх**	**четырём**	**четы́ре (четырёх)***	**четырьмя́**	**четырёх**

* If animate.

The numerals from 5 to 20 and also 30 are declined like feminine nouns ending in **-ь.** Thus:

Nom. and acc.:	**пять**	**вóсемь**	**двенáдцать**	**трúдцать**
gen., dat., prep.:	**пятú**	**восьмú**	**двенáдцати**	**тридцатú**
instr.:	**пятью́**	**восемью́**	**двенáдцатью**	**тридцатью́**

40, 90 and 100 have only two declension forms:

Nom. and acc.:	**сóрок**	**девянóсто**	**сто**
gen., dat., instr., prep.:	**сорокá**	**девянóста**	**ста**

50, 60, 70, 80.—Both parts of the numeral are declined:

Nom.: **пятьдеся́т** gen.: **пятúдесяти** dat.: **пятúдесяти** acc.: **пятьдеся́т**

instr.: **пятьюдесятью** prep.: **пятúдесяти**

200, 300, 400.—Both parts are declined:

nom.	gen.	dat.	acc.	instr.	prep.
двéсти	**двухсóт**	**двумстáм**	**двéсти***	**двумястáми**	**двухстáх**
трúста	**трёхсóт**	**трёмстáм**	**трúста***	**тремястáми**	**трёхстáх**
четы́реста	**четырёхсóт**	**четырёмстáм**	**четы́реста***	**четырьмястáми**	**четырёхстáх**

* If animate, the accusative is like the genitive: **двухсóт, трёхсóт, четырёхсóт.**

500, 600, 700, 800, 900.—Both parts are declined; the first part like **пять, шесть** etc., the other like the second part of **двéсти:**

nom.	gen.	dat.	acc.	instr.	prep.
пятьсóт	**пятисóт**	**пятистáм**	**пятьсóт**	**пятьюстáми**	**пятистáх**
шестьсóт	**шестисóт**	**шестистáм**	**шестьсóт**	**шестьюстáми**	**шестистáх**
etc.					

Collective Numerals

Nom.	**óба**	**óбе**	**двóе**	**трóе**	**пя́теро**	**чéтверо**
Gen.	**обóих**	**обéих**	**двои́х**	**трои́х**	**пятеры́х**	**четверы́х**
Dat.	**обóим**	**обéим**	**двои́м**	**трои́м**	**пятеры́м**	**четверы́м**
Acc.	Like nominative if inanimate, like genitive if animate.					
Instr.	**обóими**	**обéими**	**двои́ми**	**трои́ми**	**пятеры́ми**	**четверы́ми**
Prep.	**обóих**	**обéих**	**двои́х**	**трои́х**	**пятеры́х**	**четверы́х**

In the same way are declined **шéстеро, сéмеро, вóсьмеро** etc.

The collective numerals **пятóк** ("five"), **деся́ток** ("ten"), **дю́жина** ("dozen") and **сóтня** ("hundred") are declined as nouns.

Fractional Numerals

полови́на ("a half") is declined like a feminine noun ending in **-а; треть** ("one third") and **че́тверть** ("a quarter") are declined like feminine nouns ending in **-ь.** The other fractional numbers consist of two parts of which the first is declined while the second part always remains in the genitive plural:

две пя́тых ("two fifths"), gen.: **двух пя́тых,** dat.: **двум пя́тым** etc.; **три восьмы́х** ("three eights"), gen.: **трёх восьмы́х,** dat.: **трём восьмы́м** etc.

полтора́ (masc.) and **полторы́** (fem.) ("one and a half") are declined:

полтора́ (рубля́)	**полторы́ (копе́йки)**
полу́тора (рубле́й)	**полу́тора (копе́ек)**
полу́тора (рубля́м)	**полу́тора (копе́йкам)**
полтора́ (рубля́)	**полторы́ (копе́йки)**
полу́тора (рубля́ми)	**полу́тора (копе́йками)**
о полу́тора (рубля́х)	**о полу́тора (копе́йках)**

Ordinal Numerals are declined like adjectives.

DECLENSION OF ADJECTIVES, PARTICIPLES AND ORDINAL NUMERALS

Remember that the accusative singular of the masculine gender and the accusative plural of all genders is like the nominative (singular or plural respectively) if the adjective refers to an inanimate object, but it is like the genitive if it refers to an animate being.

1. Stem ending in a hard consonant.

до́брый ("good, kind"), **больно́й** ("sick"), **пе́рвый** ("first"), **второ́й** ("second").

Singular

	Nom.	Gen.	Dat.	Acc.	Instr.	Prep.
Masc.	**-ый (-ой)**	**-ого**	**-ому**	**-ый (-ой)** **-ого**	**-ым**	**-ом**
Fem.	**-ая**	**-ой**	**-ой**	**-ую**	**-ой (-ою)**	**-ой**
Neut.	**-ое**	**-ого**	**-ому**	**-ое**	**-ым**	**-ом**

Plural

All genders	**-ые**	**-ых**	**-ым**	**-ые** **-ых**	**-ыми**	**-ых**

2. Stem ending in a guttural (г, к, х).

стро́гий ("strict"), **ру́сский** ("Russian"), **ти́хий** ("quiet").

Singular

	Nom.	Gen.	Dat.	Acc.	Instr.	Prep.
Masc.	**-ий**	**-ого**	**-ому**	**-ий** **-ого**	**-им**	**-ом**
Fem.	**-ая**	**-ой**	**-ой**	**-ую**	**-ой (-ою)**	**-ой**
Neut.	**-ое**	**-ого**	**-ому**	**-ое**	**-им**	**-ом**

Plural

	Nom.	Gen.	Dat.	Acc.	Instr.	Prep.
All genders	**-ие**	**-их**	**-им**	**-ие** **-их**	**-ими**	**-их**

---

3. Stem ending in a soft consonant.

си́ний ("blue").

Singular

	Nom.	Gen.	Dat.	Acc.	Instr.	Prep.
Masc.	**-ий**	**-его**	**-ему**	**-ий** **-его**	**-им**	**-ем**
Fem.	**-яя**	**-ей**	**-ей**	**-юю**	**-ей (-ею)**	**-ей**
Neut.	**-ее**	**-его**	**-ему**	**-ее**	**-им**	**-ем**

Plural

	Nom.	Gen.	Dat.	Acc.	Instr.	Prep.
All genders	**-ие**	**-их**	**-им**	**-ие** **-их**	**-ими**	**-их**

---

4. Stem ending in a sibilant (ж, ч, ш, щ).

дю́жий ("sturdy"), **зря́чий** ("seeing"), **пе́ший** ("pedestrian"), **спя́щий** ("sleeping").

Singular

	Nom.	Gen.	Dat.	Acc.	Instr.	Prep.
Masc.	**-ий**	**-его**	**-ему**	**-ий** **-его**	**-им**	**-ем**
Fem.	**-ая**	**-ей**	**-ей**	**-ую**	**-ей (-ею)**	**-ей**
Neut.	**-ее**	**-его**	**-ему**	**-ее**	**-им**	**-ем**

Plural

	Nom.	Gen.	Dat.	Acc.	Instr.	Prep.
All genders	**-ие**	**-их**	**-им**	**-ие** **-их**	**-ими**	**-их**

5. Adjectives derived from the names of animals and the numeral тре́тий.

ли́сий ("fox-"), **соба́чий** ("dog-"), **ры́бий** ("fish-").

Singular

	Nom.	Gen.	Dat.	Acc.	Instr.	Prep.
Masc.	**-ий**	**-ьего**	**-ьему**	**-ий** **-ьего**	**-ьим**	**-ьем**
Fem.	**-ья**	**-ьей**	**-ьей**	**-ью**	**-ьей (-ьею)**	**-ьей**
Neut.	**-ье**	**-ьего**	**-ьему**	**-ье**	**-ьим**	**-ьем**

Plural

	Nom.	Gen.	Dat.	Acc.	Instr.	Prep.
All genders	**-ьи**	**-ьих**	**-ьим**	**-ьи** **-ьих**	**-ьими**	**-ьих**

ADJECTIVES

Full and Short Adjectives

Adjectives usually end in **-ый, -ой, -ий** (masc.), **-ая, -яя** (fem.), **-ое, -ее** (neut.). These "full" endings are mostly used attributively: **до́брый челове́к, краси́вая река́, высо́кое де́рево.**

Besides these "full" endings, adjectives denoting quality (of which degrees of comparison can be formed) also have "short" endings which are used only predicatively and only in the nominative (singular or plural). In the singular the short form for the masculine is the stem: **до́брый,** short form—**добр.** If the stem ends in two consonants which are difficult to pronounce, an **о** or **е** (ё if accented) is inserted: **кре́пкий** ("strong")—**кре́пок; тру́дный** ("difficult")—**тру́ден; у́мный** ("clever")—**умён.** For the feminine the ending is **-а** or **-я,** and for the neuter—**-о** or **-е.** In the plural the ending is **-ы** for all genders.

краси́вый дом—	a beautiful house
краси́вая ло́шадь—	a beautiful horse
краси́вое пла́тье—	a beautiful dress
краси́вые дома́, ло́шади, пла́тья—	beautiful houses, horses, dresses.
Дом краси́в—	The house is beautiful
Ло́шадь краси́ва—	The horse is beautiful
Пла́тье краси́во—	The dress is beautiful
Дома́, ло́шади, пла́тья краси́вы—	The houses, horses, dresses are beautiful

Some adjectives denoting quality (e.g. **большо́й, ма́ленький**) have no short endings. A few only exist in the short form, for instance **рад** (m.), **ра́да** (f.)—"glad".

Relative adjectives, i.e. adjectives relating to the material of which something is made (**деревя́нный**—"wooden") or denoting nationality, origine, place, time (**ру́сский**—"Russian", **зде́шний**—"local", **вече́рний**—"evening-") have the full form only, which is used both attributively and predicatively.

золото́е кольцо́—a golden ring. **Кольцо́ золото́е**—The ring is of gold.

A special category of relative adjectives are the "possessive" adjectives which indicate that something belongs to, or originates from somebody or something. They have only short endings and they are used in all cases and mostly attributively. Possessive adjectives end either in **-ий, -ья, -ье** or in **-ин** (m.), **-ина** (f.), **-ино** (n.); **-ов, -ова, -ово; -ев, -ева, -ево,** e.g.:

во́лчий вой	wolf's howl	**о́льгин зо́нтик**	Olga's umbrella
ли́сья шу́ба	fox coat	**ма́шина шля́па**	Masha's hat
коро́вье молоко́	cow's milk	**колу́мбово яйцо́**	the egg of Columbus

Many Russian family names are adjectives in form and are declined like "full" or "short" adjectives according to their endings. Names with full adjective-endings are, for instance, **Достое́вский, Толсто́й.** Names with short endings are **Сама́рин, Попо́в, Васи́льев.** Thus you say in Russian:

Я написа́л Толсто́му	I wrote (to) Tolstoy
Преступле́ние и Наказа́ние—рома́н Достое́вского	Crime and Punishment is a novel of Dostoyevsky
Беспро́волочный телегра́ф изобре-тён Попо́вым	The wireless was invented by Popov

The Comparative

The comparative can be formed in two different ways:

1) By having the adjective preceded by **бо́лее** ("more") or **ме́нее** ("less"), e.g.: **бо́лее высо́кий дом**—"the taller house", **ме́нее высо́кий дом** or **бо́лее ни́зкий дом**—"the lower house". This form can be used either attributively or predicatively.
2) Another way is to add to the stem of the adjective the ending **-ее: до́брый** ("good, kind")—**добре́е; у́мный** ("clever")—**умне́е.**

Some adjectives, especially those ending in a guttural **(г, к, х)** and also in **д, з, т, ст,** form the comparative in **-е,** whereby these consonants change into sibilants: **гро́мкий** ("loud")—**гро́мче, ни́зкий** ("low")—**ни́же, молодо́й** ("young")—**моло́же, то́лстый** ("fat")—**то́лще** etc.

The endings of the comparatives in **-ее** and **-е** never change regardless of gender or number; they can be used only predicatively: **Он, она́, они́ умне́е**—"He, she is (they are) more clever".

Some adjectives form the comparative in **-ший: бо́льший** ("bigger"), **ме́ньший** ("smaller"), **лу́чший** ("better"), **вы́сший** ("higher") etc. The prefix **по-** imparts to the comparative the meaning of "a little": **побо́льше**—"a little more", **поме́ньше**—"a little less". Sometimes this particle enhances the meaning: **Беги́ поскоре́е!**—"Run faster!", meaning "as fast as you can".

In some cases the comparative is formed, as in English, from a different stem: **хоро́ший** ("good")—**лу́чше** ("better"), **плохо́й** ("bad")—**ху́же** ("worse").

The Superlative

The superlative is usually formed by having the adjective preceded by **са́мый** (masc.), **са́мая** (fem.), **са́мое** (neut.): **са́мый у́мный**—"the cleverest", **са́мый глу́пый**—"the most stupid". With some adjectives the comparative is preceded by **са́мый: са́мый лу́чший**—"the best".

Another way of forming the superlative is by adding the endings **-ейший, -ейшая, -ейшее** to the stem. If the stem ends in a guttural **(г, к, х)**, the ending is **-айший, -айшая, -айшее** and the guttural changes into a sibilant: **высо́кий** ("high")—**высоча́йший** ("the highest"). This form has the meaning of an absolute superlative only if the object of the comparison is mentioned: **Эльбру́с высоча́йшая гора́ на Кавка́зе**—"The Elbrus is the highest mountain in the Caucasus"; but **Эльбру́с высоча́йшая гора́**—"The Elbrus is a very high mountain". **Он добре́йший челове́к**—"He is a very kind man". The prefix **пре-** imparts to the adjective the same meaning: **Он предо́брый**—"He is very kind"; **Она́ прекра́сна**—"She is (very) beautiful".

Also the comparative of some adjectives is used as a superlative: **лу́чший**—"the best", **ху́дший**—"the worst". The prefix **наи-** enhances the meaning: **наилу́чший**—"The very best". (See Note on page 196).

THE VERB

Almost all Russian verbs have two forms, called **вид**—"aspect". It is absolutely necessary to know both of them.

The IMPERFECTIVE aspect expresses an unfinished action, an action in its progress or an action which repeats itself.

The PERFECTIVE aspect expresses the completed action. This aspect has no present tense, naturally, since the present tense describes an action which is in actual progress, i.e. not completed.

A good example of the difference between these aspects can be expressed by **я пил во́дку** and **я вы́пил во́дку.** The former means "I was drinking some vodka", or "I drank vodka", but the latter leaves no doubt that you finished up the glass or bottle in question.

The difference in aspect is expressed in various ways, e.g.:

1) by prefixes **по-, на-, про-, с-, о-, об-, у-**

Imperf.	Perf.	Imperf.	Perf.
проси́ть	**попроси́ть**	**де́лать**	**сде́лать**
писа́ть	**написа́ть**	**чита́ть**	**прочита́ть**

2) by alteration of the vowel connecting the stem with the infinitive ending:

реша́ть	**реши́ть**	**конча́ть**	**ко́нчить**

3) by suffixes which sometimes alter the stem **-ыва, -ива, -я, -а, -ну** etc.

забыва́ть	**забы́ть**	**пры́гать**	**пры́гнуть**
разбива́ть	**разби́ть**	**понима́ть**	**поня́ть**
собира́ть	**собра́ть**		

4) by different verbs:

брать	взять	говори́ть	сказа́ть
класть	положи́ть	лови́ть	пойма́ть
бить	уда́рить		

5) simply by putting the stress on another syllable:

обреза́ть	обре́зать	рассыпа́ть	рассы́пать

There are a few verbs which have the same form for both aspects:

жени́ть	жени́ть	ра́нить	ра́нить

CONJUGATION

There are two conjugations: the First or "e" conjugation and the Second or "и" conjugation which are so called because of the predominance of the vowel **е** or **и** respectively in the endings of the present tense.

FIRST OR "e" CONJUGATION

Imperfective	Perfective

Infinitive

д е́ л а т ь	с д е́ л а т ь

Present

Imperfective		Perfective
я де́лаю	мы де́лаем	none
ты де́лаешь	вы де́лаете	
он / она́ / оно́ } де́лает	они́ де́лают	

Past

Imperfective	Perfective
я, ты, он де́лал	я, ты, он сде́лал
я, ты, она́ де́лала	я, ты, она́ сде́лала
оно́ де́лало	оно́ сде́лало
мы / вы / они́ } де́лали	мы / вы / они́ } сде́лали

Future

Imperfective		Perfective	
я бу́ду } де́лать	мы бу́дем } де́лать	я сде́лаю	мы сде́лаем
ты бу́дешь } де́лать	вы бу́дете } де́лать	ты сде́лаешь	вы сде́лаете
он / она́ / оно́ } бу́дет } де́лать	они́ бу́дут } де́лать	он / она́ / оно́ } сде́лает	они́ сде́лают

Conditional

я, ты, он де́лал бы	я, ты, он сде́лал бы
я, ты, она́ це́лала бы	я, ты, она́ сде́лала бы
оно́ де́лало бы	оно́ сде́лало бы
мы, вы, они́ } де́лали бы	мы, вы, они́ } сде́лали бы

Imperative

де́лай	сде́лай
де́лайте	сде́лайте

PARTICIPLES

Active—Present

де́лающий, -ая, -ее де́лающие	none

Active—Past

де́лавший, -ая, -ее де́лавшие	сде́лавший, -ая, -ее сде́лавшие

Passive—Present

де́лаемый, -ая, -ое де́лаемые	none

Passive—Past

де́ланный, -ая, -ое де́ланные	сде́ланный, -ая, -ое сде́ланные

GERUNDS

Present

де́лая	none

Past

де́лав (де́лавши)	сде́лав (сде́лавши)

SECOND OR "и" CONJUGATION

Imperfective	Perfective

Infinitive

д а р и́ т ь	п о д а р и́ т ь

Present

я дарю́	мы дари́м	
ты дари́шь	вы дари́те	
он, она́, оно́ } дари́т	они́ даря́т	none

Past

я, ты, он дари́л	я, ты, он подари́л
я, ты она́ дари́ла	я, ты она́ подари́ла
оно́ дари́ло	оно́ подари́ло
мы, вы, они́ } дари́ли	мы, вы, они́ } подари́ли

Future

я бу́ду } дари́ть	мы бу́дем } дари́ть	я подарю́	мы подари́м
ты бу́дешь } дари́ть	вы бу́дете } дари́ть	ты подари́шь	вы подари́те
он, она́, оно́ } бу́дет } дари́ть	они́ бу́дут } дари́ть	он, она́, оно́ } подари́т	они́ подаря́т

Conditional

я, ты, он дари́л бы	я, ты, он подари́л бы
я, ты, она́ дари́ла бы	я, ты, она́ подари́ла бы
оно́ дари́ло бы	оно́ подари́ло бы
мы, вы, они́ } дари́ли бы	мы, вы, они́ } подари́ли бы

Imperative

дари́	подари́
дари́те	подари́те

PARTICIPLES

Active—Present

даря́щий, -ая, -ее даря́щие	none

Active—Past

дари́вший, -ая, -ее дари́вшие	подари́вший, -ая, -ее подари́вшие

Passive—Present

дари́мый, -ая, -ое дари́мые	none

Passive—Past

дарённый, -ая, -ое дарённые	подарённый, -ая, -ое подарённые

GERUNDS

Present

даря́	none

Past

дари́в (дари́вши)	подари́в (подари́вши)

THE PAST

The endings of the past tense are in the singular **-л** (masc.), **-ла** (fem.) and **-ло** (neut.) irrespectively of person, and in the plural **-ли** regardless of person and gender. These endings are added to the stem of the infinitive, e.g.: **игра́-ть** ("to play"), **ма́льчик игра́-л** ("the boy was playing"), **де́вочка игра́-ла** ("the girl was playing"), **дитя́ игра́-ло** ("the child was playing"), **де́ти игра́-ли** ("the children were playing").

If the stem ends in a consonant, the **л** is omitted in the masculine, but retained in the feminine and neuter, and in the plural: **нес-ти́** ("to carry"), **нёс** (masc.), **нес-ла́** (fem.), **нес-ло́** (neut.), **нес-ли́** (plural).

Verbs whose infinitives end in **-сти** or **-чь** form the past from the stem of the present tense (perfective verbs from the stem of the future tense): **мочь** ("to be able, can"), **мог-у́** ("I can"), **мог, мог-ла́, мог-ло́, мог-ли́.** If the final consonant is **д** or **т,** this consonant is omitted: **вес-ти́** ("to lead"), **вед-у́** ("I lead"), **вёл, вела́, вело́, вели́.**

THE IMPERATIVE

Is formed from the stem of the present tense of the imperfective aspect or from the stem of the future tense of the perfective aspect of the verb to which the endings **-и** (2-nd pers. sing.) or **-ите** (2-nd pers. plur.) are added. To ascertain the stem, cut off the ending of the 3-rd person plural: **ид-у́т** ("they go"), stem—**ид,** imperative—**ид-и́, ид-и́те; бер-у́т** ("they take"), stem—**бер,** imperative—**бер-и́, бер-и́те.**

If the stem ends in a vowel, the endings **-и** and **-ите** are shortened to **-й** and **-йте: чита́-ют** ("they read"), imperative—**чита́-й, чита́-йте.**

With some verbs these endings are shortened still more to **-ь** and **-ьте: ре́ж-ут** ("they cut"), imperative—**реж-ь, ре́ж-ьте; уда́р-ят** ("they will hit"), imperative—**уда́рь, уда́рьте.**

The imperative of the first person plural is expressed by the first person plural of the indicative with a corresponding intonation: **идём!** ("let's go!"). Sometimes the particle **-те** is added (**идёмте!**) which is a more polite form of the imperative. This particle is also used when several persons are addressed.

PREPOSITIONS

Here is a list of the most common prepositions with the cases they require. Some prepositions are used with two or even three different cases which impart to them different meanings. Here is a helpful hint: more than half of the prepositions take the genitive.

без (безо) *gen.*—without   **близ** *gen.*—near

в (во) { *acc.* (denoting motion)—in, into
prep. (mere location)—in

вдоль *gen.*—along

вместо *gen.*—instead of

вне gen.—outside of

внутри *gen.*—inside, within

внутрь *gen.*—in, inwards

вόзле *gen.*—beside, by, near

вокрýг *gen.*—around

вопреки́ *gen.*—in spite of

впереди́ *gen.*—in front of

для *gen.*—for, for the sake of

до *gen.*—to, up to, as far as; until

за { *acc.* (denoting motion) / *instr.* (mere location) } —behind, across, beyond

из (изо) *gen.*—from, out of

из-за *gen.*—from behind; because of

из-под *gen.*—from under

к (ко) *dat.*—to, towards

крóме *gen.*—with the exception of

мéжду *instr.* & *gen.*—between, among

ми́мо *gen.*—past, by

на { *acc.* (denoting motion)—on, towards / *prep.* (mere position)—on, at }

над *instr.*—above

о (об, обо) { *acc.*—against (to lean against etc.) / *prep.*—about, concerning }

óколо *gen.*—by, near

от *gen.*—from

пéред (пéредо) { *acc.* (denoting motion) / *instr.* (mere location) } before, in front of

по { *dat.*—along; according to / *acc.*—up to; to, until / *prep.*—after }

под (подо) { *acc.* (denoting motion) / *instr.* (mere position) } under; near

позади́ *gen.*—behind

пóсле *gen.*—after

посреди́ *gen.*—in the midst of; among

при *prep.*—by; near; in the time of; in the presence of

прóтив *gen.*—opposite; against

ра́ди *gen.*—for the sake of

с (со) { *gen.*—from; off, away; since / *acc.*—as, about the size of / *instr.*—with }

сквозь *acc.*—through

среди́ *gen.*—between, among

у *gen.*—at, near

чéрез *acc.*—across, over; through

A LAST WORD — These are the most important points of Russian grammar. But even if you make some mistakes at first (!) don't even *hesitate* to speak. With what you know now, and by constant practice, you should soon be speaking Russian like a real **русáк!**

THE RUSSIAN ALPHABET AS WRITTEN

NOTE ON RUSSIAN HANDWRITING:

You already know the printed Russian letters. Here are the handwritten ones. As some of them resemble each other, they occasionally are written with a horizontal line over or under them, to make the difference clear. Thus, the letters **т** and **п** are frequently written with a horizontal line *above* them, while the letter **ш** is written with a line *below.*

А а	Б б	В в	Г г
Д д д	Е е	Ж ж	З з
И и	й	К к	Л л
М м	Н н	О о	П п
Р р	С с	Т т	У у
Ф ф	Х х	Ц ц	Ч ч
Ш ш	Щ щ	ъ	ы
ь	Э э	Ю ю	Я я

EXAMPLES OF RUSSIAN HANDWRITING

Человек состоит из души, тела и паспорта

(You will find this in print on page 183, line 2.)

Терпи Казак, атаманом будешь.

(See page 179, line 1.)

Незваный гость хуже татарина.

(See page 145, line 1.)

Теперь я могу говорить, читать и писать по-русски.

(See if you can decipher this yourself!)